THE CASE
AGAINST
ISRAEL'S
ENEMIES

Books by Alan Dershowitz

Is There a Right to Remain Silent? Coercive Interrogation and the Fifth Amendment after 9/11

Finding Jefferson: A Lost Letter, a Remarkable Discovery, and the First Amendment in an Age of Terrorism

Blasphemy: How the Religious Right Is Hijacking Our Declaration of Independence

Preemption: A Knife That Cuts Both Ways

What Israel Means to Me: By 80 Prominent Writers, Performers, Scholars, Politicians, and Journalists

Rights from Wrongs: A Secular Theory of the Origins of Rights

America on Trial: Inside the Legal Battles That Transformed Our Nation

The Case for Peace: How the Arab-Israeli Conflict Can Be Resolved

The Case for Israel

America Declares Independence

Why Terrorism Works: Understanding the Threat, Responding to the Challenge

Shouting Fire: Civil Liberties in a Turbulent Age

Letters to a Young Lawyer

Supreme Injustice: How the High Court Hijacked Election 2000

Genesis of Justice: Ten Stories of Biblical Injustice That Led to the Ten Commandments and Modern Law

Just Revenge

Sexual McCarthyism: Clinton, Starr, and the Emerging Constitutional Crisis

The Vanishing American Jew: In Search of Jewish Identity for the Next Century

Reasonable Doubts: The Criminal Justice System and the O.J. Simpson Case

The Abuse Excuse: And Other Cop-Outs, Sob Stories, and Evasions of Responsibility

The Advocate's Devil

Contrary to Popular Opinion

Chutzpah

Taking Liberties: A Decade of Hard Cases, Bad Laws, and Bum Raps

Reversal of Fortune: Inside the von Bülow Case

The Best Defense

Criminal Law: Theory and Process

Psychoanalysis: Psychiatry and Law

THE CASE
AGAINST
ISRAEL'S
ENEMIES

Exposing Jimmy Carter and Others
Who Stand in the Way of Peace

Alan Dershowitz

John Wiley & Sons, Inc.

Published by John Wiley & Sons, Inc., Hoboken, New Jersey
Published simultaneously in Canada

For general information about our other products and services, please contact our Customer Care Department within the United States at (800) 762–2974, outside the United States at (317) 572–3993 or fax (317) 572–4002.

Wiley also publishes its books in a variety of electronic formats. Some content that appears in print may not be available in electronic books. For more information about Wiley products, visit our web site at www.wiley.com.

Library of Congress Cataloging-in-Publication Data

Dershowitz, Alan M.
    The case against Israel's enemies : exposing Jimmy Carter and others who stand in the way of peace / Alan Dershowitz.
        p. cm.
    Includes index.
    ISBN 978-0-470-37992-9 (cloth : alk. paper)
    1. Arab-Israeli conflict–Public opinion. 2. Arab-Israeli conflict–1993—Peace–Public opinion. 3. Israel–Public opinion. 4. Public opinion–United States. 5. Public opinion–Islamic countries. I. Title.
    DS119.7.D4634 2008
    956.05–dc22   2008033318

Printed in the United States of America

10 9 8 7 6 5 4 3 2 1

This book is dedicated to Israel's constructive and nuanced critics, whose rational voices are too often drowned out by the exaggerations, demonizations, and hate-filled lies put forth by Israel's enemies. Criticism is the lifeblood of democracy and a sure sign of admiration for an imperfect democracy seeking to improve itself.

CONTENTS

ACKNOWLEDGMENTS

This book was a collaborative effort in which my student research assistants played a significant role in reviewing and critiquing the writings of Israel's enemies. The students who worked directly on the research for this book included Peter Mulcahy, Joel Pollack, Danielle Sassoon, and Chaim Kagedan.

The students who worked on my earlier writings, which have been adapted for inclusion in this book, include Mitch Webber, Aaron Voloj Dessauer, Alexander Blenkinsopp, Charles Johnson, Alexandra Katz, and Elizabeth Pugh.

I also wish to acknowledge my assistant, Sarah Neely, for shepherding the project and typing the manuscript.

Thanks also to Helen Rees, my agent, and Hana Lane, my editor, for encouraging me to write this book, and to Lisa Burstiner for her excellent copyediting.

And to my Brooklyn friends and my family who reviewed and made useful suggestions on earlier drafts, my constant appreciation.

Finally, thanks to my lecture audiences and e-mail correspondents, who convinced me that this was a book that had to be written.

Introduction

For a tiny nation of a little more than six and a half million citizens (approximately 5.3 million of whom are Jewish and 1.3 million are Muslim and Christian Arabs) living in an area roughly the size of New Jersey, Israel has proportionally more enemies than any nation on earth. No nation has been threatened more often with divestment, boycotts, and other sanctions. No nation has generated more protests against it on college and university campuses. No nation has been targeted for as much editorial abuse from the worldwide media. No nation has been subjected to more frequent threats of annihilation. No nation has had more genocidal incitements directed against its citizens.

It is remarkable indeed that a democratic nation born in response to a decision of the United Nations should still not be accepted by so many countries, groups, and individuals. No other UN member is threatened with physical destruction by other member states so openly and with so little rebuke from the General Assembly or the Security Council. Indeed, no nation, regardless of its size or the number of deaths it has caused, has been condemned as often by the UN and its constituent bodies. Simply put, no nation is hated as much as the Jewish nation.

Yet over the last sixty years, no nation in the world has contributed more per capita to the general welfare of the people of this planet than Israel. Israel has exported more lifesaving medical technology to the far-flung corners of the earth than any nation of comparable size. It has done more to protect the environment; to promote literature, music, and the arts and sciences; and to spread agricultural advances. Its scientists and engineers have secured more patents and its high-tech entrepreneurs more new listings on NASDAQ than any but the largest nations in the world. Its academics have won more international prizes, published more papers, and achieved more technological breakthroughs than any other nation of comparable size. Its students have been accepted at more elite graduate and professional schools than those of other small countries.

And Israel has learned and taught others how to fight terrorism within the rule of law. Israel has created a legal system that is the envy of the world, with a Supreme Court that stands at the pinnacle of democratic judiciaries—a court open to all with few, if any, restrictions on its jurisdiction. As America's most liberal Supreme Court justice, William Brennan, observed when he visited Israel in 1987,

> It may well be Israel, not the United States, that provides the best hope for building a jurisprudence that can protect civil liberties against the demands of national security. For it is Israel that has been facing real and serious threats to its security for the last forty years and seems destined to continue facing such threats in the foreseeable future. The struggle to establish civil liberties against the backdrop of these security threats, while difficult, promises to build bulwarks of liberty that can endure the fears and frenzy of sudden danger— bulwarks to help guarantee that a nation fighting for its survival does not sacrifice those national values that make the fight worthwhile. . . .
>
> I [would not] be surprised if in the future the protections generally afforded civil liberties during times of world danger owed much to the lessons Israel learns in its struggle to preserve simultaneously the liberties of its citizens and the security of its nation. For in this crucible of danger lies the opportunity to forge a worldwide jurisprudence of civil liberties that can withstand the turbulences of war and crisis.[1]

Israel's media have become models of openness and self-criticism, in which every perspective from the hard anti-Zionist left to the hardest right may be heard and seen. So may Israeli Arabs, many of whom do not accept the legitimacy of the Zionist state. As an Israeli friend once quipped, "Israelis and Palestinians have exactly the same free speech rights: they may both condemn the Israeli prime minister and praise the leader of Hamas."

In an otherwise critical article in the May 2008 edition of the *Atlantic,* Jeffrey Goldberg, who questions whether Israel will survive, summarized Israel's achievements over its sixty-year history:

> Israel is, by almost any measure[,] an astonishing success. It has a large, sophisticated and growing economy (its gross domestic product last year was $150 billion); the finest universities and medical centers in the Middle East; and a main city, Tel Aviv, that is a center of art, fashion, cuisine, and high culture spread along a beautiful Mediterranean beach. Israel has shown itself, with notable exceptions, to be adept at self-defense, and capable (albeit imperfectly) of protecting civil liberties during wartime. It has become a worldwide center of Jewish learning and self-expression; its strength has straightened the spines of Jews around the world; and, most consequentially, it has absorbed and enfranchised millions of previously impoverished and dispossessed Jews. Zionism may actually be the most successful national liberation movement of the 20th century.[2]

In contrast, Goldberg characterizes the Palestinians as having "perhaps the least successful national liberation movement of the 20th century," largely because of the "Arab opposition" to any Jewish state and to any two-state solution.

There is, to be sure, much to criticize with regard to Israel, just as there is with regard to every imperfect democracy (which includes all democracies). Criticism is healthy, indeed indispensable to the workings of democracy. No one should ever confuse criticism of Israel or of Israeli policies with anti-Semitism. And no one should ever accuse mere critics of Israel of anti-Semitism. If criticism of Israel or Israeli policies constituted anti-Semitism, then the highest concentration of anti-Semites would be in Israel, where *everybody* is a critic. There is an apocryphal story about an Israeli who was stranded alone on a desert island for ten years. By the time he was finally rescued, he had started four political parties, six newspapers, and two synagogues. I, too, have been a frequent critic of Israeli policies—especially, but not exclusively, with regard to the settlement and occupation policies—since the early 1970s. Yet no one has called me an anti-Semite. The claim that critics of Israel are branded anti-Semites is a straw man and a fabrication of Israel's enemies who seek to play the victim card.

Yet this big lie persists. Susannah Heshel, a professor of Jewish studies at Dartmouth, has charged, "We often hear that criticism of Israel is equivalent to anti-Semitism."[3] Michael Lerner, the editor of *Tikkun,* has made a similar charge. So has Noam Chomsky. Most recently, a vocal professor at Harvard, Lorand Matory, has made this accusation.[4] I have challenged anyone who claims that mere criticism of Israel is often labeled anti-Semitism to document that serious charge by providing actual quotations, in context, with the sources of the statements identified. No one has responded to my challenge. I am not talking about the occasional kook who writes an anonymous postcard or an e-mail. I am talking about mainstream supporters of Israel, who, it is claimed, have often equated mere criticism of Israel with anti-Semitism.

Surely that is not what Thomas Friedman of the *New York Times* did when he wrote the following: "Criticizing Israel is not anti-Semitic, and saying so is vile. But singling out Israel for opprobrium and international sanction—out of all proportion to any other party in the Middle East—is anti-Semitic, and not saying so is dishonest."[5] Nor is it what former Harvard University president Lawrence Summers did when he said, in condemning divestment petitions against Israel, "There is much to be debated about the Middle East and much in Israel's foreign and defense policy that can be and should be vigorously challenged."

Surely it is not what I have done when I have welcomed criticism of Israel, while accusing of bigotry those who would single out Israel for economic and academic capital punishment, despite the reality that Israel's human rights record is far better than that of any other country in the region and at least as good as that of any other country that has faced comparable dangers. Yet no other nation, including those with the most abysmal of human rights records, faces as much enmity. Most significantly, the intensity of the enmity directed against the Mideast's only democracy is unexplainable on any rational basis.

I will never forget how I personally experienced this hatred in March 2004. It took place in front of Faneuil Hall, the birthplace of American independence and liberty. I was receiving a justice award and delivering a talk from the podium of that historic hall on civil liberties in the age of terrorism. When I left, award in hand, I was accosted by a group of screaming, angry young men and women carrying virulently anti-Israel signs. The sign carriers were shouting epithets at me that crossed the line from civility to bigotry. "Dershowitz and Hitler, just the same, the only difference is the name." The sin that, in the opinion of the screamers, warranted this comparison between me and the man who murdered dozens of my family members was my support for Israel.

It was irrelevant to these chanters that I also support a Palestinian state, the end of the Israeli occupation, and the dismantling of most of the settlements. The protesters also shouted, "Dershowitz and Gibbels [sic], just the same, the only difference is the name"—not even knowing how to pronounce the name of the anti-Semitic Nazi butcher.

One sign carrier shouted that Jews who support Israel are worse than Nazis. Another demanded that I be tortured and killed. It was not only their words; it was the hatred in their eyes. If a dozen Boston police had not been protecting me, I have little doubt I would have been physically attacked. The protesters' eyes were ablaze with fanatical zeal.

The feminist writer Phyllis Chesler aptly describes the hatred some young people often direct against Israel and supporters of the Jewish state as "eroticized."[6] That is what I saw: passionate hatred, ecstatic hatred, orgasmic hatred. It was beyond mere differences of opinion.

When I looked into the faces of the protesters, I could imagine young Nazis in the 1930s in Hitler's Germany. They had no doubt that they were right and that I was pure evil for my support of the

Jewish state, despite my public disagreement with some of Israel's policies and despite my support for Palestinian statehood.

There was no place for nuance here. It was black and white, good versus evil, and any Jew who supported Israel was pure evil, deserving of torture, violence, and whatever fate Hitler and Goebbels deserved.

To be sure, these protesters' verbal attack on me was constitutionally protected speech, just as the Nazi march through Skokie, Illinois, was constitutionally protected speech. But the shouting was plainly calculated to intimidate. An aura of violence was in the air, and had the police not been there, I would not have been able to express any views counter to the young demonstrators'.

As it turned out, I was not able to express my opinions anyway, even in response to their outrageous mischaracterization of my viewpoint or their comparisons of me to the most evil men in the world. When I turned to answer one of the bigoted chants, as I always do in these situations, the police officer in charge gently but firmly insisted that I walk directly to my car and not engage them. It was an order, reasonably calculated to assure my safety, and it was right.

The officer climbed into my car with me and only got out a few blocks away, when we were beyond the range of violence. The intimidation had succeeded. I had been silenced, and the false and horrible message had gone unanswered in the plaza near Faneuil Hall.

That is not the way the marketplace of ideas is supposed to work. It is not the conception of liberty for which Sam and John Adams spoke so eloquently and controversially in and around Faneuil Hall more than two hundred years earlier. It was far more reminiscent of rallies conducted by Nazi thugs in Berlin seventy years ago.

The shouters know that I will not be silenced or intimidated. Their goal is to silence and intimidate others who do not get police protection and do not have access to the media. The shouters in front of Faneuil Hall wanted no views but their own to be seen and heard, because they were certain that only their views were politically correct.

They succeeded that day in front of Faneuil Hall, as they have on some university campuses, where pro-Israel speakers—including former prime ministers Ehud Barak and Benjamin Netanyahu—have been prevented from speaking by threats of violence, and where human rights heroes like Natan Sharansky have been shouted down by intolerant bigots who care nothing about human rights, except for the rights of those who share their extremist ideology.[7] But the marketplace of ideas is far too vibrant to be shut down by a bunch of self-righteous ruffians shouting ugly and threatening epithets.

I have seen similar rage from audiences I addressed on university campuses in London, Toronto, Irvine, and elsewhere. Even in Iceland, there were some protests from university students when it was announced that I had been invited to speak about legal issues.[8]

I can only imagine how much more intense the hatred of Israel must be in some Islamic universities, mosques, streets, and terrorist training camps, especially in light of the daily diet of anti-Israel and anti-Jewish hate speech to which many young Muslims are exposed. Listen to the words of widely admired imams, whose incitements are broadcast on Hamas, Hezbollah, and even Palestinian Authority television and radio. (You can actually listen to and watch these hateful messages at memri.org.) Here is a representative example from Sheik Ibrahim Mudeiris, a paid employee of the Palestinian Authority (as broadcast on Palestinian Authority TV):

> Allah warned His beloved Prophet Muhammad about the Jews, who had killed the prophets, forged their Torah, and sowed corruption throughout their history.
>
> With the establishment of the state of Israel, the entire Islamic nation was lost, because Israel is a cancer spreading through the body of the Islamic nation, and because the Jews are a virus resembling AIDS, from which the entire world suffers.
>
> You will find that the Jews were behind all the civil strife in this world. The Jews are behind the suffering of the nations. . . .
>
> They are committing worse deeds than those done to them in the Nazi war. . . .
>
> Listen to the Prophet Muhammad, who tells you about the evil end that awaits Jews. The stones and trees will want the Muslims to finish off every Jew.

Now listen to Dr. Ahmad Abu Halabiya, speaking from a large mosque in Gaza:

> Have no mercy on the Jews, no matter where they are, in any country. . . . Wherever you are, kill those Jews and those Americans who are like them. . . . They established Israel here, in the beating heart of the Arab world, in Palestine . . . to be the outpost of their civilization— and the vanguard of their army, and to be the sword of the West and the Crusaders. . . .
>
> We will not give up a single grain of soil of Palestine, from Haifa [to] Jaffa.

In addition to these broadcasts, Hamas publishes a children's magazine (posted online at www.al-fateh.net) that, according to an analysis by Memri, features

> stories, poems, riddles, puzzles, etc., [that] includes incitement to jihad and martyrdom and glorification of terrorist operations and of their planners and perpetrators, as well as characterizations of Jews as "murderers of the prophets" and laudatory descriptions of parents who encourage their sons to kill Jews. . . .
>
> Some issues feature stories with martyrdom themes, including characters who express a wish to die in battle and meet the virgins of Paradise, and parents who rejoice at their son's death in a jihad operation and celebrate by uttering cries of joy and handing out sweets.

But not all hatred emanates from young American hooligans, like those who confronted me at Faneuil Hall, or brainwashed Muslim extremists. Just go online to huffingtonpost.com, a relatively mainstream blog, and peruse the readers' comments related to Israel. Or listen to Pacifica Radio, especially the call-ins. The irrational hatred expressed by relatively well-educated people is staggering. There is nothing comparable regarding any other nation.

Nor is any other nation so routinely subjected to vilification by European politicians and diplomats. Clare Short, the former secretary of state for international development in the UK Labour government, has said that Israel will cause the end of the human race because it diverts the world's attention from the problem of global warming.[9] Not China, the United States, or other large polluters, but tiny Israel, which is one of the most environmentally conscious nations in the world.

In 2001, the ambassador of a major European Union country politely told a gathering that the current troubles in the world were all because of "that shitty little country Israel."[10] The ambassador was later identified as Daniel Bernard, who was representing France in the court of St. James's. He refused to apologize or withdraw his remark.[11] (Israel has contributed more to the world over the last sixty years than France has, not only in proportion to its population, but in absolute terms as well. France collaborated with fascism, deported its Jewish citizens to Auschwitz, fought one of the dirtiest wars in history to defend its colonial rule over Algeria, and has cynically placed its own interests over those of its allies by collaborating with some of the greatest evils in the world, such as the Iraqi and Iranian nuclear weapons programs. Moreover, Israel's Muslim population is, by every measurable standard, better off and better treated than France's. For a French diplomat to demean Israel is the height of chutzpah.)

Because of my support for Israel, I have received bigoted threatening letters from university professors, such as Robert Trivers, a Rutgers evolutionary anthropologist with a reputation for barroom brawling. He threatened to "visit" and confront me "directly" if I continued to make the case for Israel: "If you decide once again to rationalize [Israel's military actions] publicly, look forward to a visit from me. Nazis—and Nazi-like apologists such as yourself—need to be confronted directly."

Other hate mail has included more threats, swastikas, poetry, cartoons, and other drivel with tasteless erotic insinuations. I make it a point to display these hateful and threatening missives on my office door, for students and other visitors to see. Those who peruse them are shocked at their virulence. I believe it is important for my students to know what they may encounter if they become public advocates for a peaceful and just resolution of the Arab-Israeli conflict.[12] These missives are not directed at me personally. These people do not know me. They are directed at Israel *through* me because I am viewed as an advocate for the Jewish nation, which is the true object of their hatred.

I have devoted countless hours to thinking about the sources of this irrational, even "eroticized," hatred toward an admittedly imperfect democracy that is the object of such disproportionate vilification. No single explanation seems to suffice. Israel's close association with the United States, global dependence on Arab oil, or sympathy with Third World movements may all play some role. It seems likely, however, that Israel's status as the world's only Jewish state (on a planet with dozens of Islamic, Christian, Buddhist, and other religiously and ethnically defined nations) is an important factor in the hatred directed at it.

Hatred alone, of course, does not endanger a nation or a people, but hatred combined with power does, as evidenced, most tragically, by the Nazi hatred turned to genocide by German military power. Although overwhelming military power of the kind possessed by the Germans in the late 1930s and early 1940s is the most dangerous, it must never be forgotten that the Nazi war machine came to power through the use of politics, the media, religion, and even academia.

That is why these and other enemies of Israel must be answered in the open marketplace of ideas. They cannot shout down a book, although their predecessors burned books with which they disagreed. Justice Robert Jackson, the chief U.S. prosecutor at Nuremberg, paraphrased Heinrich Heine when he said that those who start by burning books often end by burning people, as the Nazis infamously did.

Today Israel faces the military power of Iran, with its unmistakable intention to develop deliverable weapons of mass destruction that are capable of burning and otherwise murdering millions. It also faces military threats, though not of an existential nature, from Hezbollah, Hamas, Syria, al-Qaeda, and perhaps other nations and groups. These military threats are enhanced by political, academic, and media threats from groups and individuals who are determined to delegitimize, demonize, and destroy Israel. For example, the false claim that Israel is an apartheid regime can have no other purpose than to subject Israel to the fate of the prior apartheid regime: namely, white South Africa. The same is true of false claims of analogy to other illegitimate and deposed Nazi, fascist, colonialist, and racist regimes. Even the argument—rarely made in good faith—for a "one-state solution" to the Israeli-Palestinian conflict is a ploy designed ultimately to turn the secular, democratic Jewish state of Israel into yet another Arab state, most likely an Islamic fundamentalist tyranny.

Israel's enemies off the battlefield—its political, academic, diplomatic, media, and religious enemies—may not pose the level of immediate physical danger that is inherent in Iran's potential nuclear weapons, Hezbollah's Katyushas, Hamas's Qassams, or Islamic jihad's suicide bombers. But the risk they do pose not only encourages Israel's military enemies but also threatens Israel's survival in more subtle but equally perilous ways. By constantly seeking to delegitimize Israel's very membership in the community of nations, Israel's nonmilitary enemies threaten the peace of the world. They destabilize public order by encouraging terrorism and rewarding those who would seek to destroy Israel (and other Western democracies) by force and violence.

When I write about Israel's enemies, as I do in this book, I include only those who despise Israel as a Jewish nation and wish it ill, not those who merely criticize specific policies or actions. I also include those who single out Israel, and Israel alone, for sanctions such as boycotts, divestiture, censorship of its advocates, and other tactics designed to delegitimize the Jewish state among the community of nations. Some, such as Mahmoud Ahmadinejad, acknowledge—indeed, proclaim—hatred toward Israel. Others deny it, but, as I will show in the pages to come, their words and actions belie their self-serving disclaimers.

Israel's most dangerous enemies are those who wield the power—political, academic, religious, and military—to challenge Israel's continued existence as a Jewish, democratic, multiethnic, and multicultural state. These include Western political leaders, led by former president Jimmy Carter, who would delegitimize Israel as an apartheid regime subject to the same fate as white South Africa; Israel's academic enemies, led by Professors Stephen Walt and John Mearsheimer, who would accuse supporters of Israel of dual loyalty and indeed disloyalty to the United States; powerful academic unions, such as those in Great Britain, which proposed (and continue to propose) a boycott of Israeli academics that threatens to isolate Israeli science, technology, and medicine; certain religious groups, such as the Presbyterian Church and the Tikkun community (led by Rabbi Michael Lerner), which would divest from Israel and Israel alone for its alleged human rights violations; media and academic extremists on the hard left and the hard right who single out Israel for special vilification; certain self-proclaimed "human rights" organizations that subject Israel to a double standard to which no other nation is held; the current Iranian regime, which threatens Israel's physical existence by its likely development of deliverable nuclear weapons that it has publicly said it would use against the Jewish state; and the emerging radical Islamic "crescent" that surrounds Israel, consisting of Iran, Syria, Hezbollah-controlled southern Lebanon, Hamas-controlled Gaza, and perhaps in the future other nations with increasingly radical Islamic populations.

The reason Jimmy Carter is so dangerous to Israel is that because of his high standing as a former president, he has mainstreamed the sort of political delegitimization and vilification of Israel that had previously been limited to the fringe left and the fringe right in the United States. If Carter's arguments remain unrebutted, it is only a matter of time before some younger mainstream American politicians pick them up and campaign against U.S. support of Israel. This would make Israel's very existence a matter of political dispute in the U.S. political system, whereas now America's support for Israel is a consensus issue in the political sphere. Were Israel to be abandoned by the United States—or even subjected to the kind of "even-handedness" that is characteristic of much of Europe—its continued existence would be imperiled. Even-handedness toward tyrannical regimes that deliberately target civilians for terrorism, as well as toward democracies that seek to protect their civilians without endangering other civilians, is the kind of immoral equivalence that characterized Swiss "even-handedness" during World War II.

What Carter threatens to do in U.S. politics, Walt and Mearsheimer seek to do in U.S. academia. Prior to the publication of their screed against the so-called Israel Lobby (which in reality includes most Americans), the kind of attack they level against Jewish influence in U.S. politics was common only among hard-leftists in American academia, such as Noam Chomsky and Norman Finkelstein, and hard-rightists, such as Pat Buchanan and Robert Novak. But Walt and Mearsheimer are mainstream American academics, representing the realist school of U.S. foreign policy. If their false and malignant thesis remains unrebutted, it, too, will threaten to become mainstream. The paradox of their approach, and why it has been so difficult to counteract, is that when American Jews and other supporters of Israel join together to oppose their perspective, such legitimate collective activity is seen by Walt and Mearsheimer as further proof of the power of the Jewish lobby. Accordingly, it is crucial for other academics to confront their arguments in the marketplace of ideas. It is also important because today's students in academia are tomorrow's leaders. That is precisely why these students are being targeted by anti-Israel extremists.

The threat posed to Israel by religious groups is more subtle, but equally dangerous. Israel's moral standing has been challenged by certain leaders of liberal Protestant denominations, as well as by some in the Catholic hierarchy and even a few Jewish religious leftists. Many evangelical Christians, on the other hand, strongly support not only Israel's right to exist, but the most extreme positions within Israel, such as continuing the occupation. They do so largely on theological grounds. This division threatens to turn the debate over Israel into a right-left theological dispute, which will make a compromise peace more difficult to achieve.

Then there is the military danger posed by Iran, which has explicitly threatened to destroy the Jewish state in the name of

Islam. This threat converts the concept of individual suicide terrorists into a suicide nation, which is willing to incur millions of casualties among its own citizens as the price of destroying a religious enemy. Former Iranian president and supposed Iranian moderate Hashemi Rafsanjani "boast[ed] that an Iranian [nuclear] attack would kill as many as five million Jews. Rafsanjani estimated that even if Israel retaliated by dropping its own nuclear bombs, Iran would probably lose only fifteen million people, which he said would be a small 'sacrifice' from among the billion Muslims in the world."[13]

The determination of the Iranian regime to destroy Israel has only increased with the ascension to power of Mahmoud Ahmadinejad, who believes that a nuclear war with Israel will hasten the arrival of the Twelfth Imam. As Charles Krauthammer has stated:

> The president of a country about to go nuclear is a confirmed believer in the coming apocalypse. Like Judaism and Christianity, Shiite Islam has its own version of the messianic return—the reappearance of the Twelfth Imam. . . .
>
> Ahmadinejad has said publicly that the main mission of the Islamic Revolution is to pave the way for the reappearance of the Twelfth Imam.[14]

On July 18, 2008, the respected Israeli historian Benny Morris published an op-ed in the *New York Times* predicting that "Israel will almost surely attack Iran's nuclear sites," and "if the attack fails, the Middle East will almost certainly face a nuclear war."

In the pages to come, I will describe, assess, and criticize Israel's enemies. I will present the case against them, much as I presented the case for Israel and for peace in my previous books. Because I have been so directly involved in several of the battles against Israel's enemies—most particularly, President Carter, Professors Walt and Mearsheimer, those who promoted the British boycott against Israeli academics, and extremist Israel-bashers among both left- and right-wing academics and pundits—this book is inevitably more personal in describing my role and that of others with whom I have worked and continue to work.

Although this "case against" book is, by its nature, more negative than my "case for" books, I remain optimistic that Israel will go on to celebrate many birthdays beyond its sixtieth and will continue to contribute disproportionately to the welfare of the world. Yet I realize that optimism is currently in short supply when it comes to the prospects for peace: in Israel, a "pessimist" is defined as someone who says, "Things can't get any worse"; an "optimist" is one who insists, "Yes, they can!" I remain optimistic that the Palestinian leadership and people will come to want their own state more than they want the destruction of the Jewish state. I remain optimistic as well that the Palestinian people will come to see that the enemies of Israel are not necessarily their friends—that the old adage "the enemy of my enemy is my friend" is often false and self-destructive. Many of Israel's most virulent enemies, such as David Duke, Pat Buchanan, and Robert Novak, do not care one whit about the welfare of the Palestinian people. They support their cause only because their perceived enemy is the Jewish state. If it were not, these bigots, who have little sympathy for other "oppressed" ethnic groups, would show nothing but contempt for the anti-American violence committed in their name. Many supporters of Israel—and I count myself among them—care deeply about the Palestinian people. I am pro-Israel and pro-Palestine. I want to see a vibrant, democratic, economically viable, peaceful Palestinian state existing side by side with Israel.

A recent talk I gave to a large audience at the University of California at Irvine was revealing in this regard. I asked audience members how many of them would count themselves as generally pro-Israel. About a hundred or so students raised their hands. I then asked these pro-Israel students how many of them would favor a Palestinian state existing in peace alongside Israel. Every single one of them raised a hand. I next asked how many audience members counted themselves as supportive of the Palestinian side. A similar number raised their hands. I asked those pro-Palestine students how many of them would support a peaceful, nonexpansionist Israel located beside a Palestinian state. Not a single person raised a hand.

The hundreds of students and faculty members who identified themselves as neither pro-Israel nor pro-Palestine saw that the willingness to reach a compromise peace that would be good for the people on both sides of the conflict—a two-state solution—was far greater on the Israeli side than on the Palestinian side. They saw that the pro-Israel students were also pro-Palestine, whereas the pro-Palestine advocates were anti-Israel. Sadly, what the students saw at Irvine was, in some respects, a microcosm of the world at large.

In that sense, this "case against" book is a positive book, because by exposing Israel's enemies as the enemies of a realistic, compromise peace, it may help to promote the kind of enduring peace that will serve the interests not only of the Israeli and the Palestinian people but of the whole world as well.

Peace is never easy to achieve, and it is not in the hands of Israel alone, as some of Israel's enemies suggest. I challenge the enemies of Israel to dispute the following propositions:

- If Israel's military enemies—Hamas, Hezbollah, Iran, and other terrorist groups and nations—were to lay down their arms, stop firing rockets, stop sending suicide bombers, and stop threatening to wipe Israel off the map, there would be peace.

- If Israel were to lay down its arms, there would be genocide.

This is the sad reality that Israel's enemies forget or ignore, when they blame Israel alone for the current situation in the Mideast. It is to these enemies we now turn, starting with former president Jimmy Carter.

1 The Case against President Jimmy Carter

I've known Jimmy Carter since February 12, 1976. That was the day the then obscure presidential candidate sent me a handwritten note from "Plains, Georgia," telling me that he had been "impressed with [my] ideas on crime and punishment," which I had expressed in a recent *New York Times Magazine* article. He asked for my help with "other ideas" that would be "very valuable to [him]" in his campaign. A "cc" on the bottom of the page to "Stu" indicated that he had sent a copy to Stuart Eisenstadt, his chief domestic assistant and a former student of mine. Stuart, who was a committed Zionist and an active member of the Atlanta Jewish community, had served as an important adviser to Carter when he was governor of Georgia. Stuart was then a leading figure in the former peanut farmer's unlikely run for president.

When I received the letter, I barely knew who Carter was, but I had always liked Stuart, who in addition to being a brilliant student was a great basketball player. So when Stuart called and told me that Carter was coming to speak at Harvard and wanted to meet me, I agreed. We met in one of Harvard's undergraduate houses, where he repeated his request for my assistance on criminal justice matters.

I immediately liked the gracious Southerner and agreed to work on his campaign. In June of that year, *Newsweek* ran a cover story on "Carter's game plan" that included a page on "the Carter brain trust."[1] I was featured in that story, with my photograph (beard, long hair, and aviator glasses) and a report that I was a key part of the brain trust and a member of Carter's "task force on criminal justice." Following Carter's election and inauguration, my name was included on several lists of lawyers the president was considering for Supreme Court appointments if any vacancies were to occur. (None did.)

When Natan (Anatoly) Sharansky was arrested in the Soviet Union in March 1977 and charged with spying for the United States, I was asked by his wife and his mother to represent him. I went to the White House to urge Carter to formally deny that Sharansky had ever spied for us. Stuart advised me that it would be a difficult sell, since no president ever admits or denies that anyone was an American spy. But after considerable efforts on Stuart's part and mine, President Carter agreed to issue an unprecedented denial, saying he was "completely convinced" that Sharansky was innocent. Carter repeated his denial after Sharansky's conviction in July 1978, declaring that the charges were "patently false."[2]

Several years later, I closely followed the Camp David meetings between Israeli prime minister Menachem Begin and Egyptian leader Anwar Sadat. My friend Aharon Barak was Israel's chief legal adviser at the talks, Stuart was an important adviser to Carter, and another former Harvard Law student, Osama El-Baz, was one of the leaders of the Egyptian negotiating team. Once peace was finally achieved, I was invited to the White House ceremony on March 26, 1979.

I campaigned for Carter during his losing reelection campaign in 1980, and I considered myself a friend and a supporter during his years of active retirement and good works. I was not then aware of some of Carter's lapses of judgment, such as his failed intervention on behalf of an ex-Nazi SS guard.[3] In 1987, the former president forwarded a letter from the daughter of Waffen-SS guard Martin Bartesch to the U.S. Department of Justice's Office of Special Investigation, which had deported Bartesch and taken away his citizenship. Bartesch had been a guard at the Mauthausen death camp whose involvement in the murder of prisoners had been documented by the Nazis themselves. After the war, he lied about his past to gain entry to the United States. His daughter's letter to the government claimed that Bartesch had "no control over his destiny" during World War II. Carter attached a note in his own hand: "I hope that, in cases like this, that special consideration can be given to affected families for humanitarian reasons. Jimmy Carter." It was the first of many humanitarian actions by Carter, siding with those who murdered Jews over those who protected Jews from being murdered.

Carter's "humanitarianism" seems to go in one direction only. His latest humanitarian intervention has taken the form of support for Hamas, which fires rockets at civilians in Sderot and other populated Israeli areas, rather than support for the victims of terrorism. On April 9, 2008, it was announced that Carter would visit Khaled Meshal, the leader of Hamas, in Damascus. He was strongly advised against doing so by the U.S. State Department, but he said that he felt "quite at ease" meeting with the leaders of the terrorist group.[4] Before his visit with Hamas, Carter had never visited Israeli victims of Hamas rockets, but he made a point of stopping briefly in Sderot to show support for victims before his meeting with Meshal. But his shallow show of support for the victims of Hamas terrorism did not stop him from calling on the European Union to break from the United States and recognize the legitimacy of Hamas, despite that group's continuing terrorism and refusal to accept Israel's existence.

The last time I saw Carter in person was in January 2006, when we were both invited to speak at the Herzliya Conference in Israel. Following his talk, I asked the first question from the audience. Although my question had a somewhat critical tone, Carter's response to me could not have been warmer or more personal. We met and talked after the session, and he told me he was going to observe the Palestinian parliamentary elections the following day, as I was also. Carter assured me that Hamas would be soundly defeated, because most Palestinians wanted peace. We parted amicably, with mutual regards to and from Stuart. Carter did not tell me that he was about to publish an explosive book titled *Palestine: Peace Not Apartheid*. Nor did he tell Stuart, his dear friend and adviser, or most of his other Jewish friends and supporters. I first learned of the title of the book from a journalist who called me for a comment. I said I didn't believe Carter would have written such a book. The journalist then e-mailed me a press release.

When I told Stuart about the forthcoming book and its incendiary title, he, too, expressed surprise and disbelief. Stuart said that he would call Carter and try to persuade him to change the title. Several other friends and colleagues did as well, to no avail. The book was published amid great fanfare and controversy, which assured its ascent on the best-seller lists. Carter announced that he had written the book and had deliberately included the explosive word *apartheid* in the title to "stimulate discussion [and] debate."[5] It was only natural that Carter would be expected to participate in that debate.

So when some hard-left professors at Brandeis University invited Carter to discuss his book on campus, the president of Brandeis, Jehuda Reinharz, proposed a debate, at Stuart's suggestion.[6] Stuart, a member of Brandeis's Board of Trustees, also put my name forward as the appropriate person to debate Carter. I had worked for Carter, admired him, and had written the first mainstream review of his book—a respectful review in which I wondered why Carter, "generally a careful man," had allowed so many errors to mar his book.[7] Carter adamantly refused to debate me, saying, "I don't want to have a conversation even indirectly with Dershowitz. There is no need for me to debate somebody who, in my opinion, knows nothing about the situation in Palestine."[8] That was, of course, untrue, as Carter well knew, since we had discussed my several visits to the Palestinian Authority during our conversation only months earlier in Herzliya.

Following is part of an op-ed piece I wrote for the *Boston Globe:*

> You can always tell when a public figure has written an indefensible book: when he refuses to debate it in the court of public opinion. . . . Carter's refusal to debate wouldn't be so strange if it weren't for the fact that he claims that he wrote the book precisely so as to start debate over the issue of the Israel-Palestine peace process. If that were really true, Carter would be thrilled to have the opportunity to debate. Authors should be accountable for their ideas and their facts. Books shouldn't be like chapel, delivered from on high and believed on faith. . . . When Jimmy Carter's ready to speak at Brandeis, or anywhere else, I'll be there.[9]

To its credit, Brandeis came up with a compromise under which Carter spoke first, left the stage, and then I followed—about half an hour later. Most of the students remained, although some from the hard left walked out on my talk. C-SPAN carried both of our talks sequentially, turning it into the functional equivalent of a virtual debate, although questions from the audience to Carter were selected in advance and filtered through a group of his supporters. During my lecture, I took live questions from the audience, including several hostile ones, and allowed each person the chance to follow up his or her question with a rebuttal.

Carter's talk at Brandeis bore little resemblance to his book and to his many television and radio interviews. It was conciliatory in tone and compromising in substance. It had all the hallmarks of having been drafted by Stuart Eisenstadt. Carter backed away from some of his claims and apologized for "improper and stupid" wording in a passage that appeared to condone Palestinian terror. I had prepared to rebut what Carter had said in his book, and so I had to quickly change my approach. "Had he written a book which was similar to what he said from the stage," I told the audience, "I do not believe there would have been much controversy." I acknowledged that Carter supported the two-state solution and the peace process but noted that his book had done Israel—and peace—much damage.

I proceeded to point out specific misstatements in his book, all of which were against Israel. I criticized the former president for supporting Yasser Arafat's decision to walk away from the Clinton-Barak offer of Palestinian statehood in all of Gaza and more than 95 percent of the West Bank. I accused Carter of having become an advocate for the maximalist Palestinian view, rather than a broker for peace. That, to my mind, was the true tragedy of a decent man who worked so hard for peace and who now in effect was pressuring the Palestinians not to accept reasonable compromise and reasonable peace.[10]

In the weeks and months following the Brandeis debate, Carter's tone became more shrill and his substantive accusations against Israel more one-sided, even bigoted. He went so far as to publicly deny that he had been invited to debate me. Speaking to an audience at George Washington University several weeks after the Brandeis event, he said that he had "never received any invitation to debate, contrary to what a Harvard professor has said."[11]

Reportage in the *Boston Globe*—which Carter has never challenged—makes it clear that he was lying: "Last month, the former president told the *Globe* he had declined an invitation from a university trustee to speak at Brandeis, because it came with the suggestion he debate Alan Dershowitz, a professor at Harvard Law School who has criticized Carter's book *Palestine: Peace Not Apartheid*."[12]

Carter was also well aware of the numerous invitations to debate that I had issued in newspapers, on television, and over the radio. He simply lied in order to protect his views from scrutiny.[13] If a lawyer engaged in such mendacity in court, he would be disciplined, if not disbarred, especially if the lie was part of a pattern of lying, as is the case with Carter. On April 22, 2008, Secretary of State Condoleezza Rice accused Carter of a similar falsehood: Carter had denied that the State Department told him not to meet with Hamas leaders. Rice was "blunt in her account" that it had.[14] "We counseled President Carter against . . . having contacts with Hamas," Rice insisted.[15]

Carter claimed to have been the victim of an orchestrated campaign of vilification, which was designed to quash any criticism of Israel. In fact, no one had objected to mere criticism of Israel, only to the support he had given to the delegitimization of the Jewish state by using the explosive and incorrect term *apartheid.*

The accusation of apartheid—an accusation Carter has never apologized for or retracted—is no mere exaggeration. It associates the Jewish state with an evil system that was declared a "crime against humanity." That phrase, used against apartheid South Africa in the 1970s, was first applied by the Allies to describe the Armenian genocide in World War I and was subsequently used by the Allies against the Nazis in World War II.[16] To accuse Israel of apartheid is therefore to strike at the foundations of the state itself. It implies—and many of those who make the accusation declare openly—that Israel is illegitimate, racist, and deserving of destruction. Just as the apartheid system in South Africa had to be dismantled entirely, the analogy posits, "apartheid Israel" must be utterly destroyed. It also suggests that academic boycotts and divestment campaigns, the tools used against apartheid South Africa, are appropriate for use against Israel.

Carter, despite the title of his book, offered no shred of evidence to prove that Israel practices apartheid. Search through the pages carefully, and you will find the word *apartheid* mentioned only three times. Carter does not even define what the term means. Jeffrey Goldberg, reviewing Carter's book for the *Washington Post,* accused Carter of using "bait and switch" tactics, by failing to prove what he alleges.[17] Sometimes you really can tell a book by its cover, or at least by its phony title. Carter even admits, toward the end of his book, that the term *apartheid* is problematic: the situation in Israel today "is unlike that in South Africa—not racism, but the acquisition of land."[18] He does not add that Israel gained control of that territory in a defensive war, that it has long offered to trade land for peace, and that it has pulled its settlers and soldiers off much of these lands in genuine good faith.

The Israel-apartheid analogy is a fraud, one that Carter per-petuates by citing imaginary sources. At Brandeis, he claimed that South Africa's Nelson Mandela had "used the same description."[19] Carter appeared to be citing a fake memorandum from "Nelson Mandela" that was written by Arjan El-Fassed, an Arab journalist living in the Netherlands.[20] Anti-Israel activists often circulate the memorandum, pretending it is authentic, as does Carter, who has personal access to Mandela and has to know that the quote was made up.[21]

What is most striking about Carter's use of the word *apartheid* is his refusal to apply such labels to countries that actually deserve it. The Arab dictatorship in Sudan, for example, has murdered hundreds of thousands of black Muslims in the western province of Darfur. Its government-backed militia, the *janjaweed,* has dis-placed millions of people and used systematic rape as a weapon of terror. Yet when Carter visited Darfur in October 2007, he vehemently objected to the use of the term *genocide* to describe what was happening in Darfur. He said, "There is a legal defini-tion of genocide and Darfur does not meet that legal standard. The atrocities were horrible but I do not think it qualifies to be called genocide."[22] He said this in the presence of a "group of elders," including Archbishop Desmond Tutu. Carter added, "If you read the law textbooks . . . you'll see very clearly that it's not genocide and to call it genocide falsely just to exaggerate a horrible situation—I don't think it helps."[23] Carter was wrong. The UN Convention on the Prevention and Punishment of the Crime of Genocide of 1948 defines genocide as killing "with intent to destroy, in whole or in part, a national, ethnical, racial or religious group." Clearly, that is precisely what is happening in Darfur, but because the slaughter is being conducted with the support of Arab governments, the hard left that Carter has come to represent has refused to con-demn it as genocide. Experienced prosecutors at the International Criminal Court in the Hague have a different view of the law.

Carter is wrong on apartheid, too. The International Convention on the Suppression and Punishment of the Crime of Apartheid of 1973 defines *apartheid* as "inhuman acts committed for the purpose of establishing and maintaining domination by one racial group of persons over any other racial group of persons." That definition was reaffirmed by the Rome Statute of the International Criminal Court in 2002: "'The crime of apartheid' means inhumane acts . . . committed in the context of an institutionalized regime of systematic oppression and domination by one racial group over any other racial group or groups and committed with the intention of maintaining that regime." That might describe the policies of Sudan's Arab regime against black Darfuris. It has no relevance at all to the Israeli-Palestinian conflict, which Carter acknowledges is not based on racism, but rather, he claims, on "acquisition of land." Racism is the sine qua non of apartheid, and without it the word has no accepted meaning except as an inflammatory provocation. The Jews of Israel are multiracial, multiethnic, and multireligious, comprising Europeans, Africans, Ethiopians, Yemenites, Georgians, and other groups. Israelis are not a "racial group." They are not even a uniform religious group. Some actively practice Judaism, many do not. More than a million Israelis practice other religions. But Israel, unlike its neighboring Arab nations, does not use religious coercion; neither is there segregation or discrimination against minorities who are not Jewish.

Yet Carter reserves his legal "expertise" for Israel alone. Before we examine the reason behind Carter's double standard, it is worth noting that his book is filled with errors of fact as well as of law, in addition to those regarding the false charge of "apartheid." As I wrote in one review, "Mr. Carter's book is so filled with simple mistakes of fact and deliberate omissions that were it a brief filed in a court of law, it would be struck and its author sanctioned for misleading the court. Mr. Carter too is guilty of misleading the court of public opinion."[24] Other reviewers also pointed to numerous factual errors in Carter's slim volume. Yet Carter brazenly told the *Washington Post* that "most critics have not seriously disputed or even mentioned the facts."[25] This is simply a lie and Carter knows it. He also lied when he told Larry King that "everything in the book, I might say, is completely accurate."[26] A mere listing of all of Mr. Carter's mistakes and omissions would fill a volume the size of his book. The appendix to this book lists dozens of simple factual errors, all of which could easily have been caught and corrected by a first-year college student tasked to find the truth. But truth was obviously not Carter's goal, since all of his errors paint Israel in a false, negative light. For example, Carter states that Israel carried out a preemptive strike against Jordan in the 1967 conflict.[27] But historians agree that Jordan struck first, after Israel pleaded with King Hussein not to join the war. In addition to such naked and malevolent errors, Carter is guilty of omitting key facts and context. He criticizes Israel's attack on Iraq's Osirak nuclear reactor in 1981 without mentioning that it was the site of Saddam Hussein's nuclear weapons program, that Iran had already attacked the site the year before, and that the UN had failed to take any action to prevent Iraq from acquiring nuclear weapons. Carter also fails to mention that Iraqi leaders had said that the nuclear bombs Iraq planned to build were specifically intended for use against Israel alone.

Carter criticizes Israel for refusing to accept UN Security Council Resolution 242 but leaves out the fact that Israel did, in fact, approve the resolution's "land for peace" formula, while the Arab states categorically rejected it. At Khartoum in August 1967, the Arab states issued their infamous "three no's"—"no peace, no recognition, no negotiation."[28] Palestinian leader Yasser Arafat did not even accept Resolution 242 until 1988, under heavy U.S. pressure. Israel has consistently defended and maintained sites that are holy to Christians and Muslims, as well as Jewish sites, while Jordan destroyed synagogues—including an ancient site that was the Jewish equivalent of the Dome of the Rock—and other Jewish institutions as soon as it conquered the Jewish Quarter of Jerusalem in 1948.[29] Yet Carter attacks Israel's administration of these sites, disregarding Israel's long record of careful stewardship and the Palestinian Authority's record of failure.[30] In recent years, Palestinians have destroyed Jewish holy sites and burned Christian churches, but Carter ignores these events.

Carter also misrepresents negotiations between Israel and the Palestinians. He labels one map the "Israeli Interpretation" of the Clinton parameters of December 2001, when in fact that map is the actual U.S. proposal, which Israel agreed to but the Palestinians did not.[31] (Carter was also accused of misusing maps from Dennis Ross's book *The Missing Peace* without attribution.)

Other errors include Carter's false claim that the Palestinians have long accepted a two-state solution and Israel has rejected it, when in fact the opposite is true; his grim depiction of the Israeli legal system, which in actuality leads the world in human rights jurisprudence, and whose Supreme Court is trusted even by Israel's harshest critics; and his claim that the Second Lebanon War started when Hezbollah "captured" two Israeli soldiers, when they were really kidnapped by the terrorists.[32] Hezbollah has not even provided a single sign that the soldiers are alive. If the Israeli soldiers had in fact been "captured," then their captors would have been required to abide by the provisions of the Geneva Convention relative to the Treatment of Prisoners of War.[33] But Hezbollah—and Hamas, which is still holding Israeli soldier Gilad Shalit—has made no effort to comply with international law. In both cases, Israel's soldiers were illegally kidnapped, and their fate remains largely unknown. Carter is simply, plainly, and malevolently wrong.

The list of errors goes on. Carter notes that "Christian and Muslim Arabs had continued to live in this same land since Roman times" but leaves out the fact that Jews have lived in Jerusalem (where they were a majority since the first modern census), Hebron, Tzfat, and other cities for far longer—continuously, in many cases. He also ignores the expulsion of hundreds of thousands of Jews from Arab lands in the years since 1948. He hardly touches on the fact that Israel accepted the UN partition plan in 1947, while the Palestinians and the Arabs rejected it. He claims that Israel has caused an "exodus of Christians from the Holy Land," when there is actually a net *influx* of Christians (including Christian Arabs) into Israel. He disregards the Islamization of the Palestinian Authority by Hamas and the rise of Hezbollah in southern Lebanon, both of which are the primary factors driving Christian emigration from the region.

Carter's mistakes aren't limited to Israel. He claims that "dialogue on controversial issues is a privilege to be extended only as a reward for subservient behavior and withheld from those who reject U.S. demands"—a gross exaggeration that confuses terrorist states such as Iran and Syria, which the United States does isolate with states such as Saudi Arabia, Egypt, France, and China, with which the United States disagrees but consults all the time.

Most egregious of all is Carter's use of the word *apartheid* and other terms associated with it. He fails to describe the apartheid system in South Africa, which does not remotely resemble Israel—the pervasive racial segregation laws; the censorship of the media; the banning of political parties; the torture and murder of human rights activists in detention; the indoctrination of children with racial ideology; the removal of voting rights from blacks; the use of the death penalty for political crimes; and so on. His omission is obviously willful, because any accurate description of real apartheid would make it clear to the reader that the word applies far more precisely to Palestinian governance than to Israeli governance, even on the West Bank.

All of these terrible features of apartheid were well known to those of us who were active in the antiapartheid movement. When Nelson Mandela was in prison, I was one of the lawyers enlisted to work for his release. When I was invited to speak in South Africa in the 1980s, I refused to go, because the apartheid government said it would offer me a visa only if I did not criticize its policies. Jimmy Carter should know the difference, too. It was during his term in the White House that the United States joined the international arms embargo against South Africa (although it did not take part in the economic sanctions until Congress passed and President Ronald Reagan signed the Comprehensive Anti-Apartheid Act in 1986). President Carter spoke against apartheid while still vigorously opposing a Palestinian state.[34]

As Rhoda Kadalie and Julia Bertelsmann, two black South African women, wrote recently,

> Israel is not an apartheid state. . . . Arab citizens of Israel can vote and serve in the Knesset; black South Africans could not vote until 1994. There are no laws in Israel that discriminate against Arab citizens or separate them from Jews. . . . South Africa had a job reservation policy for white people; Israel has adopted pro-Arab affirmative action

measures in some sectors. Israeli schools, universities and hospitals make no distinction between Jews and Arabs. An Arab citizen who brings a case before an Israeli court will have that case decided on the basis of merit, not ethnicity. This was never the case for blacks under apartheid.[35]

Kadalie and Bertelsmann are critical of Israel's policies in the occupied territories but add that "racism and discrimination do not form the rationale for Israel's policies and actions. . . . In the West Bank, measures such as the ugly security barrier have been used to prevent suicide bombings and attacks on civilians, not to enforce any racist ideology. Without the ongoing conflict and the tendency of Palestinian leaders to resort to violence, these would not exist."[36]

At a recent concert by Daniel Barenboim with an orchestra composed of Israelis and Palestinians held at the Young Men's Christian Association in Jerusalem, I sat next to an Israeli Arab who was Israel's minister of culture. This is a cabinet position. The audience, too, was a mixture of Israelis and Palestinians, many from the West Bank. Hardly a feature of real apartheid!

Carter ignores these realities, and in wrongly exploiting the apartheid analogy, he has devalued the antiapartheid struggle itself. According to Congressman John Conyers, who helped found the Congressional Black Caucus, applying the word *apartheid* to Israel belittles real racism and apartheid; the word "does not serve the cause of peace, and the use of it against the Jewish people in particular, who have been victims of the worst kind of discrimination, discrimination resulting in death, is offensive and wrong."[37]

The apartheid analogy is not the only analogy Carter abuses. When he was asked by Chris Matthews in a live television interview whether he believed that Israel's "persecution" of Palestinians was "even worse . . . than a place like Rwanda," Carter answered, "Yes. I think—yes."[38] The comparison is obscene. Nearly one million civilians were murdered in a matter of weeks during the Rwandan genocide. The number of Israelis and Palestinians killed during any comparable period of time has, at worst, been in the hundreds, nearly all the direct result of Palestinian terrorism and Israeli efforts to stop it. The Rwandan victims never had a chance to prevent the killing. In contrast, the Palestinians have repeatedly chosen violence instead of negotiations and have refused to sign or honor any peace deal, from the generous terms of the Peel Commission in 1937 until the present day. To compare Rwanda to Israel is insulting not only to Israel, but to the memory of the Rwandan victims, who were brutally raped, tortured, mutilated, and murdered by soldiers and machete-wielding militias and civilians in what can only be described as a genocide.

Carter has backtracked on his Rwanda analogy, saying that he did not want to debate "ancient history about Rwanda."[39] But the "genocide" bell cannot be un-rung. When you use the example of Rwanda in the context of a debate about human rights, it is commonly understood that you are referring to genocide. Similarly, the example of South Africa refers to racial segregation and political oppression. Carter uses these analogies, although he knows they do not fit, precisely because of such connotations. Yet he criticizes others for using the word *genocide* to characterize the mass killings in Darfur. This is not merely hypocrisy; it is double-standard bigotry.

When called upon to defend his arguments, Carter has refused—because he knows he cannot. Instead, he has resorted to a crude tactic with a long, infamous history: namely, blaming Jews for his own shortcomings. To Carter, the problem is not his unsubstantiated claims or the relentless hatred of Israel's enemies that has blocked peace for years; rather, it is covert Jewish domination and disloyalty. Carter claimed, for example, that the United States sides with Israel for the following reason: "because of powerful political, economic, and religious forces in the U.S., Israeli government decisions are rarely questioned or condemned, voices from Jerusalem dominate our media, and most American citizens are unaware of circumstances in the occupied territories."[40] This is untrue. The grievances of Palestinians dominate news coverage in the United States, as well as in European and Middle Eastern media. On U.S. campuses, the issue of Palestinian rights pushes more urgent and pressing human rights issues Darfur, Zimbabwe, Tibet—to the margins. No other occupied or victimized group receives as much attention per capita as the Palestinians, despite their refusal to accept offers to end the occupation in exchange for peace. The radical anti-Israel academic Beshara Doumani, for example, writing in a recent issue of the *Journal of Palestine Studies*—hardly a pro-Israel publication—acknowledged, "For a variety of reasons, the world has paid more attention to this conflict than to any other in modern history. This attention can turn the weaknesses of Palestinians into sources of strength."[41]

The accusations that Jews control the media and that they use their "political, economic, and religious forces" against the countries in which they live has a long and sordid history. They have been the staple of extremist Jew-haters throughout history. To read them in the words of a former U.S. president is sad and disgraceful.

Initially, I defended Carter against accusations of anti-Semitism. I wrote in the *Jerusalem Post*, "In his book, *Palestine: Peace Not Apartheid*, Carter unfairly, one-sidedly, ahistorically—even indecently—condemns Israeli policies, but in my view he does not cross the line into overt anti-Semitism."[42] His attacks on Israel, vehement and ill-informed though they were, were not in themselves anti-Semitic. The problem, I noted, was what Carter had said to defend his book whenever his bogus factual claims have been challenged. On *Larry King Live*, for example, Carter claimed that "the oppression of the Palestinians by Israeli forces in the occupied territories is horrendous. And it's not something that has been acknowledged or even discussed in this country. . . . It is not debated at all in this country."[43] When King asked Carter to explain why, Carter evaded the question. "I don't know," he said. But he repeated his claim at every opportunity. "For the last 30 years," he wrote in the *Los Angeles Times* in December 2006, "I have witnessed and experienced the severe restraints on any free and balanced discussion of the facts."[44] But no one has prevented him from making his opinions known, even without basis in fact.

Carter's claim of a thirty-year-silence would include his entire presidential term, which began in January 1977. Thus, he expects the world to believe, without proof, that even when he held the most influential office in the mightiest country on the planet, he was being censored by "powerful political, economic, and religious forces." This is the stuff of ranting conspiracy theorists, not former presidents or Nobel laureates.

As Walt and Mearsheimer had done, Carter points the finger at the "Israel lobby": "This reluctance to criticize any policies of the Israeli government is because of the extraordinary lobbying efforts of the American-Israel Public Affairs Committee and the absence of any significant contrary voices," Carter claimed.[45] He added, "It would be almost politically suicidal for members of Congress to espouse a balanced position between Israel and Palestine, to suggest that Israel comply with international law or to speak in defense of justice or human rights for Palestinians. Very few would ever deign to visit the Palestinian cities of Ramallah, Nablus, Hebron, Gaza City, or even Bethlehem and talk to the beleaguered residents." This claim is demonstrable nonsense. Many U.S. leaders and public representatives have visited the West Bank and Gaza and offered support for Palestinian rights and goals. Carter did not limit his accusations to the "Israel lobby." He also stated, falsely, that "book reviews in the mainstream media have been written mostly by representatives of Jewish organizations."[46] He must know this to be a lie, unless he believes that all Jews are somehow "representatives" of Jewish organizations. The most critical reviews were written by Michael Kinsley, Ethan Bronner, Jeffrey Goldberg, and me. None of us are representatives of Jewish organizations—unless he believes that all Jews belong to some uniform and organized conspiracy. On NBC's *Meet the Press*, Carter claimed that the "Jewish lobby"—a term even Walt and Mearsheimer eschew—was part of the problem, never defining what he meant but leaving a clear implication of dual loyalty against "Jewish" Americans.[47]

One is left to conclude, sadly, that Jimmy Carter has resorted to one of the oldest and deadliest conspiracy theories—the myth of Jewish money, power, and control—to defend his indefensible claims. I had given him the benefit of the doubt, but I can do so no longer. One of the telltale signs of Carter's descent into scapegoating is how loudly he complains about being accused—unjustly, he says—of anti-Jewish prejudice. He told his audience at Brandeis, "This is the first time that I've ever been called . . . an anti-Semite."[48] That is not quite true, and he certainly knows that his harshest critics have made such accusations before.[49] Journalists Andrew and Leslie Cockburn, who generally sympathize with Carter's views on Israel, reported that when Carter was told that Israeli leader Menachem Begin was advising Carter's political opponents, Carter said, "If I get back in . . . I'm going to fuck the Jews."[50] During the 1976 Democratic primaries, he said of Jewish voters, "[Senator Henry] Jackson has all the Jews anyway. We get the Christians."[51] But Carter now finds it useful to paint himself as a victim, to make his own views seem more credible, and to silence his critics by portraying them as intolerant toward any criticism of Israel.

Ironically, while Carter makes use of anti-Semitic stereotypes, especially regarding money, it is he who has been bought off by millions of dollars in donations from Arab governments that refuse to recognize Israel and from Arab rulers who actively promote Jew-hatred in the Middle East and elsewhere. Investigative journalists have revealed the extent to which Carter has been "bought and paid for" by Arab and Islamic money. The Carter Center, a philanthropic foundation that the former president started after leaving office, has received donations in excess of $1 million from Saudi Arabia, the United Arab Emirates, and the Sultanate of Oman; and groups and individuals with close ties to these governments, including OPEC, the Saudi Binladin Group, and the late Saudi king Fahd, a "founder" member of the center.[52] Other founders included the late Agha Hasan Abedi, whose Bank of Credit and Commerce International (BCCI) was an elaborate criminal enterprise fronted by Saudi billionaire Gaith Pharaon. As journalist Rachel Ehrenfeld noted in an exposé of Carter's funders, BCCI had ideological goals: building "the best bridge to help the world of Islam, and the best way to fight the evil influence of the Zionists."[53] And these are only the donations we know about. Ehrenfeld has documented other contributions of a more personal nature, including Saudi funds that rescued Carter's failing peanut farm in 1976. Some donations have gone to Carter's presidential library and various other Carter projects. These sources have aims directly at odds with U.S. foreign policy and American values at home.

Carter has also accepted half a million dollars and an award from Sheik Zayed bin Sultan al-Nahyan, then the ruler of the United Arab Emirates.[54] Zayed's Center for Coordination and Follow-Up was the Arab League's official think tank until 2003. During that time, it promoted Holocaust denial, 9/11 conspiracy theories, and anti-Semitic claims that "Zionists," not Nazis, had killed the Jews of Europe.[55] When a student discovered that Harvard Divinity School had accepted $2.5 million from Zayed, the school returned the money. Not so Jimmy Carter, who admitted to his audience at Brandeis that he gave Zayed's money to the Carter Center and refused to give it back, even once the views of his patron were exposed.[56] Upon receiving the money from Zayed, Carter gave a speech in which he proclaimed, "This award has special significance for me because it is named for my personal friend, Sheik Zayed bin Sultan al-Nahyan." Carter said that donations from "Mideast Arab nations" represent a small percentage of his foundation's overall budget, although he refuses to disclose financial reports that would allow an independent check of this dubious claim. Regardless, the donations have been enough to buy his silence on human rights abuses throughout the Arab and Islamic world. The Carter Center, since receiving payoffs from Saudi sources, has said little about Saudi Arabia's abuse of women, non-Muslims, and prisoners, or about the autocratic rule of the Saudi regime. Indeed, an examination of the Carter Center's human rights activities reveals that while it devotes a disproportionately large amount of attention to Israel, it says and does little about the Sudan, Iran, or North Korea, to name just a few places with far more pressing rights problems. It refuses to scrutinize the record of its contributors in the Arab world or question the near-total absence of democracy there.

Carter seems to recognize this kind of prejudice only when it serves his interest to do so. In a speech to the UN Human Rights Council in March 2007, he observed that its "singular focus on the violations committed by Israel, while failing to address with the same vigor serious human rights abuses in many other parts of the world, has been counterproductive" (not immoral or bigoted—just "counterproductive").[57] Yet he is unwilling or unable to admit that he himself is often guilty of such bias. Nor has he tried to correct it because his silence has been fully paid for. Once again, he is speaking out of both sides of his mouth.

A particularly striking example of this is Carter's refusal to recognize and condemn Palestinian terror against Israel with the moral fervor he reserves for Israeli actions. Shortly before the Brandeis event, he appeared on Al-Jazeera television to discuss his book and claimed that Palestinian rockets from Gaza that target Israeli civilians are not "terrorism": "I don't really consider . . . I wasn't equating the Palestinian missiles with terrorism."[58] These are antipersonnel rockets aimed at Israeli towns, schools, shopping malls, and hospitals, but to Carter they are not terrorism. Carter did criticize suicide bombings on Israeli buses. In an apparent attempt to appease his audience, however, he refused to condemn suicide bombings on moral grounds. Instead, he focused on the tactical and propaganda disadvantages for the Palestinian cause: "Such acts create a rejection of the Palestinians among those who care about them. It turns the world away from sympathy and support for the Palestinian people. That's why I said that acts of terrorism like I just described are suicidal for the popularity and support for the Palestinian cause."[59] Carter also suggested that the deliberate targeting of Israeli children by Palestinian terrorists was morally equivalent to Israel's accidental killing of Palestinian children (who are, in some cases, armed) in legitimate attempts to stop terror. (I discuss in detail, in chapter 5, the deliberate use of human shields by Israel's military enemies as a way of forcing Israel to the terrible choice of not responding to rocket attacks on its civilians or, by responding, risking the deaths of some Palestinian civilians. Carter implicitly encourages this unlawful tactic by declaring those who fire the rockets morally equivalent to those who try to prevent the rockets from being fired.)

Journalist Joseph Lelyveld has generally supported Carter's attempts to draw analogies between Israel and apartheid South Africa, although he has also argued that Carter's use of the term was "basically a slogan, not reasoned argument." Yet even he noted that Carter failed to show empathy for Israeli victims of terror. "Carter condemns the dispatching of suicide bombers into crowds of Jewish civilians," he wrote, "but does so coolly, tersely, almost clinically, stressing that such attacks are counterproductive, without conveying the kind of visceral horror that the phenomenon arouses among Israel's supporters and many others as well. He's capable of such feelings when he turns to the [Israeli] settlements."[60] Carter's refusal to morally condemn terrorism against Israeli civilians, which even rights groups that are generally hostile to Israel (such as Amnesty International and Human Rights Watch) have recognized as "war crimes" and "crimes against humanity," highlights the shallowness of his human rights record—a shallowness that goes back to the beginning of his political career. In Georgia state politics, Carter eagerly sought racist voters. According to several Georgians interviewed on a PBS documentary,

> He courted the racist vote. There were some radio ads that he ran in 1970. He said that "Unlike Sanders, I am not trying to get the" and he sort of slid over whether it was "block" or "black" vote. But it sort of meant the same thing. . . .
>
> Carter himself was not a segregationist in 1970. But he did say things that the segregationists wanted to hear. He was opposed to busing. He was in favor of private schools. He said that he would invite segregationist governor George Wallace to come to Georgia to give a speech.[61]

Carter was a latecomer to human rights, only discovering the cause during his 1976 presidential run. As one journalist has noted, "Carter was also initially cold to the subject of human rights. His 1975 book *Why Not the Best?* issued as a launching pad for his presidential campaign, makes no mention of it. Nor did he utter a word about human rights during the 1976 primaries. It was only in the course of hammering out the Democratic Party's platform that his interest was kindled."[62]

Though Carter's presidency was generally seen as a high-water mark for human rights causes, he has been condemned by rights groups for a number of the decisions he made during his term. In 1977, for example, Carter gave millions of dollars in military assistance, as well as aircraft, to the Indonesian regime of General Suharto, which had invaded East Timor only two years earlier.[63] According to Amnesty International, that invasion and its after math resulted in the deaths of two hundred thousand people—one third of the population—who "were killed or died of starvation or disease."[64] Carter also reversed his administration's policy toward the Moroccan regime in 1979 and began to permit arms sales that allowed Morocco to maintain control of annexed Western Sahara, which it still occupies today.[65] His administration recognized the Khmer Rouge as Cambodia's legitimate rulers *after* the leader Pol Pot had slaughtered millions of people and his murderous government had been pushed out in 1979. Carter also sent arms through Saudi Arabia to the mujahideen in Afghanistan, whose fighters would later form the backbone of the Taliban and al-Qaeda. As Carter himself admitted, "We channeled assistance for those freedom fighters through Saudi Arabia, through Egypt and other places."[66] His most dramatic action on behalf of human rights—canceling the participation of U.S. athletes in the 1980 Olympics to protest the Soviet invasion of Afghanistan—is now widely regarded as having backfired and strengthened the hands of the Taliban and al-Qaeda. It did not stop Soviet tanks from rolling into Afghanistan. It helped the Taliban gain a propaganda victory. The rise of al-Qaeda (as well as the success of the ayatollahs in Iran) has been traced by some pundits to Carter's misguided foreign policy decisions.

As is typical of Jimmy Carter, the ex-president has now disclaimed responsibility for the 1980 Olympics fiasco, blaming it on the Olympic Committee, which he states was "independent of government control." That is total nonsense, since Carter threatened to revoke the passport of any U.S. athlete who defied his boycott and went to the games.[67]

Carter also bears some responsibility for the current, dreadful human rights and strategic situation in Iran. In an editorial that was critical of Carter's April 2008 meetings with Hamas leaders, in direct contradiction of U.S. policy, the *Boston Globe*—which is generally supportive of Carter—asked the following pointedly rhetorical question: "How would he have reacted if his predecessors made similar gestures while he was toasting the Shah of Iran on New Year's Eve 1977 as 'an island of stability,' or when he had the Pentagon tell Iranian generals to allow Ayatollah Khomeini to return to Iran, or when he provoked the seizure of American hostages by permitting the exiled shah to receive medical treatment in the United States?"[68]

One can explain or contextualize some of these actions by noting that they occurred against the backdrop of the cold war, in which both the United States and the Soviet Union backed unsavory client regimes. But Carter has continued to appease rogue states since then. In the mid-1990s, when a diplomatic confrontation erupted over North Korea's nuclear program, Carter intervened, expressing sympathy for dictator Kim Jong-Il and ensuring that the final agreement blocked the option of sanctions.[69] This flawed deal, which North Korea never lived up to, broke down several years later. The truth is that in his term as president and in the years since, Carter has rarely honored the principles of human rights against which he judges Israel—and Israel alone. His one-sided criticism has exposed the hypocrisy of his stance.

It would appear that Carter also bears considerable personal animus toward Israel and Israelis. On the one hand, Israel is central to his presidential legacy. Without that famous handshake on the White House lawn, Carter's presidency might be remembered only for the Iran hostage crisis, economic stagnation, and the "misery index." On the other hand, Carter seems to resent the Jewish state and its leaders. Carter certainly has some Israeli friends and supporters, mostly on the left wing of the Israeli political spectrum. He is, for example, a member of the international board of governors of the Peres Center for Peace, a pet project of Israel's long-time Labor stalwart (and current president) Shimon Peres. (So, however, is Desmond M. Tutu, who has joined anti-Israel extremists in likening Israel to apartheid South Africa.) But here is what Peres had to say about Carter's book: "To say there is apartheid, my God, what sort of an expression is that? . . . For Jimmy Carter to say that this is apartheid is for me a shock." Peres also said that Carter was "mistaken" in his claim that Hamas had unilaterally stopped terror attacks against Israel: "I mean, who is firing the missiles day in and day out every day?"[70]

Nor is Carter's dislike of Israel limited to the Israeli right wing. Rather, it is aimed at Israel itself and stems in part from his religious convictions. While many evangelical Christians are ardent—some might say too ardent—supporters of Israel, Carter's own evangelical worldview has led him to the belief that Israel is deserving of punishment because Israeli Jews are not all strictly religious. When Carter met Israeli prime minister Golda Meir, for example, he scolded her about Israel's largely "secular" culture, then said that "Israel was punished whenever its leaders turned away from devout worship of God."[71] Most observers of the Middle East would agree that religion has made conflicts far worse. But Carter frowns upon Israel's liberal, tolerant society; it falls short of his biblical ideal. Carter openly links his particular Christianity to the belief that it is his personal mission to restore true faith to the Holy Land. In many ways, the target of his book is not only Israel but also the mainstream evangelical community. That may partly account for the way he has defended his views so passionately, even when the facts are against him. His argument is grounded in faith, not reason.

One result of Carter's religious prejudice is that he always holds Israel to an impossibly high standard—one, as I have shown, that he never applies to Israel's neighbors. Carter does not care that he judges Israel more harshly than any other nation (or, for that matter, to his own administration). So does the Bible, after all.

This religious bias—and Carter's eagerness to read himself into the prophetic tradition—twists his view of reality. He cannot accept contemporary Israel or Israeli Jews for what they are. He is open, for example, about his dislike for Menachem Begin.[72] And he rarely shows affection for Israelis other than those who share his views. Contrast that with his friendliness toward the secularist Syrian dictator and mass murderer Hafez al-Assad or toward Yasser Arafat, a secular leader who was responsible for hundreds of American and Israeli deaths. Listen to the warmth with which he described a meeting with the man who directly ordered the cold-blooded murder of two U.S. diplomats and hundreds of other innocent civilians:

> Rosalynn and I met with Yasir Arafat in Gaza City, where he was staying with his wife, Suha, and their little daughter. The baby, dressed in a beautiful pink suit, came readily to sit on my lap, where I practiced the same wiles that had been successful with our children and grandchildren. A lot of photographs were taken, and then the photographers asked that Arafat hold his daughter for a while. When he took her, the child screamed loudly and reached out her hands to me, bringing jovial admonitions to the presidential candidate to stay at home enough to become acquainted with his own child.[73]

There is something profoundly unsettling about Carter's coziness with a man who, even then, was involved in terror activities and incitement against Israeli civilians—especially when contrasted with Carter's coolness toward nearly all Israeli leaders.

According to journalist Douglas Brinkley, Carter once told Arafat that he considered the Palestinians' plight his own "obsession."[74] Brinkley also wrote that both Carter and Arafat enjoyed a "shared belief that they were both ordained to be peacemakers by God." He quoted a speech that Carter wrote for Arafat that described "the excessive suffering of the Palestinians," implying that alternatives to "excessive" patience might be legitimate. Carter has never shown Israeli leaders such indulgence.

During his visit to the Mideast in 2008, Carter made a point to visit the grave of Yasser Arafat, laying a wreath and calling the mass-murderer of innocent children, women, and men—including Americans—a "dear friend." He did not visit the graves of any of Arafat's victims or of Yitzhak Rabin.

Carter's ego is also at stake. As Lelyveld—again, a sympathetic reviewer—notes, Carter spends much of his book talking about himself. "The man's ego is full of vigor," Lelyveld concludes.[75] Carter is still disgruntled about his landslide loss in 1980 to Ronald Reagan and claims all would have gone well had he remained in office. He told the *New York Times* in 2003, "Had I been elected to a second term, with the prestige and authority and influence and reputation I had in the region, we could have moved to a final solution."[76] This clumsy, counterfactual comment ignores the effect of Palestinian terrorism. Carter also routinely blames every administration that followed his own for failing to resolve the conflict. Even the *Economist* noted that Carter wrote his book as if he felt he'd been "had" by the Israelis he was negotiating with at Camp David, blaming them (and them alone) for the continued strife in the region. The review concluded that Carter's book is "simplistic and one-sided as charged."[77]

In fact, Carter's interventions in recent Israeli-Palestinian negotiations may have actually prolonged the violence. Carter argues in his book that it was Israeli Prime Minister Ehud Barak, not Arafat, who walked away from negotiations at Camp David in July 2000. This contradicts the published recollections of President Bill Clinton and U.S. negotiator Dennis Ross, who were actually there.[78] Clinton is reportedly furious at Carter for accepting Arafat's account over his.[79] Carter willfully distorts the narrative in order to shift the blame for the collapse of the peace process away from the Palestinians. Other radical anti-Israel commentators have made similar attempts to blame Israel. Bending the facts to justify their hatred of the Jewish state is their stock in trade. But it is possible that Carter may have had another motive for supporting the false, revisionist account: he may have wished to hide the extent to which he himself advised Arafat to reject Israeli offers and walk away from the table.

There is a wealth of circumstantial evidence to suggest that Carter indeed gave Arafat such advice. We know that Carter has

a long history of inserting himself into America's international negotiations, often to the disadvantage of the sitting U.S. administration.
We also know that Carter opposed—and occasionally undermined—
U.S. policy toward North Korea, Iraq, Syria, and Cuba, among
other rogue states. In addition, we know, according to Brinkley,
that Arafat had approached Carter for help in improving the PLO's
(Palestine Liberation Organization) image in the United States. We
also know that Carter actually prepared texts for Arafat to use. And
we know—because Carter tells us in his book—that he believes,
"There was no possibility that any Palestinian leader could accept
such terms [the ones offered at Camp David] and survive."[80]

On the basis of this evidence, I and several students have put
to Carter the following specific questions, which he has refused to
answer:

- Was Carter asked his advice by Yasser Arafat, or anyone else
  in the Palestinian Authority, regarding whether to accept or
  reject the offer of Palestinian statehood proposed by President
  Clinton and Israeli Prime Minister Ehud Barak at Camp David
  and/or Taba?

- If not, did Carter offer any advice on this or related issues or
  express any views about the matter before the end of January
  2001?

- If he gave any such advice, what exactly was it?

- Did he say before or at the time of these negotiations what
  we know he said thereafter, namely that "There was no possibility that any Palestinian leader could accept such terms
  and survive"? (What does this say about Carter's views of the
  Palestinian people?)

One of three possibilities must be true. First, it is possible
that Arafat did not seek or Carter did not offer Arafat—directly
or indirectly—any advice about Israel's offers at Camp David,
despite the fact that Carter was advising Arafat about his image in
the United States, and despite the connection between Carter's
own successful mediation efforts at Camp David and the new

Camp David talks. This possibility seems extremely unlikely, especially in light of the importance to Arafat's image in the United States of any decision he might make about the Clinton proposals. The other two possibilities consider the likelihood that Carter did advise Arafat. Either Carter told Arafat to do what he really thought Arafat should do—namely, to walk away from Israel's historic offer—or else he told Arafat to do the opposite of what he believed was best: accept the offer and expose himself to the risk of assassination. Carter must have been relieved when Arafat chose self-preservation over continuing the negotiations.

It is hard to believe that Carter would have withheld his advice or masked his true feelings if he believed Arafat's life was at stake. After all, if Arafat had agreed to Israel's terms or made a counteroffer that allowed talks to continue, thereby legitimizing Israel's opening bargaining position, and he had then been assassinated by Palestinian extremists, Carter would have felt deep regret. (Recall his visit to his dear friend's grave.)

Only Carter knows the truth, and only Carter can tell us, since Arafat died in 2004. I—and others—have repeatedly asked Carter these questions.

Carter has yet to provide answers, despite having promised his audience at Brandeis that he would be happy to respond to any remaining questions that could not be answered during his lecture. In dozens of appearances since then, across the United States and around the world, he has failed to comment on the compelling evidence of his intervention, nor has he attempted to refute it.

It is not hard to see why Carter would want to hide any part he played in encouraging Arafat to scuttle the peace talks. The consequences of Arafat's decision were devastating. The prediction of Saudi Arabia's Prince Bandar—that walking away would be a crime against Palestinians and all Arabs—came to sad fruition. Had Arafat accepted Israel's proposal or even offered a reasonable counterproposal that recognized the need for both sides to compromise, there would have been no second intifada, no suicide bombings, no Israeli raids, and no checkpoints or security barriers. Instead, there would be an independent Palestinian state alongside Israel, and four thousand Israelis and Palestinians would still be alive.

Whether Carter advised Arafat or not, one thing is certain: his book has fed the anti-Israel hatred that helps keep the conflict going. He has granted undue legitimacy to the claims of a once-marginal group of extremists that has sought for years to equate Israel with apartheid South Africa. That was the goal, for example, of radical activists at the disastrous UN World Conference against Racism in 2001. The conference, which was held in the South African city of Durban, ought to have been an occasion for celebrating the end of apartheid and South Africa's happy entry into the family of democratic nations. Instead, it became an anti-Semitic carnival of hatred that embarrassed the UN and shocked the free world. The attempt by radical organizations to link Israel and apartheid was largely to blame. The final declaration of the nongovernmental organizations that had gathered in Durban accused Israel of "racist methods amounting to Israel's brand of apartheid," "racist crimes against humanity," and "genocide and practices of ethnic cleansing." Though devoting several paragraphs to Israel, the declaration included only one single, solitary sentence on racism and human rights abuses in the Arab Middle East: "Arabs as a Semitic people have also suffered from alternative forms of anti-Semitism, manifesting itself as anti Arab discrimination and for those Arabs who are Muslim, also as Islamophobia."[81] This document was so offensive and one-sided, even by the standards of the UN, that then UN High Commissioner for Human Rights Mary Robinson—not a friend of Israel's by any standard—refused to commend it to the official delegates of UN member states. It was the first time, she said, that she "was not able to commend a document in its entirety," pointing specifically to the paragraphs that equated Israel's policies with apartheid and genocide.[82]

Carter's book has now made such notions acceptable within the mainstream of political discourse. Though Carter has recently been careful to apply the term *apartheid* to the West Bank and not to Israel as a whole, few of the extremists who endorse his book—including white supremacists such as David Duke and left-wing charlatans like Norman Finkelstein—care to acknowledge such hair-splitting. They are delighted that it is now less taboo than it once was to assign Israel to the same pariah category that once applied to apartheid South Africa, and which South Africa escaped only by dismantling its government and forming a new unitary state. Similarly, opponents of Israel do not want a two-state solution or an end to occupation: they want a "South African solution" that would end the existence of Israel.

Carter has given hard-line opponents of Israel the opportunity to spread their own rejectionist messages. The Council on American Islamic Relations, for example, which has been linked to terror groups, mailed Carter's book to public libraries throughout the United States.[83] Radical groups frequently cite Carter's book—not to support his call for renewed negotiations, but to support their calls for Israel's isolation and delegitimization. Churches that share Carter's religious hostility to Israel now feel that they may use anti-Israel rhetoric to justify classic anti-Jewish bigotry. In October 2007, for example, Boston's historic Old South Church hosted a conference endorsing the Israel-apartheid analogy. Quotes from Carter were featured in the program, and Archbishop Tutu delivered a keynote address accusing Jews of "fighting against God."[84]

Tutu has taken a prominent role within what Kadalie and Bertelsmann call the "cottage industry that exploits the Israel-apartheid analogy for personal and political gain."[85] Tutu has compared the struggle against apartheid in South Africa to the Palestinian struggle against Israel. "Yesterday's South African township dwellers can tell you about today's life in the Occupied Territories," he wrote in 2002.[86] Like Mearsheimer and Walt, he has also attacked Israel's supporters in the United States; Tutu went further, however, referring explicitly to the "Jewish lobby" and suggesting a comparison between the power of the Jews today and that of Hitler and other powerful leaders of the past: "People are scared in this country [the United States], to say wrong is wrong because the Jewish lobby is powerful—very powerful. Well, so what? For goodness sake, this is God's world! We live in a moral universe. The apartheid government was very powerful, but today it no longer exists. Hitler, Mussolini, Stalin, Pinochet, Milosevic, and Idi Amin were all powerful, but in the end they bit the dust."[87]

Tutu's fellow South African John Dugard has exploited the Israel-apartheid analogy for years, much to the delight of the Arab dictatorships that were instrumental in appointing him the UN Commission on Human Rights special rapporteur on the situation of human rights in the occupied Palestinian territories. Dugard's only job was to condemn alleged Israeli human rights abuses against Palestinians, not the other way around. As he admitted in his 2007 report to the UN Human Rights Council, "I shall not consider the violation of human rights caused by Palestinian suicide bombers. Nor shall I consider the violation of human rights caused by the political conflict between Fatah and Hamas in the OPT [Occupied Palestinian Territories]. . . . My mandate precludes me from examining them." Citing Carter's book, Dugard contended that "Israel's practices and policies in the OPT are frequently likened to those of apartheid South Africa."[88] Dugard had to admit that "the two regimes are different," so in order to make the Israel-apartheid analogy seem to fit, he redefined Jews as a "racial group."[89] Ironically, the last time Jews were defined as a "race" was in Nazi Germany. That is how low defenders of Carter's analogy are prepared to stoop. "Can it seriously be denied," Dugard asked, "that the purpose of such action is to establish and maintain domination by one racial group (Jews) over another racial group (Palestinians) and systematically oppressing them?"[90]

Speaking at Harvard's Kennedy School of Government later that year, Dugard seemed to condone Palestinian terrorism: "Without justifying it [suicide bombing], I think one can understand it."[91] He reiterated that view in his final report to the UN Human Rights Council in 2008: "While such acts cannot be justified, they must be understood as being a painful but inevitable consequence of colonialism, apartheid or occupation."[92] He then went on to compare Palestinian terror against Israeli civilians to European resistance to Nazi occupation in World War II. In a similar vein, Dugard's successor, Richard Falk, recently compared the situation in the territories to the Nazi Holocaust.[93] (More on this in chapter 4.)

Carter's book has given aid and comfort to such bigots. But if Carter had intended to shift the attitudes of ordinary Americans away from Israel, however, his book must be judged a dismal failure. Survey data released in May 2007, shortly after his book's successful run at the top of the best-seller lists, indicated that more than two-thirds of Americans supported Israel—the highest level ever recorded—while fewer Americans than ever said they supported the Palestinians.[94] The leadership of Carter's own Democratic Party, including Speaker of the House Nancy Pelosi and presidential candidates Hillary Clinton and Barack Obama, disagreed explicitly with Carter's views while reaffirming their support for Israel's security and for the two-state solution. The Bush administration pressed ahead with the roadmap for peace and a Palestinian state.

Carter's claims have found resonance among some overseas audiences that are more hostile to Israel. Yet the international community correctly rejected Carter's view of Hamas's rockets and supported Israel's refusal to negotiate with it while it pursued the annihilation of the Jewish state through terror, despite Carter's insistence that the European Union break with the United States over this issue. Though Carter may have achieved commercial success and strengthened the radical fringe, his book was a political failure.

Yet we ought not dismiss the long-term effects of *Palestine: Peace Not Apartheid*. The analogy between Israel and apartheid South Africa fuels anti-Semitism in the Arab world and features frequently in the forums of the United Nations. Carter's ideas allow the enemies of peace to cast their views and goals as reasonable and legitimate. The encouragement that Carter continues to provide to Arab regimes that reject Israel and to extremists who seek to undermine support for Israel in the West has left a stain on his legacy. Equally, his distortion of historical facts and his resort to execrable anti-Jewish motifs have tarnished his image as an elder statesman. If he advised Arafat to reject Israel's peace offer, as seems likely, he may be remembered not as a Nobel peace laureate but as a vain and destructive meddler.

I once worked with Jimmy Carter, and I once admired him. He is not someone I would have wanted to oppose, especially over the security and legitimacy of Israel. But it was he who has written a book with a title deliberately designed to provoke debate. Yet he refuses to debate, engage, or even acknowledge his critics. In the July 20, 2008, issue of *New York* magazine, Carter said, "I don't read Dershowitz." This from a man who describes such mass murderers and terrorists as Khaled Mashal, Yasser Arafat, and Hafez al-Assad as "very nice," and with whom he has always been willing to engage.

However substantial some of his achievements, Carter has done his best to undo them. For that, he, and not Israel, must stand in the dock and face the judgment of history. He must be exposed as an enemy of a compromise peace, an inciter of Palestinian extremism, and an apologist for those who would continue to employ terror in an effort to destroy the Jewish state.

In an article titled "The Sad End of Jimmy Carter," the French intellectual and journalist Bernard-Henri Lévy asks, "So what happened to this man?" In response, he suggests vanity, loss of touch, and "a variant of self-hatred."[95] Whatever the reason or reasons for Jimmy Carter's recent descent into the gutter of bigotry, history will not judge him kindly.

2 The Case against Professors John Mearsheimer and Stephen Walt

Although Stephen M. Walt teaches at Harvard's Kennedy School of Government, I hardly know him. I recall meeting him only once, when he moderated a talk I gave to the Wexner fellows, a group of Israeli mid-career government officials who come to Harvard for a year of study. Professor Walt seemed like a fair and decent man. He holds the Robert and Renée Belfer Chair in International Affairs, which was established at Harvard by a prominent Jewish real estate mogul in New York who was active in support of Israel and other Jewish causes.

Under the heading "It's a small world," it turns out that in the early 1970s I had represented—on a pro bono basis—a young man who had been accused of making a smoke bomb that had been planted in the offices of the world-famous music impresario Sol Hurok. The group behind the smoke bomb was the radical Jewish Defense League (JDL). The JDL opposed Hurok's importation of musicians from the Soviet Union, which was oppressing Jews and refusing to allow them to emigrate to Israel. The bomb was an immoral and stupid form of protest, and although the bomb had been designed merely to annoy and not to hurt, one woman suffocated from the smoke. She was a twenty-seven-year-old assistant in the Hurok office—and was the sister of Robert Belfer's wife. Those who made and planted the smoke bomb were charged with felony murder and faced the death penalty. I was asked to defend the bomb maker because no one else was willing to take the case. After a series of legal and constitutional maneuvers, I managed to win an appellate reversal, and all of the defendants went free. I took no pleasure in the victory, but the government had engaged in massive constitutional violations, and the Court of Appeal dismissed all charges.[1]

As you might imagine, the Belfers were understandably enraged—not only at the defendants who had killed their loved one, but at the court that had freed them and at me for having argued successfully on their behalf. I was told by a former dean of Harvard Law School that the Belfer chair and the Belfer building were both donated to the Harvard Kennedy School instead of the law school solely because I was on the law school faculty.

I can only imagine, therefore, how conflicted the Belfers must have felt when the man who holds the chair bearing their name began his vicious attack against "the Israel Lobby" in March 2006. The Belfers are prominent advocates of the U.S.-Israel relationship and therefore part of what Walt and Mearsheimer called "the Israel Lobby." The Belfers certainly must have disapproved of what Walt and his coauthor, John J. Mearsheimer of the University of Chicago, said in the "working paper" they released on the Kennedy School's Web site.[2] And I am equally certain that the Belfers must have approved of the content of my counterattack, our past disagreements notwithstanding.

On the day the Mearsheimer-Walt screed appeared on the Web, I dropped everything I was doing and began to write a rebuttal. I assembled a group of students and assigned them the task of researching every claim Walt and Mearsheimer had made in support of their accusations against the "Israel Lobby." Among their many claims, addressed in my reply, are the following:[3]

- That the "Israel Lobby," a cabal whose "core" is "American Jews," has a "stranglehold" on the mainstream media in the United States, as well as on the government, think tanks, and academia.[4]

- That the "Israel Lobby," led by the American-Israel Public Affairs Committee (AIPAC)—which the authors describe as "a de facto agent of a foreign government"—places Israel ahead of U.S. interests.[5]

- That Jews who make political contributions use their "money" to blackmail government officials, while "Jewish philanthropists" exercise "influence" over academic opinion and "police" academic programs.[6]

- That congressional staffers who are Jewish "look at certain issues in terms of their Jewishness," rather than as Americans, leading their bosses astray and betraying the trust of the voters.[7]

- That the "Israel Lobby" works against the United States because Israel's interests are not just different from but are actually opposed to America's; because America's "terrorism problem" stems from its "all[iance] with Israel"; because Israel drags the United States into unnecessary confrontations with Arab states; and because Israel spied on the United States during the cold war, feeding information to the Soviet Union, America's enemy. (A complete lie.)[8]

- That Israel cannot even claim U.S. support on principled or moral grounds because the "creation of Israel entailed a moral crime against the Palestinian people," including "massacres . . . and rapes by Jews." That Israel is not a true democracy, but a highly deficient one in which "citizenship is based on the principle of blood kinship" among Jews and only Jews.[9]

- That Israel's supporters form a protean, powerful network—which the authors identified throughout their paper with a capital "L"—that is primarily made up of Jews, and which manipulates the United States into "fighting, dying . . . and paying" for Israel's own narrow interests.[10]

• That "the Lobby" was responsible for the U.S. war against Iraq and is pushing the United States to fight Iran, Syria, and other countries.

To summarize: Mearsheimer and Walt accuse American Jews of creating a mechanism of political and social control in order to further their loyalty to Israel—which, Mearsheimer and Walt imply, trumped American Jews' loyalty to the United States—by steering U.S. foreign policy in directions that suited Israel's and not America's interests. American Jews and their friends are not only disloyal, Mearsheimer and Walt suggest, but dangerous to the United States.

If this sounds familiar, it is. It is a modern version of the oldest charge against Jews, dating back to the Book of Exodus and Pharaoh's instruction to the Egyptians as to why they should enslave the people of Israel: "Come on, let us deal wisely with them; lest they multiply, and it come to pass, that, when there falleth out any war, they join also unto our enemies, and fight against us, and so get them up out of the land."[11] It is a charge that has been repeated throughout the ages, hidden by Mearsheimer and Walt behind a facade of erudition that purports to reject anti-Semitism but copies its classic archetype. It is parroted by hard-left radicals such as Alexander Cockburn and far-right reactionaries like David Duke. It is disseminated daily by official media in the Arab and Muslim world.

The accusations leveled by Mearsheimer and Walt share the same themes as the notorious *Protocols of the Elders of Zion*, the czarist forgery whose motifs became a staple of anti-Semitic propaganda. They echo the accusations made by Nazi publications and the America First propaganda of the 1930s and early 1940s, as well as the official anti-Semitism of the Soviet Union under Stalin. Even David Duke noted, "The Harvard report contains little new information. I and a few other American commentators have for years been making the same assertions as this paper."[12] It "validates every point I have been making," Duke added.[13] All that was different was the stature of the authors and their universities, which gave undeserved credibility to the oldest and most shameless of lies.

The original Mearsheimer-Walt paper generated so much interest that within a few months it had been downloaded from the Kennedy School of Government's Web site more than 275,000 times.[14] The heavy traffic prompted Mearsheimer and Walt to prepare a book, *The Israel Lobby and U.S. Foreign Policy,* which they published the following year, and which remained a best-seller for months thereafter. (Despite their whining about not being able to publish their original paper in the United States—"I do not believe that we could have gotten it published in the United States," said Mearsheimer; "publishers told us that it was virtually impossible to get the piece published in the United States"; "the whole subject of the Israel lobby and American foreign policy is a third-rail issue"; "publishers understand that if they publish a piece like ours it would cause them all sorts of problems"—they apparently received a large advance for their book from their U.S. publisher.[15]) So much, one would have thought, for the contention that the Israel lobby manipulates the media. As I observed at the time,

> One has to wonder just how powerful this Israel Lobby is if, since exposing the Lobby and decrying its tactics and objectives, Walt and Mearsheimer have become international celebrities and campus rockstars. In fact, things have gotten so bad for Walt and Mearsheimer that just last week the *Forward* announced their book deal with Farrar, Straus and Giroux to publish an expanded version of their Israel Lobby paper.[16]

"As expected," the authors state in the book's preface, "the essay initially generated a firestorm of criticism from prominent groups or individuals in the lobby, and we were denounced as anti-Semites by the Anti-Defamation League and by writers in the *Jerusalem Post, New York Sun, Wall Street Journal* and *Washington*

Post."[17] They do not acknowledge the scathing criticism the essay received from non-Jewish academics and others who are not part of "The Israel Lobby." Nor do they cite the glee with which their essay was received by avowed anti-Semites, who cited it as proof of their rabid Jewish conspiracy theories. Alongside Duke and his white supremacists, the essay's enthusiastic distributors included, for example, Hamas and the Muslim Brotherhood, which direct violent attacks and incitement against Jews in Israel and elsewhere.[18]

The authors complain of "guilt by association," but they frequently chose such associations. Walt, for example, was the keynote speaker at a "Middle East/North Africa" conference at Harvard in the fall of 2007 that refused to include campus Israel groups, even when the pro-Israel groups complained to the deans.[19] And shortly after the release of their book, both Mearsheimer and Walt addressed the Council on American-Islamic Relations (CAIR), a radical organization linked in the past to Hamas that cheers Islamic terror against Israel and the United States.[20]

In their book, Mearsheimer and Walt sharpen their attack but leave it essentially unchanged. They acknowledge some of the concerns that critics of their essay have raised about anti-Semitism, declaring, "Let us be clear: we categorically reject all of these anti-Semitic claims." They also dropped some sources whose credibility had been questioned, such as former DePaul University professor Norman Finkelstein.[21] Yet the three basic pillars of their argument remain: that support for Israel is bad for U.S. interests, that "the lobby" (now in lowercase, to present the appearance of moderation) is "the principal reason for that support," and that "the lobby" maintains that support through a largely Jewish network that twists the arms of politicians and uses the media to prod a gullible U.S. public to war.[22]

One reason Mearsheimer and Walt's argument has generated so much interest is its timing. In 2003, as the United States went to war in Iraq, the majority of Americans backed President George W. Bush's decision to invade.[23] By 2007, when *The Israel Lobby and U.S. Foreign Policy* hit bookshelves, the war had become very unpopular.[74] In the interim, Democrats failed to dislodge Bush from power or use their control of Congress to stop the war. Though principled defenders of the U.S. mission in Iraq remained vocal, many Americans wondered how and why the Iraq War had been authorized, and why it had not been ended, despite Republican declarations of victory and Democratic promises of withdrawal. The truth is that the United States suffered a failure of political leadership, on both sides of the aisle. But for some Americans, the simple truth was not enough. They needed scapegoats.

Conspiracy theories began to spread, such as the claim that the government had withheld the full truth about the September 11 terror attacks—a claim endorsed by some celebrities and "intellectuals" who ought to have known better. Mearsheimer and Walt entered this murky marketplace of bad ideas, peddling a theory that absolved U.S. voters and politicians of their own poor judgment leading up to Iraq. These conspiratorial approaches to history and current events are not what Americans expect to hear from senior academics at the nation's top universities. They evoke what Professor Richard Hofstadter described in his famous essay "The Paranoid Style in American Politics," in which extremists of the left and the right project wild visions of the power of small, identifiable demographic groups.[25] The trademark of conspiracy theories is that they purport to explain far more than a single phenomenon and can be constantly adjusted to fit inconvenient facts. Thus Mearsheimer and Walt place an astonishing array of individuals in "the lobby"—leaving out some highly critical supporters of Israel but including Jews and others who agree on virtually nothing except, the authors tell us, that Israel's interests are paramount.

Mearsheimer and Walt claim that they do not "blame the Jews" for the Iraq War. Yet they still say that the role played by "groups in the lobby" was "necessary" for the war to take place.[26] It is telling that the cover of their book consists of the U.S. flag in the colors of the Israeli blue-and-white, implying that "the lobby" controls not only U.S. foreign policy, but the United States itself. That is the classic conspiratorial mind-set.

Had Mearsheimer and Walt merely argued the first part of their thesis—that support for Israel is not in America's best interests—their essay and their book would have been far less controversial. They still would have provoked a great deal of debate, as well as opposition from the many experts and ordinary Americans who believe that support for Israel is good for U.S. goals and for American values. But the opposite view, often described as the "realist" view, is a respected school of thought in policy circles. Mearsheimer and Walt were themselves once considered leaders of the "realist" school, which argues that states seek to maximize their power, rather than pursue moral aims, in their foreign relations. In the Middle East, realists have often backed stronger relations with Arab states that supply the United States with oil.

What provoked widespread outrage was the second part of their argument—that "the lobby" is the main reason for U.S. support of Israel, and that "the lobby" effectively controlled U.S. politics. Not only do Mearsheimer and Walt fail to prove these claims, but they also dismiss legitimate criticism of their essay as evidence of the lobby at work—again, the circular logic that is typical of conspiracy theorists.

As I show in my initial response to their essay, Mearsheimer and Walt are guilty of three major kinds of errors. First, they use quotes taken out of context. For example, they manipulate a quote by Israeli prime minister David Ben-Gurion to suggest that he favored expelling Arabs from Palestine by "brutal compulsion."[27] In fact, Ben-Gurion said that an evacuation of Arabs should not be "part of our programme" precisely because it would require such compulsion.[28] Mearsheimer and Walt protest that they have not misquoted Ben-Gurion, claiming that he favored a program of "transfer." Yet they characteristically cite only such evidence as supports their claim.[29] This was the second kind of error: misstating basic facts, such as saying that Israeli citizenship is based on "blood kinship." The third kind of error is the use of false but convenient logical fallacies, such as the idea that cooperation between the United States and Israel is proof of the power of "the lobby," or that "the mere existence of the lobby" shows that "support for Israel is not in the American national interest."[30] These kinds of errors persist in their book.

Between publishing their essay and finishing *The Israel Lobby and U.S. Foreign Policy,* Mearsheimer and Walt attempt to address criticisms of their work in a paper titled "Setting the Record Straight" that still appears on their publisher's Web site.[31] In their paper, they acknowledge a number of errors in their original essay and admit that "there are places where our choice of words could have been clearer or more nuanced."[32] What is even more interesting are the errors they refuse to admit. For example, they protest, "We never said that the lobby was 'all-powerful' and did not imply that it gets its way on every issue."[33] In their original essay, however, they describe "the Lobby" as "unmatched" in its power.[34] They fail to provide any examples of "the Lobby" losing a political battle, although Israel's supporters have lost many, especially to the lobby representing Saudi Arabia—a country with almost no grass-roots support among Americans that yet has enormous influence over U.S. foreign policy. Mearsheimer and Walt also do not acknowledge that they were wrong about increased anti-Semitism in France and continue to claim that it is "declining."[35] Yet data collected separately by the French government and the Jewish community confirm that anti-Jewish attacks are on the rise, and many French Jews have chosen to emigrate to Israel and other places as a result.[36]

Throughout their original essay, their responses to their critics, and their book, Mearsheimer and Walt claim that the "evidence" they refer to is "not controversial."[37] This is a tactic used by Noam Chomsky, Norman Finkelstein, and other hard-line opponents of Israel: they state, without proof, that their most far-fetched and distorted claims are accepted by everyone without question. It is also a tactic I have encountered in the courtroom. It is typical of prosecutors who know they have a weak case against the defendant but want to dazzle the jury into believing the case is open-and-shut. Such claims usually fall apart under cross-examination or when the defense has an opportunity to present its own witnesses.

That is why good prosecutors don't stretch their evidence farther than it can legitimately reach.

Mearsheimer and Walt would fail a first-year criminal law class. They admit that they did not conduct any interviews and rely heavily on newspaper articles to make their case against "the lobby."[38] Their charge that Israel pushed the Bush administration to go to war in Iraq, for example, is based entirely on opinion articles in the popular press. That does not qualify as evidence.[39] Nor are they faithful to counterevidence from the same sources, such as reports that Israeli prime minister Ariel Sharon advised President Bush *not* to invade Iraq, or that groups such as AIPAC also expressed misgivings about the war.[40] Yossi Alpher documented Sharon's interaction with Bush in the *Forward:*

> Publicly, Sharon played the silent ally; he neither criticized nor supported the Iraq adventure. . . .
>
> But sometime prior to March 2003, Sharon told Bush privately in no uncertain terms what he thought about the Iraq plan. Sharon's words—revealed here for the first time—constituted a friendly but pointed warning to Bush. Sharon acknowledged that Saddam Hussein was an "acute threat" to the Middle East and that he believed Saddam possessed weapons of mass destruction.
>
> Yet according to one knowledgeable source, Sharon nevertheless advised Bush not to occupy Iraq. According to another source— Danny Ayalon, who was Israel's ambassador to the United States at the time of the Iraq invasion, and who sat in on the Bush-Sharon meetings—Sharon told Bush that Israel would not "push one way or another" regarding the Iraq scheme.
>
> According to both sources, Sharon warned Bush that if he insisted on occupying Iraq, he should at least abandon his plan to implant democracy in this part of the world. "In terms of culture and tradition, the Arab world is not built for democratization," Ayalon recalls Sharon advising.
>
> Be sure, Sharon added, not to go into Iraq without a viable exit strategy. And ready a counter-insurgency strategy if you expect to rule Iraq, which will eventually have to be partitioned into its component parts. Finally, Sharon told Bush, please remember that you will conquer, occupy and leave, but we have to remain in this part of the world.[41]

Alpher's reporting is confirmed by my own experience. I met Ariel Sharon just before the Iraq War, and he told me that he was opposed to it and had advised President Bush against it. Indeed, much of the historical evidence that we have access to suggests that the incumbent Israeli leaders and policymakers at the time were skeptical of, if not outright opposed to, a U.S. invasion and occupation of Iraq.[42] The fact that the Israelis refrained from publicly opposing the United States or from pressing their objections too strongly underlines the fact that it is the United States that dominates the close relationship between the two countries and not the other way around.

Mearsheimer and Walt ignore this and other bodies of evidence. One does not expect professors at America's best universities to offer such flimsy, poorly supported arguments. Mearsheimer and Walt's claims do not meet a legal standard of proof or even an academic standard of probability. They consider the least likely explanation—that U.S. policy is controlled by an "agent for a foreign government"—to be the only possible explanation, rejecting hard evidence to the contrary.

It is worth closely examining Mearsheimer and Walt's methods, which are contrary to the standards of serious scholarship. One of the authors admitted that "none of the evidence [in the original paper] represents original documentation or is derived from independent interviews."[43] This is startling, given that academics are judged by the quality of their original research. In addition, in several places Mearsheimer and Walt cite primary sources when it is quite clear that they have not actually found the particular quotes or information they use in those sources. In one such example, they cite a quotation from Max Frankel's autobiography, *The Times of My Life and My Life with the Times*: "I was much more deeply devoted to Israel than I dared to assert." This quotation is one of several that appear (usually out of context) with depressing regularity on extremist, conspiracy theory Web sites that repeat many of the same charges that Mearsheimer and Walt make. It seems unlikely that they have actually read Frankel's lengthy autobiography and happened to come across this one controversial quote. It is far more probable that they simply lifted the quote from a rather less reputable secondary source. They also cite primary sources incorrectly. For example, they refer to page 99 of the Steve Cox translation of Nahum Goldmann's memoir, *The Jewish Paradox* (discussed further on). They do not cite the source correctly, however; rather than citing their actual secondary source, they simply cut-and-pasted the citation they found there. The authors do not contest these claims in "Setting the Record Straight" and repeat many of these misleading citations (including the Frankel and Cox citations) in their book.[44]

Without primary sources to draw on, Mearsheimer and Walt rely heavily on secondhand hearsay "evidence," which they often obtained from questionable sources. Their initial essay, for example, uses "evidence" from extremist anti-Israel and anti-American Web sites such as CounterPunch.org and from discredited academics such as Finkelstein.[45]

They also cite so-called evidence that is commonly featured on radical sites of the far left and the far right and make arguments not altogether different from those found on neo-Nazi sites such as nukeisrael.com.[46] Mearsheimer and Walt complain that this is "guilt by association" and deny that they share the same views as the owners of these sites.[47] I accept that they do not share such views; I have never said that they do. It is appropriate, however, to ask what checks they employ when they borrow "evidence" from such sites—whether they accept it at face value or subject it to scrutiny. Take, for example, another Ben-Gurion quote they use in their essay and their book: "If I was an Arab leader I would never make terms with Israel. That is natural: we have taken their country. . . . Why should they accept that?"[48]

This quote appears on numerous anti-Israel and anti-Semitic Web sites.[49] It is, in fact, an out-of-context secondary account of a late-night conversation between Ben Gurion and Nahum Goldmann, recounted by Goldmann in his 1978 memoir, *The Jewish Paradox*. After Mearsheimer and Walt produced this quote in their original essay, I pointed out that they had left out the end of Goldmann's account of his conversation: "That was Ben-Gurion all over: he had told me that so as to show me how well he knew in his heart that Israel could not exist without peace with the Arabs."[50] Mearsheimer and Walt also failed to include any contrary quotes from Ben-Gurion. For example, in 1948, Ben-Gurion said, "An Arab has also the right to be elected president of the state, should he be elected by all. If in America a Jew or a black cannot become president of the state—I do not believe in the quality of its civil rights."[51] This statement was made at the very moment in which, according to the anti-Israel polemicists Mearsheimer and Walt cite, Ben-Gurion was contemplating the expulsion of the Palestinian Arabs. Mearsheimer and Walt attempt to dismiss such contrary evidence by arguing that "Ben-Gurion was not rejecting this policy; he was simply noting that the Zionists should not openly proclaim it."[52]

But when it comes to the open proclamations of Arab leaders that their explicit aims in war were to destroy Israel and exterminate its Jewish population, Mearsheimer and Walt rush to excuse them. "There is no question that some Arab leaders talked about 'driving the Jews into the Sea' during the 1948 war," they argue, "but this was mainly rhetoric designed to appease their publics."[53] Their willingness to infer the worst about Israel's leaders and the best about Israel's Arab enemies demonstrates the determined way in which Mearsheimer and Walt abuse the historical record. It is this outright bias that makes their use of "evidence" commonly found on extremist Web sites, without further context or investigation of such material, relevant to an evaluation of their scholarship.

Other questionable sources include Noam Chomsky, whose own history of hateful anti-Americanism includes such claims as "If the Nuremberg laws were applied today, then every Post-War American president would have to be hanged."[54] They also cite CounterPunch's Alexander Cockburn, who is noted for referring to "the shared enthusiasm of the Fuehrer and all U.S. Presidents (with the possible exception of Warren Harding) for mass murder as an appropriate expression of national policy."[55]

The attitude of Walt and Mearsheimer toward reputable sources is not much better. In their book, for example, they cite the research of University of Chicago professor Robert Pape, who has attempted to show that suicide terrorists share a common goal of pushing foreign armies off lands that the terrorists consider their own.[56] They use Pape's research to argue that al-Qaeda's campaign of terror against the United States is motivated by anger at the Israeli occupation of Palestinian lands. But not even Pape believes that theory and has specifically denied that al-Qaeda is chiefly motivated by Israel.[57] Like most other scholars, he agrees that al-Qaeda emerged in opposition to the presence of "infidel" U.S. forces in the Middle East.

In addition, Mearsheimer and Walt present historical facts without their context in order to convey the most damning image of Israel possible. In their essay, they note Israel's "quick and easy victories" in various wars to demonstrate Israel's military strength. Yet they do not explain how or why these wars came about. In their book, they provide false explanations and rely almost entirely on the work of revisionist historians, while repeating the claims of Arab propagandists. Regarding the Six-Day War in 1967, they wrote that Israel "was not preempting an impending attack when it struck the first blow on June 5, 1967. Instead, it was launching a preventive war—a war aimed at affecting the balance of power over time—or, as Menachem Begin put it, 'a war of choice.'"[58] This claim, which again manipulates a quote out of context, is completely untrue, as I have demonstrated elsewhere, and relies on discredited or disputed accounts.[59] For example, they use Tom Segev's work to support a claim that Israel went to war to achieve territorial and strategic ambitions.[60] But Michael Oren, widely regarded as the most authoritative historian of the war—and who, unlike Segev, reads Arabic and relies on Arab as well as Israeli sources—dismisses Segev's account and accuses Segev of "twisting his text to meet a revisionist agenda."[61] What is important here is not only the merit or otherwise of Segev's work, but rather the fact that Mearsheimer and Walt depend entirely on such sources.

In discussing the central topic of their book—"the lobby" and how it works—they also resort to such intellectual sleight-of-hand. Their favorite technique is to cite opinions as facts. Faced with evidence, for example, that AIPAC (the American-Israel Public Affairs Committee) is not actually the most powerful lobby group in the United States, they quote a former congressman who once claimed, "There's no lobby group that matches it."[62] Perhaps the most pernicious trick is the way Mearsheimer and Walt use their broad definition of "the lobby" to blame *all* pro-Israel groups for things done by only some of them. Their chief target, for example, is AIPAC. But AIPAC never encouraged the United States to go to war in Iraq, as the authors well know, so they shift their attack to the neoconservatives in the Bush administration, claiming that they are all part of "the lobby."[63] This is not serious scholarship. It is a naked attempt to distort reality.

In addition, Mearsheimer and Walt's original essay is riddled with factual errors, some of which the authors themselves later acknowledged, and for which they were widely criticized. An editorial in the *Forward* stated, "Countless facts are simply wrong. Long stretches of argument are implausible, at times almost comically so. . . . An undergraduate submitting work like this would be laughed out of class."[64] Despite admitting some of their mistakes, Mearsheimer and Walt protested that "to claim that the paper was sloppy is implausible."[65] They argued that their prior reputations should dispel doubts about the accuracy of their current research: "We have each written three scholarly books and published numerous articles over the past twenty-plus years. . . . Is it likely that we would suddenly choose this moment and this issue to produce our first piece of sloppy scholarship?" I ask the same question about why their work is so sloppy and so error-filled only in one direction—against Israel. They owe a better answer than simply to re-ask the question in a self-serving manner.

Facts are either right or wrong, regardless of the prestige of the person citing them. It is precisely because Mearsheimer and Walt were previously held in such esteem that their one-sided mistakes are so shocking. The question that naturally arises is why they would choose to risk their reputations by publishing such poor work. The answer is that they have actually enhanced their reputations among Israel-haters and far-left and far-right ideologues and have become far more sought after as paid lecturers than they were in the past.

In my initial response to Mearsheimer and Walt's essay, I addressed only a few of their most egregious errors. The authors have now responded to these and other criticisms, and it is worth examining whether they have done so satisfactorily, as well as whether they are any more faithful to the facts in their best-selling book.

1. "By contrast, Israel was explicitly founded as a Jewish state and citizenship is based on the principle of blood kinship." This accusation ignores the fact that 1.2 million Arabs are Israeli citizens, making up about 20 percent of the total population, and that they are guaranteed rights equal to those of Jewish Israelis. In addition, the reference to "blood" evokes imagery used in neo-Nazi propaganda. Mearsheimer and Walt acknowledge that their wording was "awkward," yet maintain that their "basic point was correct."[66] They argue that Israeli citizenship is indeed based on "blood kinship," since Israel is a Jewish state and Jewishness is determined by "maternal ancestry." But Jewishness is relevant only to citizenship acquired under Israel's Law of Return, which was designed (and has been invoked) to provide a haven for Jews, as well as to non-Jewish relatives of Jews, from persecution.[67] Indeed, thousands of former Soviet citizens who emigrated to Israel and became Israeli citizens are not Jewish by any religious definition of the term; one of the fastest-growing churches in Israel is the Russian Orthodox faith.

Mearsheimer and Walt repeat their error in their book, confusing Israel's character as a Jewish state with its laws regarding citizenship. The most relevant law, which Mearsheimer and Walt ignore, is not the Law of Return but Israel's Nationality Law of 1952, which grants citizenship in many ways, including residency, military service, and naturalization, that have nothing to do with "blood kinship."[68]

2. "The United States has a terrorism problem in good part because it is so closely allied with Israel, not the other way around. . . . There is no question, for example, that many al Qaeda leaders, including [Osama] bin Laden, are motivated by Israel's presence in Jerusalem and the plight of the Palestinians."[69] What is interesting about this accusation is that the authors seem to assume that it is natural, if not appropriate, for bin Laden and other terrorists to react to the United States in this way. They seem to absolve al-Qaeda of any responsibility for the "rage of anti-American terrorists."[70] Essentially, Mearsheimer and Walt blame the United States for terror attacks against itself by third parties who have no direct connection to the Palestinians.

   Mearsheimer and Walt are also factually wrong here. The first and second fatwas issued by Osama bin Laden, in 1996 and 1998, respectively, established that his primary grievance was the U.S. military presence in the Arabian peninsula: "First, for over seven years the United States has been occupying the lands of Islam in the holiest of places, the Arabian Peninsula, plundering its riches, dictating to its rulers, humiliating its people, terrorizing its neighbors, and turning its bases in the Peninsula into a spearhead through which to fight the neighboring Muslim peoples."[71]

   Mearsheimer and Walt do not explore the way in which hatred of Israel and the United States is carefully constructed in many Arab societies to deflect potential challenges to these countries' autocratic governments. Their argument is as ludicrous as the idea that the United States alone was responsible for the cold war, or that British foreign policy was the root cause of Hitler's fascism and aggression.

3. "Contrary to popular belief, the Zionists had larger, better-equipped, and better-led forces during the 1947–49 War of Independence."[72] Here, in addition to my criticism, Mearsheimer and Walt are challenged by none other than Benny Morris, the revisionist Israeli historian whose work they relied on so heavily.

In a devastating response, Morris wrote in the *New Republic,*

Like many pro-Arab propagandists at work today, Mearsheimer and Walt often cite my own books, sometimes quoting directly from them, in apparent corroboration of their arguments. Yet their work is a travesty of the history that I have studied and written for the past two decades. Their work is riddled with shoddiness and defiled by mendacity. Were *The Israel Lobby and U.S. Foreign Policy* an actual person, I would have to say that he did not have a single honest bone in his body.[73]

Morris points out that "the Arabs probably had an overall edge in men-under-arms" during most of the first stage of the 1947–1949 war, and that in the same period "the Palestinians probably had an edge in light arms, the main armaments."[74] In the war's second stage, "the Arab side began with an overwhelming . . . advantage in equipment and firepower," Morris notes. As for the number of soldiers, Morris wrote, the picture was "murky" because "Israel's archives are open . . . but the archives of all the Arab states, which are dictatorships, remain closed." Israeli forces outnumbered Arab forces late in the war, but the Israeli figures include "both combat troops . . . and rear echelon units," whereas the number of Arab soldiers in rear units remains a matter of speculation.

Because Mearsheimer and Walt have done no original research, they struggled to respond to Morris. They attempt to use his past statements against him, such as his assertion that "the stronger side, in fact, won" the war.[75] In so doing, they confuse the superior *performance* of the Israeli forces—whose strength Morris readily acknowledges—with superior *numbers.* They also leave out the crucial fact that Israel lost 1 percent of its population, many of them civilians and survivors of the Holocaust, in repelling the genocidal attacks of the Arab invaders. These errors persist in the book as well. And again (as with Carter), all of their errors go one way—against Israel.

4. "Israeli officials have long claimed that the Arabs fled because their leaders told them to, but careful scholarship (much of it by Israeli historians like Morris) have demolished this myth."[76] Mearsheimer and Walt distort Morris's work, implying that because he says that not *all* refugees were told to leave by Arab leaders, *none* were. But Morris acknowledges that some Palestinians were, in fact, instructed by Arab leaders to flee. "In some areas Arab commanders ordered the villagers to evacuate to clear the ground for military purposes or to prevent surrender," he observes. "More than half a dozen villages—just north of Jerusalem and in the Lower Galilee—were abandoned during these months as a result of such orders."[77]

Since Mearsheimer and Walt's book borrows so heavily, albeit selectively, from Morris's account in *1948 and After,* perhaps they ought to have paid closer attention to his criticism of historians who "avoid the rich world of nuance and deny multiple causation" and are drawn to a "single-cause explanation" that "must . . . bow before the needs, or presumed needs, of current political battle and propaganda."[78]

5. "But the creation of Israel involved additional crimes against a largely innocent third party: the Palestinians." In my response, I note the active collaboration of the Palestinian leadership with Hitler, which Mearsheimer and Walt continue to ignore. (More on this in chapter 6.) I add that Palestinians have joined Arab states in attempting to destroy Israel at its birth, which would indeed, if successful, have been a "moral crime." Mearsheimer and Walt's response is that "it was virtually impossible for the Zionists to create a Jewish state in a land filled with Palestinians without committing crimes against them."[79] This absurd statement denies the peaceful, lawful settlement of Jewish communities in Palestine, as well as the legal foundations of Israeli sovereignty in UN resolutions and international law.

The authors claim that they believe in Israel's right to exist, and that they "believe the history of the Jewish people and the norm of national self-determination provide ample justification for a Jewish state."[80] There is no way to reconcile that belief with the view that the creation of Israel was a "moral crime"—unless the authors themselves feel that the "moral crime" against Palestinians was, and is, justified.

6. "The mainstream Zionist leadership was not interested in establishing a bi-national state or accepting a permanent partition of Palestine."[81] This statement is grossly misleading and is contradicted by the fact that the Zionist leadership accepted the principle of partition every time it was offered by the international community. Mearsheimer and Walt claim that this was just a "tactical maneuver."[82] The truth is that sovereignty was always more important than quantity of land to Jewish leaders.

   As far as the binational state is concerned, the only parties to suggest a binational state or even a single democratic state were Jewish parties. Admittedly, these were small groupings within the Zionist movement, but at various times even Ben-Gurion and the Revisionist leader Ze'ev Jabotinsky considered different versions of a federal state that would have combined Jewish and Arab subnational units.[83] In contrast, the Palestinian Arabs not only rejected partition, but they also rejected the binational state when it was presented by the minority on the UN Special Committee on Palestine. Yet Mearsheimer and Walt continue to claim that the "mainstream Zionist leadership" rejected compromise.[84]

7. "Pressure from extremist violence and the growing Palestinian population has forced subsequent Israeli leaders to disengage from some of the occupied territories and to explore territorial compromise, but no Israeli government has been willing to offer the Palestinians a viable state of their own. Even Prime Minister Ehud Barak's purportedly generous offer at Camp David in July 2000 would only have given the Palestinians a disarmed and dismembered set of 'Bantustans' under de facto Israeli control."[85]

In my response, I describe this as "Mearsheimer and Walt's boldest misstatement" and show how they have misquoted Barak. Interestingly, Mearsheimer and Walt never attempt to defend their statement. The reference to "Bantustans" does not appear in their book, and it is not among the errors they apologize for in "Setting the Record Straight." They have corrected the error but refuse to be held to account for the sloppiness of their scholarship. They also willfully misrepresent the geographic realities. They do not cite the map Dennis Ross published in his book *The Missing Peace*, which contrasts the "Palestinian Characterization of the Final Proposal at Camp David" with the "Map Reflecting Actual Proposal at Camp David."[86] The second map, which depicts President Bill Clinton's proposals and which Yasser Arafat rejected, shows a contiguous Palestinian state in the West Bank. Saudi Prince Bandar was so astounded by the generosity of Israel's offer at Camp David that he told Arafat in no uncertain terms, "If we lose this opportunity, it is not going to be a tragedy. This is going to be a crime."[87] Mearsheimer and Walt choose to repeat Arafat's lie over the word of virtually everyone else at Camp David and the published maps that prove exactly what it was that Arafat turned down.[88] Yet they insist on characterizing their demonstrably false description as "uncontroversial."[89]

8. "Neither America nor Israel could be blackmailed by a nuclear-armed rogue [Iran], because the blackmailer could not carry out the threat without receiving overwhelming retaliation. The danger of a 'nuclear handoff' to terrorists is equally remote, because a rogue state could not be sure the transfer would be undetected or that it would not be blamed and punished afterwards."[90] Mearsheimer and Walt continue to understate the danger of a nuclear Iran, and in their book they use the Iran issue to propound some of their wildest conspiratorial fantasies. For example, "Israel and the lobby . . . are the central forces behind all the talk in the Bush administration and on Capitol Hill about using

military force to destroy Iran's nuclear facilities."[91] Not "some," but "all." Not Dick Cheney, but Ehud Olmert. Not George W. Bush, but Benjamin Netanyahu.

It was not for nothing that one of Mearsheimer's colleagues (not a member of any Israel Lobby) called the original essay "piss-poor, monocausal social science."[92] In their book, the authors continue the same pattern of blaming Israel for America's wars—past, present, and future. In addition to minimizing Iran's nuclear ambitions, they say nothing at all about Iran's dismal human rights record. They ignore the fundamentalist religious nature of its leadership, whitewashing Iranian President Mahmoud Ahmadinejad's threat to "wipe Israel off the map." He is not the only Iranian leader to have threatened Israel with nuclear destruction. In 2001, former Iranian president Hashemi Rafsanjani, who is considered the father of Iran's nuclear program, told a crowd in Tehran, "If a day comes when the world of Islam is duly equipped with the arms Israel has in its possession, the strategy of colonialism would face a stalemate because application of an atomic bomb would not leave any thing in Israel but the same thing would just produce damages in the Muslim world."[93] These "realists" are determined to ignore reality.

9. "There is also a strong norm against criticizing Israeli policy, and Jewish-American leaders rarely support putting pressure on Israel."[94] My response is, "If the authors believe that American Jews are reluctant to criticize Israel or to try to pressure Israeli public officials, they are not familiar with the American Jewish community, which thrives on controversy."[95]

In their book, Mearsheimer and Walt seek to bolster their argument with stories of disputes within and among Jewish organizations over criticism of Israel. They succeed in showing that criticism of Israel is sometimes controversial. Ironically, they also highlight the enduring vigor of debate within the Jewish community. Few other groups in the

United States promote such constant internal dissent, and so publicly. Yet Mearsheimer and Walt, while acknowledging the internal diversity of "the lobby," often write about it as if it behaved monolithically. They even include me in "the lobby," without disclosing my publicly expressed disapproval of Israeli settlements, as well as of other Israeli policies, since the early 1970s.

10. The Lobby is engaged in a "campaign to eliminate criticism of Israel from college campuses."[96] If the success of Mearsheimer and Walt's essay and book proves anything, it is that universities are where radical critics of Israel thrive. Even the authors, in an unguarded moment, admit as much: "The Lobby has had the most difficulty stifling debate about Israel on college campuses," they wrote.[97] Anti-Israel professors continue to dominate Middle East studies programs across the country. The "free speech" argument has become the last recourse of anti-Israel academics who cannot win a debate based on facts. They do not want free speech for all views, but only special protection for their own. Much of what they describe as "censorship" is just ordinary counterspeech from people who disagree with them. Recently, for example, an anthropology professor at Harvard named J. Lorand Matory—whose field is West Africa, not the Middle East—tried to convince the Harvard faculty to pass a special resolution endorsing "civil dialogue" on matters relating to Israel. He claimed that critics of Israel "tremble in fear" on campus and that anti-Israel speakers are forbidden to speak at Harvard.[98] In response, I produced a list of dozens of anti-Israel speakers who had been welcomed at Harvard. Matory's motion failed. Ironically, it was Matory himself who led the charge against former Harvard president Lawrence Summers when he made controversial remarks about the performance of women in scientific fields. Matory also bore considerable hostility toward Summers for the university president's strong and principled stance against divestment campaigns and academic boycotts against Israel.[99] Matory's

no-confidence motions and backroom politicking paid off when Summers finally resigned. For academics like Matory, the goal is "free speech for me, but not for thee!"

There are many other glaring factual errors in Mearsheimer and Walt's final product, multiplied and spread out across 355 pages of text. I focused on the previous ten because these are the few that I highlight in my initial response. Mearsheimer and Walt have had ample opportunity to rebut my criticism. That they have failed to do so convincingly is a further indictment of their views.

There is, to be sure, an increase in sophistication from their first essay through their response to their critics and finally their book. In a few areas, their claims have become more accurate; in many others, their errors have become far worse. This was clearly an experience of "learning by doing" for the authors, who had no prior expertise in the area. Unfortunately, they do not seem to have learned much.

But let us suppose, for argument's sake, that Mearsheimer and Walt had all of their facts straight and that their scholarship was sound. Even then, their hypothesis is not able to overcome the fatally flawed logic at its core. Their argument begins with the following claim: "Indeed, the mere existence of the Lobby suggests that unconditional support for Israel is not in the American national interest. If it was, one would not need an organized special interest group to bring it about."[100] This is one of the dumbest statements I have ever seen in print, certainly by academics. By the same reasoning, the existence of the American Association of Retired Persons (AARP) proves that the rights of the elderly are not in America's interest. And so, too, with African American rights, as "proved" by the existence of the NAACP (National Association of Colored People); or civil liberties (ACLU—the American Civil Liberties Union); or a clean environment (Sierra Club); and so on.

Almost every cause, worthy or otherwise, has a lobby. Many foreign governments employ lobbyists in Washington. But only the pro-Israel lobby is singled out as being contrary to national well-being. This is not only illogical; it is also pure bigotry.

Another fallacy committed throughout Mearsheimer and Walt's work on this topic is to assume that negative claims about Jews or the lobby are true and require no further proof if the statements are made by Jews. I call this fallacy the "proof by ethnic admission." For example, in their original paper and again in their book, they cite former AIPAC leader (1974–1980) Morris Amitay: "There are a lot of guys at the working level up here [on Capitol Hill] . . . who just happen to be Jewish, who are willing . . . to look at certain issues in terms of their Jewishness."[101]

That is a sweeping, grave generalization—but it is only one uncorroborated quote, from one person, who had a professional interest in playing up his influence in Washington. This tactic is the classic ad hominem fallacy, in which the authors ask their readers to judge the identity of the source, not the logic of the argument. Turning the tables, one might claim that Mearsheimer and Walt's criticism of Israel is unfounded simply because other anti-Israel radicals, such as Chomsky and Finkelstein, have criticized their work (or, conversely, to believe that if Chomsky and Finkelstein—who are wrong about so many things—disagree with the authors, then Mearsheimer and Walt must be right). Mearsheimer and Walt complain that they are victims of "guilt by association" because David Duke agrees with them, yet the bulk of their argument against "the lobby" consists of exactly such associations.

Mearsheimer and Walt also commit the elementary logical error of confusing correlation with causation. This is their strategy, for example, in attempting to prove that "the lobby" was the key factor in causing the United States to invade Iraq. In their original paper, the authors state, "By February 2003, a *Washington Post* headline summarized the situation: 'Bush and Sharon Nearly Identical on Mideast Policy.' The main reason for this switch is the lobby." But Mearsheimer and Walt never prove this conclusory assertion. They do not consider evidence or eliminate alternative explanations; rather, they simply assert that the least likely explanation, and the most damaging from Israel's point of view, is the correct one. The facts, however, prove that it is the incorrect one: The Israeli government, its prime minister, AIPAC, and most American Jews did not favor the invasion and the occupation of Iraq. Those decisions were made by the Bush administration, despite the contrary views of the "Israel Lobby."

In response to this criticism, the authors have claimed, "We did show causation. We showed in considerable detail that Bush did not always share Sharon's worldview, and that it was pressure from the lobby that forced Bush to adopt Sharon's views."[102] They did nothing of the sort. They certainly did not consider more plausible explanations. In the period they cite (2001–2003), the Palestinians repeatedly broke promises to the United States that they would stop engaging in acts of terror. But Mearsheimer and Walt take Arafat's protestations of innocence at face value and blame "the lobby" for all outcomes.[103] They ignore the fact that Arafat was caught red-handed smuggling weapons by the boatload in the *Karine A* affair and then lied about it to President Bush's face, which the Bush administration could not ignore and which undermined efforts to rehabilitate the Palestinian leadership in American eyes.[104]

Given the small size of the U.S. Jewish population, the broad support among American Jews for a two-state solution to the Israeli-Palestinian conflict, and the heavy opposition to the Iraq War in the American Jewish community—all facts that Mearsheimer and Walt admit to be true—it would seem odd to assign responsibility for U.S. foreign policy to pro-Israel activists and Jewish organizations. Yet that is exactly what Mearsheimer and Walt do. On the basis of fallacious arguments, misleading claims of fact, and shoddy methods of research, they attempt to assert that the least likely explanation is in fact the only possible one: that "the lobby" has a "stranglehold" on U.S. foreign policy and on the United States itself.

My Harvard colleague Professor Ruth Wisse—with whom I have many political disagreements—correctly noted that Mearsheimer and Walt not only slander American Jews, but show "contempt" for non-Jewish Americans, who must be "gullible and stupid" to be so easily manipulated into supporting Israel.[105]

If Mearsheimer and Walt had been truly interested in understanding the strength of domestic interest groups that advocate close U.S. relations with Israel, they ought to have begun by analyzing those cases where U.S. and Israeli interests clearly diverge. That is where the activity of lobbyist groups would be most apparent and their success (or lack thereof) best measured and analyzed. That is the way political scientists would address the question. But Mearsheimer and Walt avoid posing the problem this way by assuming that Israel and the United States actually have few interests in common. They then apply circular logic to claim that "the lobby" is the only reason the United States and Israel adopt common foreign policy positions. They do not even bother to test the opposite hypothesis, which is a sign of their intellectual laziness or prejudice or both.

There are, in fact, issues on which pro-Israel activists have disagreed with the U.S. government. In many cases—from the 1981 sale of U.S. Airborne Warning and Control System (AWACS) jets to Saudi Arabia, to the failed attempts to convince the United States to move its embassy from Tel Aviv to Jerusalem—pro-Israel groups have been unable to bring U.S. policymakers to their point of view. But there are a few exceptions to this trend, such as the long, drawn-out debate in the early 1990s about loan guarantees for Israel, that the authors could have studied in depth but did not.

Next, they would have had to conduct original research, such as interviews, analysis of government documents, financial audits of lobby groups, and so on, in order to obtain a complete picture of the policy process. From this wealth of primary sources they would have needed to identify the most important individual actors, the most effective groups, the most essential relationships, and the most effective lobbying strategies—if indeed domestic lobby groups had managed to shift U.S. policy in any of the examples under scrutiny.

They would have had to consider the observations of experienced policymakers such as David Gergen, Walt's colleague at the Kennedy School (also not part of any Israel Lobby), who responded to "The Israel Lobby" working paper as follows:

Over the course of four tours in the White House, I never once saw a decision in the Oval Office to tilt U.S. foreign policy in favor of Israel at the expense of America's interest. Other than Richard Nixon—who occasionally said terrible things about Jews, despite the number on his team—I can't remember any president even talking about an Israeli lobby. Perhaps I have forgotten, but I can remember plenty of conversations about the power of the American gun lobby, environmentalists, evangelicals, small-business owners, and teachers unions.[106]

Gergen added,

Not only are these charges wildly at variance with what I have personally witnessed in the Oval Office over the years, but they also impugn the loyalty and the unstinting service to America's national security by public figures like Dennis Ross, Martin Indyk, and many others. As a Christian, let me add that it is also wrong and unfair to call into question the loyalty of millions of American Jews who have faithfully supported Israel while also working tirelessly and generously to advance America's cause, both at home and abroad. They are among our finest citizens and should be praised, not pilloried.[107]

In "Setting the Record Straight," Mearsheimer and Walt attempt to dismiss Gergen's criticisms by claiming "that he was not an important player in the formation of U.S. Middle East policy."[108] They then cite the supposedly differing opinion of former secretary of state George Shultz, who once wrote about "Israel's leverage in Congress" regarding a military aid package that the legislature supported but President Reagan opposed.[109] The problem, again, is that Mearsheimer and Walt quote their sources selectively. Shultz has, in fact, been one of the most important critics of Mearsheimer and Walt's claims. In his foreword to Anti-Defamation League director Abraham H. Foxman's recent book, *The Deadliest Lies: The Israel Lobby and the Myth of Jewish Control*, Shultz wrote,

We are a great nation, and our government officials invariably include brilliant, experienced, tough-minded people. Mostly, we make good decisions. But when we make a wrong decision—even one that is rec-ommended by Israel and supported by American Jewish groups—it is our decision, and one for which we alone are responsible. We are not babes in the woods, easily convinced to support Israel's or any other state's agenda. We act in our own interests.[110]

If Mearsheimer and Walt had wanted to conduct a serious investigation, they would have taken the full range of Shultz's observations into account.

They would also have discounted political actors that had no influence or marginal impact. They would have compiled a thorough list of other factors: anti-Israel lobby groups, lobbyists from the oil and defense industries, and external variables such as the U.S. economy or unexpected events abroad. They would have shown that each of these factors, in turn, was not among the causal forces at work. In addition, they would have accounted for the growing phenomenon of censorship of pro-Israel commentary in the U.S. media—a trend helped along, no doubt, by accusa-tions of pro-Israel bias that leave editors eager to tip the scales back toward an ostensibly "balanced" position. Recently, *Ms.* magazine refused to run an ad by the American Jewish Congress (AJC) featuring three of Israel's prominent female leaders and the caption "This is Israel." One reason reportedly given by the maga-zine was that the ad would "cause a lot of opposition" and "create a firestorm."[111] Similarly, the New York radio station WQXR has twice rejected weekly advertisements run by the AJC, even when these ads have used quotes from the *New York Times,* which owns the station.[112] To evaluate Mearsheimer and Walt's claims about media bias, incidents such as these would need to be taken into account in a comprehensive survey of editorial behavior across U.S. newsrooms. That is the kind of serious research and analysis required by a project of this scale.

Instead, Mearsheimer and Walt prepared and circulated a paper devoid of academic merit and replete with errors, faulty logic, and bias that could not be cured by the incantation of boilerplate disclaimers against anti-Semitism. Then, once their work had been thoroughly criticized, they did it again, this time in book form, at ten times the length. Their commercial success cannot mask their intellectual failure. Like Jimmy Carter, Mearsheimer and Walt lack the courage to debate me or any other serious critic of their work (I have extended an invitation to them to debate, but to this date they have yet to agree). Ironically, they have attempted to hide from scrutiny by labeling their critics intolerant, using the same ad hominem attacks that they claim they are victims of. They refer to me, for example, as being "often quick to brand Israel's critics as anti-Semites," without offering a shred of proof.[113] The charge is totally false, as they could have learned by reading chapter 14 of my book *The Case for Peace: How the Arab-Israeli Conflict Can Be Solved,* where I catalogue in detail thirty factors that distinguish most criticism of Israel that is not anti-Semitic from the kind of bigotry that is.

I have never called Mearsheimer or Walt anti-Semitic. I have always been prepared to give them the benefit of the doubt. But I have raised legitimate questions about the motivations of two leading scholars of international relations who seem prepared to sacrifice their hard-won reputations on such shoddy work—work that they could well have foreseen would give a boost to unabashed anti-Semitic bigots.

Mearsheimer and Walt "concede" that their argument is "not consistent with realism," the approach to international relations they were both previously known for.[114] In fact, they have yielded to a kind of moral solipsism, which assigns total responsibility to the United States and its domestic politics for anything that happens in the world, even for the spread of anti-Americanism itself, ignoring the conscious, strategic decisions of terrorists and rogue states that threaten the United States and Israel alike.

Abraham H. Foxman, the national director of the Anti-Defamation League—part of "the lobby," according to Mearsheimer and Walt—offered them a "simple remedy" for the pro-Israel direction of U.S. foreign policy: "Win the policy debate!"[115] But they refused to try and said, "Trying to weaken the lobby directly is not going to work."[116]

Thus, they do not actually want an open debate. They simply want to wrap themselves in the thin comfort that conspiracy theory provides. They are no longer realists; they are hate-mongers who have given up on scholarly debate and the democratic process in order to become rock-star heroes of anti-Israel extremists. Perhaps this is not anti-Semitism but misanthropy. Either way, *The Israel Lobby and U.S. Foreign Policy* and the essays preceding it have done enormous damage to the search for real, lasting peace and understanding in the Middle East.

3 The Case against Boycotting Israeli Academics and Divesting from Israeli Businesses

The boycott and divestment movements against Israel grow directly out of the false charge that Israel is an "apartheid" state. The "other" apartheid state, white South Africa, was subjected to boycott and divestment campaigns, which contributed to its demise. It follows therefore, in the perverted minds of those who consider Israel the Jewish equivalent of white South Africa, that the same tactics should be used. That is part of the reason why Jimmy Carter's accusation of apartheid against Israel is so dangerous, and why it is so important to rebut it in the marketplace of ideas.

The recent efforts to impose an academic boycott against Israel (and only Israel) began with a letter printed in the *Guardian* (UK) in April 2002. That letter, written by Professor Steven Rose (himself Jewish) of the Open University and his wife, Professor Hilary Rose of Bradford University, called for "a moratorium" at "both [a] national and European level . . . upon any further [grant and contract] support for Israeli academics and universities." The letter was signed by 125 academics, many of them third-rate lecturers at third-rate colleges.

The letter sparked an outcry that intensified when one of its sig-natories fired two scholars from her academic journal solely because they were Israelis.[1] In doing so, she acted not only immorally, but illegally as well, but she didn't seem to care. "I deplore the Israeli state," the firing professor said in an interview. "[The fired scholars] knew that was how I felt and that they would have to go because of the current situation. . . . It is horrific what is going on there. Many of us would like to talk about it as some kind of Holocaust, which the world will eventually wake up to, much too late, of course, as they did with the last one."[2] This outrageous comparison was made shortly after Israel had offered the Palestinians statehood in all of Gaza and more than 95 percent of the West Bank, in exchange for peace, and Yasser Arafat responded with suicide bombers.

By October 2002, the number of signatories exceeded a thousand[3]— again, mostly obscure academics from marginal schools. Similar calls were published in France, Italy, Australia, and the United States; meanwhile, the British Association of University Teachers adopted the Rose letter, while NATFHE (National Association of Teachers in Further and Higher Education), the lecturers' union, adopted, according to the *Guardian*, "an even stronger resolution," which called for a "straight boycott of all links between universities in the United Kingdom and those in Israel."[4]

By December 2002, again as reported by the *Guardian*, "evidence [was] growing that a British boycott of Israeli academ-ics [was] gathering pace." "In interviews with *The Guardian*, British and Israeli academics listed various instances in which vis-its, research projects and publication of articles had already been blocked."[5] Among these:

> Dr. Oren Yiftachel, a left-wing Israeli academic at Ben Gurion University, complained that an article he had co-authored with a Palestinian was initially rejected by the respected British Journal *Political Geography*. He said it was returned to him unopened with a note stating that *Political Geography* could not accept a submission from Israel. . . . After months of negotiation, the article is to be published but only after [he] agreed to make substantial revisions, including making a comparison between his homeland and apartheid South Africa.

He refused to submit to such McCarthyism, and the article was ultimately published in August 2004, more than two years after he first submitted it.[6]

According to Professor Paul Zinger, the outgoing head of the Israeli Science Foundation, "Every year we send most of our research papers abroad for reference. We send out about 7,000 papers a year. This year, for the first time, we had people writing back, about 25 of them, saying 'We refuse to look at these.'"[7] Three months later, the *Boston Globe* reported that the foundation had "seen the number of its research workshops fall by half," although some blamed the threat of terrorism for the decline.[8]

In early 2003, the *Boston Globe* reported that Israeli concern over the boycott was increasing, especially as it took "on an emotional cast for many Israelis . . . since the Feb. 1 death of Israeli astronaut Ilan Ramon aboard the space shuttle *Columbia*, because Ramon has become a symbol of the scientific exchanges that the boycott seeks to halt." One of the three French universities to officially join the boycott was almost immediately forced to retreat from the policy in reaction to sustained protest by Israeli and other scholars. "Tens of thousands of Europeans and Americans . . . signed anti-boycott petitions," while the secretary general of the Palestinian Academy for Science and Technology declared his opposition to the boycotts.[9] Still, boycott supporters claimed to be "gaining ground, particularly with the actions at the three French universities" that joined the boycott effort during the winter of 2002 to 2003.[10]

That spring, the British Association of University Teachers (AUT), which had previously supported the Rose letter, announced that it would vote on a motion "[urging] all UK institutions of higher education, all AUT local associations and all AUT members to review immediately, with a view to severing, any academic links they may have with official Israeli institutions, including universities." The motion was hugely controversial from the start, even among the union's leadership, which "recommended that the call for action is rejected, although it has defended its decision to debate a boycott of Israel."[11]

The following week, union members defeated the motion by a 2–1 margin, saying, "Such a ban would harm progressive Israeli academics campaigning against the Sharon government." The speaker for the executive, who was against the motion, said, "Israeli universities are largely funded by the state but they are not organized by the state. . . . We should work as closely as possible with those progressive forces both in Israel and in Palestine to hasten the day when we have two independent free states." The union instead "passed a series of motions committing the union to affiliating with the Trade Union Friends of Palestine group, to establishing links with Palestinian universities, and to campaigning for UK institutions to twin with Palestinian institutions."[12]

Despite the high-profile failure of the AUT motion, other British groups joined the boycott call in 2004. The Anglican Peace and Justice Network, an "influential" group within the Anglican Church, announced in September "a boycott of Israel and firms that do business there in protest at the occupation."[13]

Also in 2004, an Oxford University teacher, Andrew Wilkie, told an Israeli PhD applicant, "I am sure you are perfectly nice at a personal level, but no way would I take on somebody who had served in the Israeli army."[14] Wilkie was suspended by Oxford.

Calls for an academic boycott resurfaced in the spring of 2005. Three years after the initial Rose letter, the 49,000-member AUT again decided to debate, according to the *Guardian*, "whether to adopt a form of the boycott as official union policy." This new motion, "proposed by Birmingham and Open Universities," called for "the establishment of a British Committee for Universities in Palestine," a call for a boycott "that excludes Israelis who are critical of their government's actions"—a disloyalty oath—and the circulation of a statement in support of a boycott, written by a group of Palestinian academic unions and NGOs (nongovernmental organizations), to all members.[15] Another motion surfaced that would specifically boycott "Hebrew University, Bar Ilans [*sic*] University, and Haifa University, in protest over their government's action against Palestinians, and the universities' alleged complicity in elements of that."[16]

The AUT ultimately voted to boycott Haifa University, with support from Ilan Pappé, a radical anti-Zionist professor there, and Bar-Ilan University, allowing "an exception only for those academics at the two schools who declare opposition to Israeli policies toward the Palestinians."[17] The motion passed narrowly, 96 to 92. The *New York Times* reported, "Using language lifted from a Palestinian call to action, the British motions framed the boycott as a 'contribution to the struggle to end Israel's occupation, colonization and system of apartheid.'"[18]

At about the time the AUT was voting on the boycott of the two Israeli universities, I was scheduled to receive an honorary doctorate from one of the institutions that was a prime subject of the proposed boycott, Bar-Ilan University in Ramat Gan, Israel. I decided that in accepting the honor, I would do my best imitation of John F. Kennedy's greetings to the citizens of Berlin. "Today, ich bin Bar-Ilaner," I announced. (It was even more appropriate than I thought because I learned that Bar-Ilan University was named after a great scholar who had Hebraized his name from its original "Berlin.") My point was that henceforth, I would be subject to any boycott that covered any professors from Bar-Ilan or other Israeli universities that might be boycotted. I would refuse to participate in any academic events from which Israelis were boycotted. On several occasions, when I was invited to take part in conferences at British universities, I proposed several highly qualified Israeli academics for inclusion in the conference. When they were not invited, I refused to be a party to the event. I also declined an invitation from the former mayor of London—a notorious anti-Israel bigot—to participate in an event, after I inquired whether any Israeli academics were being invited and got a nonresponsive answer.

This was my individualized "retail" way of fighting against anti-Israel bias. It made me feel good, but it did not have much impact on the more general problem. Before long, however, the opportunity arose for a more "wholesale" response to growing efforts to organize a widespread academic boycott of all Israeli professors, researchers, scholars, scientists, and other professionals—at least, all who were Jewish and would not take a "disloyalty" oath to oppose Israeli policies.

The pro-boycott members of the union continued their campaign through the British Committee for Universities in Palestine.[19] Following suit, a union of British architects also threatened a boycott motion. The *Independent* reported that "The Church of England's general synod voted to divest church funds from companies profiting from Israel's illegal occupation of Palestinian territory" and, in particular, targeted the company Caterpillar, whose bulldozers were "used to demolish Palestinian homes." ("Caterpillar says the U.S. military sold them to Israel, but the church will sell its pound 2.5m of shares anyway.")[20]

In May 2006, the 67,000-member NATFHE yet again revived the debate, considering a boycott motion. This resolution "cite[d]," according to the *New York Times*, "'Israeli apartheid policies including construction of the exclusion wall, and discriminatory educational practices'" and also "'invite[d] members to consider their own responsibility for ensuring equity and nondiscrimination in contacts with Israeli educational institutions or individuals, and to consider the appropriateness of a boycott of those that do not publicly dissociate themselves from such policies.'"[21] While this is broader than the AUT motion, which called for the boycott of just two universities, the NATFHE motion was advisory instead of compulsory. The union adopted the motion at its annual conference on May 29, by a vote of 106–71, with 21 abstentions.[22]

The merger of the NATFHE and the AUT into a new union three days after the vote rendered the motion obsolete, although some argued that it set a precedent for the new union.[23] Harvard president Lawrence H. Summers immediately condemned the boycott motion, saying, "There is much that should be—indeed that must be—debated regarding Israeli policy. And all views can be, should be and will be expressed by those in academic life. However, the academic boycott resolution passed by the British professors' union in the way that it singles out Israel is in my judgment anti-Semitic in both effect and in intent."[24] "He added," according to the *Financial Times*, "that he hoped the decision would be repudiated 'in the strongest possible terms' by scholars around the world."

Steven Rose, the drafter of the initial boycott call, responded that Summers's remarks were "grotesque. . . . There is nothing anti-Semitic about putting pressure on Israeli institutors [*sic?*] and their academic staff to fight against the illegal and anti-human-rights policies of the Israeli state. When Israeli academic institutions and staff protest for the academic freedom of their academic colleagues in Palestine then I will feel more sympathetic to them."[25] The two unions successfully merged to form the University and College Union (UCU). Several months passed with little boycott news. Then, in April, Britain's largest union of journalists (the 40,000-member National Union of Journalists) voted to boycott Israeli goods.[26] This was followed closely by a call from British members of the World Medical Association for the expulsion of the Israel Medical Association from the larger organization, despite the fact that Israeli medicine had contributed more to world health than had British medicine (the quality of which is in sharp decline).[27]

Finally, in May 2007, the 116,000-member UCU considered a new boycott motion at its first annual meeting. As reported in the *Financial Times*, the new motion

> condemns illegal settlements and the "denial of educational rights for Palestinians by invasions, closures, checkpoints, curfews, and shootings and arrests of teachers, lecturers and students." It continues: "Congress condemns the complicity of Israeli academia in the occupation, which has provoked a call from Palestinian trade unions for a comprehensive and consistent international boycott of all Israeli academic institutions." An amendment to another motion also calls for academic projects to be cut off until Israel "abides by UN resolutions."[28]

The *Financial Times* noted that there were "grumblings from rank-and-file members who complained that the union was turning its back on bread-and-butter issues like pay and conditions, while absorbed in the boycott row."[29]

Still, the delegates voted 158–99 in favor of the boycott motion. Union leadership "insisted, though, that rules endorsed in a separate resolution earlier on Wednesday would forestall any immediate moves" toward "[severing] academic contacts and exchanges . . . between British and Israeli academic institutions."[30] Britain's largest labor union, the 1.3 million–member group Unison, followed suit in June by endorsing a motion urging, as reported in the *New York Times,* "'concerted and sustained pressure upon Israel,' including 'an economic, cultural, academic and sporting boycott,' to force its withdrawal from Palestinian areas."[31]

These unions (and other institutions) did not call for boycotts against any other countries, such as China (which has occupied Tibet for half a century and denies academic freedom to Tibetan critics, among other abuses), Russia (which has brutally suppressed the Chechens), North Korea (which is probably the most repressive, closed, and tyrannical state on earth), Sudan (whose state-sponsored militia has murdered almost half a million people and displaced or raped many more), Iran (an oppressive theocracy and a supporter of terrorism whose president often threatens genocide against Israel), or tyrannical regimes in Myanmar, Saudi Arabia, Cuba, Syria, Belarus, Libya, Zimbabwe, and so on. Indeed, some of the most vocal champions of the boycott against Israel actively support and justify repressive measures taken by Cuba, China, Zimbabwe, and other tyrannies favored by the hard left, thus demonstrating that the boycott against Israel has little to do with academic freedom. Indeed, Palestinians in the West Bank have more academic freedom and other educational opportunities than do academics in any Arab or Muslim country. Only Israel, which is among the freest nations in the world, was selectively subjected to these sanctions.

These union activists couldn't care less about academic freedom or any other kind of freedom, for that matter. Nor do they care much about the actual plight of the Palestinians. If they did, they would be supporting the Palestinian Authority (PA) in its efforts to make peace with Israel based on mutual compromise, rather than assisting Hamas in its futile efforts to destroy Israel as well as the PA.

What the activists are obsessed with is Israel, which they apparently despise without regard to what the Jewish state actually does or fails to do. The fact that this boycott effort was undertaken at precisely the time when Israel ended the occupation of Gaza and is reaching out to the PA and even to Syria in an effort to make peace suggests that the boycott is not intended to protest specific Israeli policies or actions, but rather to delegitimize and demonize Israel as a democratic Jewish nation. One union activist said on a BBC radio show that "Israel is worse than Stalinist Russia."

The boycotters know that Israel, without oil or other natural resources, lives by its universities, research centers, and other academic institutions. Israeli scientists, on a per capita basis, hold more patents than any other nationality in the world, have more start-up companies listed on NASDAQ, and export more medical technology.[32]

Israelis have received more Nobel and other international academic prizes than have citizens of all the Arab and Muslim nations combined.[33] Cutting Israel's academics off from collaboration with other academics would deal a death blow to the Israeli high-tech economy, and it would also set back medical research and academic collaboration throughout the world.

Moreover, many Israeli academics, precisely those who would be boycotted, are at the forefront in advocating peace efforts. They, perhaps more than others, understand the "peace dividend" that the world would reap if Israeli military expenses could be cut and the money devoted to vital scientific research.

It is more than ironic that those who advocate an academic boycott argue that Israel is guilty of imposing "collective punishment" on Palestinians by closing the borders of Gaza to prevent the importation of lethal anti-personell rockets that target Israeli civilians. Yet the proposed academic boycott itself is a stark form of collective punishment against *all* Israeli academics—indeed against the entire world which would suffer from the scientific and medical losses that would result from such a boycott.

At that point Professor Steven Weinberg, who won the Nobel Prize in Physics in 1979, and I decided to organize a response to the boycott proposal, based on what I had done in Bar-Ilan in 2005. I drafted the following petition:

> We are academics, scholars, researchers and professionals of differing religious and political perspectives. We all agree that singling out Israelis for an academic boycott is wrong. To show our solidarity with our Israeli academics in this matter, we, the undersigned, hereby declare ourselves to be Israeli academics for purposes of any academic boycott. We will regard ourselves as Israeli academics and decline to participate in any activity from which Israeli academics are excluded.

We expected a handful of Nobel Prize winners and several hundred other academics to join us in declaring ourselves Israeli academics for purposes of any boycott. We began to circulate the petition, through the good offices of Scholars for Peace in the Mideast, on June 4, 2007. On July 30, 2007, the *Jerusalem Post* carried the following headline: "UK Academic Boycott Backlash Grows: Dershowitz-Led Petition Reaches 10,000 Signatures in Seven Weeks." These signatures included thirty-two Nobel Prize winners and fifty-three college and university presidents worldwide.[34]

The American Jewish Committee sponsored another petition, signed by 286 American university presidents, which it printed in a full-page advertisement in the *New York Times*.[35] The ad appeared under the title "Boycott Israeli Universities? Boycott Ours, Too!" and included a statement from Columbia University president Lee Bollinger:

> As a citizen, I am profoundly disturbed by the recent vote by Britain's new University and College Union to advance a boycott against Israeli academic institutions. As a university professor and president, I find this idea utterly antithetical to the fundamental values of the academy, where we will not hold intellectual exchange hostage to the political disagreements of the moment. In seeking to quarantine Israeli universities and scholars, this vote threatens every university committed to fostering scholarly and cultural exchanges that lead to enlightenment, empathy, and a much-needed international marketplace of ideas. If the British UCU is intent on pursuing its deeply misguided policy, then it should add Columbia to its boycott list, for we do not intend to draw distinctions between our mission and that of the universities you are seeking to punish. Boycott us, then, for we gladly stand together with our many colleagues in British, American

and Israeli universities against such intellectually shoddy and politically biased attempts to hijack the central mission of higher education.

On August 5, fifty-six Nobel laureates, led by Elie Wiesel and including the Dalai Lama, also took out an ad in the *New York Times* expressing their opposition to the boycott. That advertisement included this statement:

> We, the undersigned Nobel Laureates, deplore the shameful proposal of the University and College Union to boycott contact and exchanges with Israeli educators and academic institutions. We also deplore a similar move by Unison and its 1.3 million public service employees. Not only do such boycotts pander to hardliners, they also glorify prejudice and bigotry. The cherished principle of academic freedom must not be undermined.[36]

In addition, Britain's Liberal Democrat Party criticized the UCU and passed a motion condemning it at the party's annual meeting in September.[37]

To increase the pressure on the boycotters, I said that we would sue anyone who participated in a boycott based on national origin or religion. I teamed up with one of England's most distinguished attorneys, Anthony Julius, and enlisted a hundred other lawyers to help break the boycott.

The *Guardian* reported on our warning in a long article that included the following:

> Mr. Dershowitz has threatened to "devastate and bankrupt" those he believes are acting against Israeli universities. . . . [He] told the *Guardian* that if the boycott call is endorsed by the UCU branches there would be retribution. . . . "If the union goes ahead with this immoral petition, it will destroy British academia," Mr. Dershowitz said. "We will isolate them from the rest of the world."

Together, we wrote an op-ed piece for the *Times* of London, in which we demonstrated parallels between this boycott and previous anti-Jewish boycotts that were undoubtedly motivated by anti-Semitism.[38] We argued that academic boycotts violate two important principles: "The first principle is that academics do not discriminate against colleagues on the basis of factors that are irrelevant to their academic work. There are three justifications for the principle: the advance of science is potentially of benefit to all mankind; the value of a given contribution to science ought to be judged on its own merits; scientists' cooperation transcends race, citizenship, religion." We then addressed the important principle of freedom of expression: "To limit or deny self-expression is . . . an attack at the root of what it is to be human. It is not sufficient for my freedom of expression for me simply to be free to speak. What matters to me is that people should also be free to hear me. Boycotts put a barrier in front of the speaker. When he addresses another, that other turns away."

We then turned to the motive underlying the campaign: "There is an edge of malice to their campaign. Their desire to hurt, to punish, outstrips their ability even to identify with any precision their targets—all Israeli universities without exception? All academics within those universities? Israeli academics in non-Israeli universities? They cannot say. And so the question arises—does this malice have a name? To be blunt, is it anti-Semitic?"

We went on to demonstrate direct parallels between this boycott and previous ones directed against Jews:

> The academic boycott resonates with earlier boycotts of Jews, whether those of medieval Europe or the Third Reich. The history of anti-Semitism is in part the history of boycotts of Jews. Each boycott derives from a principle of exclusion: Jews and/or the Jewish State are to be excluded from public life, from the community of nations, because they are dangerous and malign. We see an essential continuity here, but even if we are wrong about this, the boycott has indeed been an essential tool of anti-Semites for at least a thousand years. And who but the crassest of individuals, those least sensitive to the burden of anti-Semitism's history on Jews, would wish to impose precisely that sanction on the Jewish State today? . . .
>
> The desire to destroy Jews has been reconfigured as the desire to destroy or dismantle the Jewish State. Boycotters may have Jewish friends, they may be Jews themselves—but in supporting a boycott they have put themselves in anti-Semitism's camp.

Ultimately, on September 28, the UCU dropped its boycott call after consulting with its lawyers, who said, according to the *Guardian,* that "a boycott call ran the risk of infringing discrimination legislation."[39] "It would be beyond the union's powers and unlawful for the union, directly or indirectly, to call for, or to implement, a boycott by the union and its members of any kind of Israeli universities and other academic institutions; and that the use of union funds directly or indirectly to further such a boycott would also be unlawful," they said.[40] Proponents of the boycott blamed its defeat on our threat of legal action and vowed to reintroduce it until it succeeded.[41]

The UCU's general secretary, who had opposed the motion during the vote, was quoted as saying, "I hope this decision will allow all to move forwards [*sic*] and focus on what is our primary objective, the representation of our members." Sue Blackwell, a prominent supporter of the boycott, said of the legal decision (without irony), "It is quite ridiculous. It is cowardice. It is outrageous and an attack on academic freedom." The British minister for higher education, Bill Rammell, said, "An academic boycott would not have done anything to further the Middle East peace process, in fact the reverse."[42]

In March 2008, the National Executive Committee of the University College Union revived its campaign for an academic boycott of Israel. The motion was offered by a hard-left member of the Socialist Worker Party. The bombshell was that this motion was seconded by Linda Newman, the recently elected president of the union who had campaigned for the presidency on a platform promising to *oppose* the boycott. This is what she had told a group called Engage, which rejects academic boycotts, during the campaign: "I felt that the boycott would be ineffective and I did not believe that it was supported by a majority of members. . . . I will seek to promote and gain support from UCU for increased links between Israeli and Palestine [*sic*] academics."[43]

Yet she now favors an academic boycott of Israel and Israel alone. As one opponent of the boycott said, "I wouldn't bet on there being motions on the situation in Darfur or Tibet, but it is a certainty that there will be ones criticizing Israel."[44]

On May 28, 2008, the UCU passed a motion asking its members to "consider the moral and political implications of educational links with Israeli institutions, and to discuss the occupation with individuals and institutions concerned, including Israeli colleagues with whom they are collaborating" and to discuss "the appropriateness of continued educational links with Israeli academic institutions."[45] The passage of this motion was widely understood as the opening salvo of a renewed effort to impose a full-blown academic boycott against Israeli universities and academics. As a result, the SPME reopened its anti-boycott petition the same day, and by June 2, 2008, it had 11,973 signatures. The anti-boycott legal team is also gearing up for an all-out legal attack on any bigoted boycott based on national origin, religion, or any other invidious and illegal criteria.

If there is ever a firm decision by a British union to boycott Israeli universities or academics, the result will be a massive refusal by American academics to have anything to do with those engaging in the boycott. British universities are already in a steep decline academically, largely because of the politicization of Britain's powerful academic unions. A boycott *by* British academics would thus result in a self-inflicted boycott *of* those British academics. This will only increase the deterioration of what were once great institutions of learning. No one wants that to happen. Academics and scientists should collaborate with one another in the interests of promoting knowledge. The goal of those of us who oppose the boycott has always been to defeat the proposals for an academic boycott against Israel and to assure that those radicals who are pushing it will be delegitimized in the eyes of the vast majority of British academics who will not want to see their union hijacked by single-issue bigots.

In addition to the failed—at least, thus far—British academic boycott of Israel, there have been efforts to boycott Israeli journalists, artists, architects, and others.

The utter hypocrisy of the British National Union of Journalists, which voted in 2007 to boycott only Israel, became evident in

the face of the union's silence over moves by Venezuelan dictator Hugo Chavez to suppress dissent by the media in his leftist
regime. General Pervez Musharraf of Pakistan, too, has imposed
massive press censorship, as has President Robert Mugabe of
Zimbabwe. In many other of the hard left's favored countries—
Cuba, China, Iran, and North Korea—suppression of the press is
routine, and imprisonment of journalists is common. But there
is not a peep about these countries from the British National
Union of Journalists, which seems to admire tyranny and condemn democracy and openness. Only Israel, which has among
the freest presses of the world, is being targeted for sanctions.
Even Arab and Muslim journalists have more freedom of the
press in Israel than they do in most Arab or Muslim nations.
While Palestinian terrorist groups murder, kidnap, and threaten
journalists, the British union exempts the Palestinian Authority
and the censorious Hamas from its journalistic sanctions. The
reason is obvious. The British union cares less about journalists
or freedom of the press than it does about blindly condemning
the Jewish state.

The Presbyterian Church has also joined this orgy of hypocrisy.
The General Assembly of that church has voted to divest from only
one country in the world. No, it was not China, which has occupied Tibet for half a century and continues to deny basic human
rights to its own citizens. No, it was not Iran, which threatens
nuclear holocaust, executes dissenters, and denies religious freedom to Christians and Jews. No, it was not North Korea, Libya,
Russia, Sudan, Cuba, Myanmar, Zimbabwe, or Belarus. It was—
you guessed it—Israel, the only democracy in the Middle East and
America's most reliable ally in a troubled part of the world.

The way it will work is simple: A blacklist will be prepared
for the church's leaders, showing companies that earn more than
$1 million annually from investments in Israel or that invest more
than $1 million a year in Israel. The Presbyterians plan to divest
from any company on the list, with a handful of exemptions for
companies that deal in education, social welfare programs, and
construction. At the same time, they will presumably continue to

invest in companies that sell to China, Sudan, Cuba, and Iran, all of which are instruments of repression, discrimination, and death.

How did the church come to such a ludicrous, wrongheaded position? Just look at the resolution itself, which bursts with bigotry and ignorance. It effectively blames the Israelis for the Palestinian slaughter of civilians by asserting that the occupation is the root of terrorism.[46] This canard ignores the reality that the Palestinian leadership opted for murder and violence as the tactic of choice well before there was any occupation and that the leaders of Hamas, Hezbollah, and Islamic jihad have vowed to continue murdering Jews after the occupation ends, as long as the Jewish state exists.

The Presbyterian resolution effectively calls for the end of Israel by insisting on "the right of [Palestinian] refugees to return to their homeland." This is a well-known euphemism for turning Israel from a Jewish state into another state with a Palestinian majority. (Jordan is the other state with a Palestinian majority.)

The Presbyterian resolution also condemns Israel's military actions taken in defense of its civilians. It claims, without an iota of proof and against all of the available evidence, that Israel commits "horrific acts of violence and deadly attacks on innocent people," when the truth is that Israel, like the United States, goes to extraordinary lengths to avoid killing innocent people. It equates Israel's targeting of terrorists with the Palestinian targeting of civilians.

In a speech delivered in Harvard's Memorial Church in 2002, the then-president of Harvard University, Lawrence Summers, included the singling out of Israel for divestment as an example of "actions that are anti-Semitic in their effect, if not in their intent." The one-sided maneuvers of the Presbyterian Church fit into this category.

Divestment also encourages the continued use of terrorism by Palestinian leaders, who see that when Israel responds to their terrorism, it causes an important church to punish Israel.

I do not believe that a majority of the 2.5 million Presbyterians in the United States want their church used to support terrorism.

But they are now on notice that their church has been hijacked and its name misused in the service of an immoral tactic.

Balanced criticism of Israel and of specific policies of its government is proper and essential to democratic governance. But the Presbyterian resolution is so anti-Israel in its rhetoric and so ignorant of the realities on the ground that it can only be explained by the kind of bigotry that the Presbyterian Church itself condemned in 1987, when it acknowledged its long history of anti-Semitism and promised "never again to participate in, to contribute to, or (insofar as we are able) to allow the persecution or denigration of Jews."

Unless the church rescinds this immoral, sinful, and biased attack on the Jewish state, it will once again be "participating in" and "contributing to" bigotry and the encouragement of terrorism. In June 2008, the church leadership revised a draft statement that had condemned anti-Semitism, turning it instead into "a blueprint for how to engage in anti-Israel activity without being accused of anti-Semitism."[47]

When challenged about the church's unfair proposal for selective divestment against Israel and Israel alone, some Presbyterian leaders point to the fact that selective divestment against Israel is backed by Rabbi Michael Lerner of *Tikkun* magazine. "If a rabbi supports divestment against Israel, then it can't be anti-Semitic," is the claim.

Lerner advocates a targeted divestment campaign against "specific firms that actively contribute to the enforcement of the Occupation." Which occupation? Not the occupation of Tibet by China. Not the occupation of Kurdistan by Syria, Iraq, and Turkey. Not the occupation of Chechnya by Russia. No, only *the* Occupation—the one by Israel, which it offered to end in 2000 and 2001 and which it is in the process of ending now. In his magazine, Lerner has urged "local Tikkun Communities" (his self-aggrandizing capitalization) to initiate "targeted divestment campaigns" against Israel and *only* Israel. He has urged his "followers"—he styles himself as something of a guru with a cult following—to support and join with the Presbyterians in their malevolent divestment campaign. The reason given by Lerner for endorsing the Presbyterian divestment campaign is even more sinister and troubling: "to counter the false and misleading charges that these targeted campaigns [against Israel alone] are anti-Semitic."[48] In other words, his actions are specifically calculated to lend legitimacy to the Presbyterian divestment campaign. Lerner's thinking, such as it is, seems to be that if Jews like him favor sanctions directed against only Israel, then it can't possibly be anti-Semitic. That is about as logical as the discredited argument made by some Arab representatives to the UN, which supported the "Zionism equals racism" resolution that stated that the Arabs could not be anti-Semites because they, too, are Semites. But as Karl Marx and Norman Finkelstein have proved, even a Jew can be an anti-Semite, and now Michael Lerner has shown that even a rabbi can take part in anti-Semitic actions.

My friend and colleague Robert Brustein—the prominent writer, critic, professor, and director—should get the last word on the subject of boycotts in general and artistic boycotts in particular. Here is what he wrote in response to an effort to implement "a world-wide call for a cultural boycott of the state of Israel":

> Even in regard to the most repressive regimes, which Israel clearly is not, democratic countries have never considered boycotting their artists or scholars. Apartheid South Africa would have rejoiced if Athol Fugard, Alan Paton, Pieter Dirk Uys, or J.M. Coetzee had been excluded by the rest of the civilized world. Did the US close its doors to Bertolt Brecht, Kurt Weill, or Thomas Mann because they were born in a country currently dominated by the Nazi Party? Would we have denied visiting rights to Brodsky, Sharansky, Solzynetsin, Shostakovich, or Prokofiev, because of Stalin's genocide?
>
> Israel has arguably been over-reacting to Palestinian provocation, but it has unarguably been mightily provoked. Imagine how the US would have behaved if Mexico lobbed rockets daily into Texas or Southern California. The impulse to demonize a mid-Eastern tiny country, surrounded by a much larger population that has long been dedicated to its total destruction, is something that could only have been conceived in the minds of the "progressive" academic left, which for years has been indistinguishable in behavior, if not in ideology, from the reactionary right. Leave this sort of thing to British academics. They have a much longer history of anti-Semitism.[49]

4 The Case against the Anti-Israel Hard Left and Hard Right

How can you still be a liberal, in the face of the obvious liberal bias against Israel? This is the most frequent question I am asked by pro-Israel audience members in my speeches around the country. The question, however, is based on a false premise: liberals are not, as a group, biased against Israel; radicals are. Many radicals of both the hard left and the hard right tend to hate Israel.[1] This is not the only thing the hard left and the hard right have in common. They both have a tendency toward knee-jerk, superficial, hate-filled scapegoating. Historically, Jews have always been caught between "the black and the red," as one pundit put it. Jews are victimized by the extreme ideologies of fascism and communism (even though many original Bolsheviks were of Jewish origin). Hitler and Stalin both denounced and murdered Jews. Jews tend to thrive in centrist political environments in which individual merit is appreciated and people are judged by their accomplishments, not by some ideological or racial test.

It should not be surprising, therefore, that the Jewish state is also caught between the red of the radical left and the black of the reactionary right.

This hard left—often represented by people of Jewish origin, such as Noam Chomsky, Norman Finkelstein, Richard Falk, and Tony Kushner—usually reviles Israel, comparing it to Nazi Germany. The hard right—represented by Patrick Buchanan, Robert Novak, and David Duke—equally despises Israel and frequently compares it to the Stalinist Soviet Union. Sometimes it's hard to tell the hard left and the hard right apart from their rhetoric about Israel.

The Hard Left

The hard-left attack against Jewish nationalism began with Karl Marx, who, though himself of Jewish origin, was a classic anti-Semite. His stereotyping of Jews and his rabid hatred of all things Jewish are hard to distinguish from the beliefs of Adolf Hitler. An anti-Semite from the "religious right" whose views were strikingly parallel to Marx's was Fyodor Dostoyevsky.[2] Marx equated Judaism and "the chimerical nationality of the Jew" with greed and materialism. "What is the profane basis of Judaism?" he asked. "*Practical* need, *self-interest*. What is the world cult of the Jew? *Huckstering*. What is his worldly god? *Money*." Judaism, according to Marx, was not merely the religion of the Jews, but an affliction ailing society that must be eliminated. "It is from its own entrails that civil society ceaselessly engenders the Jew." He urged Jewish emancipation on the grounds that "The *social* emancipation of the Jew is the *emancipation* of *society from Judaism*."[3]

Marx's most outrageous claims prefigured those made in the notorious czarist forgery the *Protocols of the Elders of Zion*. Listen to the bigoted nonsense Marx spewed: "The contradiction which exists between the effective political power of the Jews and his political rights, is the contradiction between politics and the power of money in general. Politics is in principle superior to the power of money, but in practice it has become its bondsman." He advanced a conspiracy theory of Jewish power and control, predicting that Judaism would "attain universal domination and could turn alienated man and alienated nature into *alienable*, saleable objects, in thrall to egoistic need and huckstering."[4]

Literary scholar Stephen J. Greenblatt, in his essay "Marlowe, Marx, and Anti-Semitism," suggests a connection between Marx's own Jewish background and his anti-Semitism. Greenblatt points to Marx's "sharp, even hysterical, denial of his religious background" as demonstrating his eagerness "to prove that he is in no way excusing or forgiving the Jews."[5]

It is interesting to compare current attitudes among some Jewish academics of the radical left with Marx's use of Judaism as a lens for his broader criticisms and his "hysterical" effort to dissociate himself from Judaism and Jewish nationalism. For these contemporary thinkers, dissociating from Zionism (the current manifestation of Jewish nationalism) has become a "litmus test" for acceptability by the hard left.[6] Unlike Marx, however, some of them emphasize their Jewishness while rejecting Jewish nationalism. They point to their Jewish identity to discredit accusations that their ideas are anti-Semitic (claiming that as Jews, they can't be anti-Semites), to establish their special right to criticize Israel, and to give added stress to the evils of Zionism (claiming that if we, as Jews, are troubled by Zionism, then it must be really bad). Few of these Israel-haters are Jewish in any real sense, other than their parentage. They are Jewish on their "parents' side," as a friend of mine who became a Buddhist described himself. Yet they accentuate their Jewish heritage (their names and connections to the Holocaust) to gain credibility for their Israel bashing. By rejecting Zionism, they prove their commitment to the values of the hard left, as well as their lack of dual loyalty. (Similarly, early American Reform Jews and some British elite Jews defined Judaism as a religion and rejected Jewish nationalism, eager to prove their patriotism and fearing charges of dual loyalty.) This chapter will explore in greater detail the anti-Zionist expressions of these academics—an anti-Zionism that sometimes moves over the line to the sort of anti-Semitism expressed by Marx.

I begin with Professor Israel Shahak, an influential academic who taught at Hebrew University until his death in 2001.

Shahak—an Israeli Holocaust survivor, who excoriated Israel as well as Judaism—acknowledged his intellectual debt to Marx: "Marx was quite right when he characterised [classical Judaism] as dominated by profit-seeking." Echoing Marx, Shahak was recycling the stereotype of the greedy Jew, "motivated by the spirit of profit." "It is actually true that the Jewish religious establishment does have a strong tendency to chicanery and graft, due to the corrupting influence of the Orthodox Jewish religion."[7]

Shahak ignored, as Marx did, the disproportionate contributions of Jews to both Jewish and non-Jewish charities, as well as the heavy involvement of Jews in do-gooder and progressive causes. This is the way of the anti-Semite: to blame all Jews, or Judaism, for the evil practices of some Jews, but not to credit Jews or Judaism for the good deeds of many Jews.

Shahak also extended Marx's conspiracy theory to Israel, claiming that the Jewish state is a danger to the world and that American Jews wield a disproportionate and dangerous influence over U.S. policy toward Israel. "In my view," he wrote, "Israel as a Jewish state constitutes a danger not only to itself and its inhabitants, but to all Jews and to all other peoples and states in the Middle East and beyond." The danger, he explained, is Israel's "ideologically motivated pursuit of territorial expansion and the inevitable series of wars resulting from this aim." This threat, according to Shahak, "will continue to grow, as long as two currently operating developments are being strengthened: the increase in the Jewish character of Israel and the increase in its power, particularly in nuclear power. Another ominous factor is that Israeli influence in the USA political establishment is also increasing."[8]

Decrying Israeli territorial expansion, Shahak dismissed the analogy of Israel to apartheid South Africa on the grounds that Israel is more racist and a worse human rights violator, because under apartheid, 13 percent of the land was given to the blacks, whereas under Zionism, no land would ever be given to the Arabs: "'Jewish ideology' demands that no part of the Land of Israel can be recognised as 'belonging' to non-Jews. . . . The principle of the Redemption of the Land demands that ideally *all* the land, and not merely, say, 87 per cent, will in time be 'redeemed,' that is, become owned by Jews."[9]

This is total nonsense, as evidenced by Israel's decision to leave the Gaza Strip and its offer to vacate more than 95 percent of the West Bank in exchange for peace. The vast majority of Israelis are against "territorial expansion" and are "ideologically motivated" toward living in peace with their Arab neighbors, but Shahak attributed the views of a tiny minority of religious extremists to "the Jewish character of Israel" and to Jews in general. Once again, he followed the well-trodden path of earlier anti-Semites such as Marx: attributing to "the Jews,"—or, in this case, "the Israelis"—views rejected by the vast majority of Jews and Israelis. For ideologists like Shahak, facts are irrelevant. Their ideology is their only "truth."

Oblivious to history, Shahak argued that the Jewish state not only poses a greater threat than anti-Semitism, but it has *already inflicted* more persecution than anti-Semitic regimes: "The extent of the persecution and discrimination against non-Jews inflicted by the 'Jewish state' with the support of organised diaspora Jews is also enormously greater than the suffering inflicted on Jews by regimes hostile to them." Shahak wrote this ahistorical nonsense within fifty years of the murder of more than six million Jews by "regimes hostile to them"—namely, Nazi Germany and the Stalinist Soviet Union. Emphasizing that he was writing "as an Israeli Jew" and a survivor of Bergen-Belsen, Shahak wielded his Jewish identity to claim immunity for trivializing Nazi atrocities and demonizing Israel.[10]

Shahak likened Judaism to anti-Semitism on the alleged grounds that Orthodox Judaism is inherently racist and discriminatory against Gentiles. He based his conclusion on the following alleged observation of one anonymous "ultra-religious Jew" and an unidentified "rabbinical court":

> I had personally witnessed an ultra-religious Jew refuse to allow his phone to be used on the Sabbath in order to call an ambulance for a non-Jew who happened to have collapsed in his Jerusalem neighborhood. Instead of simply publishing the incident in the press,

I asked for a meeting with the members of the Rabbinical Court of Jerusalem, which is composed of rabbis nominated by the State of Israel. I asked them whether such behavior was consistent with their interpretation of Jewish religion. They answered that the Jew in question had behaved correctly, indeed piously, and backed their statement by referring me to a passage in an authoritative compendium of Talmud laws, written in this century.[11]

Shahak then generalized and stereotyped from this one questionable incident the "more general conclusion" that Jews have a "compulsion to do evil, to cheat and to deceive and, while keeping one's hands quite clean of violence, to corrupt whole peoples and drive them to oppression and murder. . . . As for Gentiles, the basic Talmudic principle is that their lives *must not* be saved, although it is forbidden to murder them outright."[12]

This, too, is total nonsense, reflecting Shahak's abysmal ignorance of the complex teachings of the Talmud, which place a premium on human life. I have asked dozens of Orthodox rabbis about Shahak's characterization of Talmudic principles, and not a single one agreed with it.

Shahak apparently borrowed his distorted views of Judaism directly from Stalinist "zionology." Stalin commissioned former Jews who had studied the Torah and the Talmud to distort or invent the most extreme view of Judaism and present it as mainstream.[13] The Nazis did the same thing.

The absurdity of Shahak's depiction of Jewish religion is exemplified by his claim that Judaism involves devil worship. Without citing a Talmudic source, Shahak claimed that the blessing over Jewish ritual washing involves "worshiping Satan."[14]

Why, you may be wondering, have I devoted so much space to this obscure academic who died in 2001 and whose claims about Judaism and Israel are clearly absurd and bigoted? Unfortunately, the absurdity of his writing is not as clear to others. Because Shahak was a Jew, an Israeli, and a survivor of the Holocaust, his grotesquely distorted views on Judaism, Israel, and the Holocaust have been given far more credence than they would deserve on their own merits—or demerits. In fact, Noam Chomsky, the world's most cited anti-Israel academic and possibly the most influential academic in the world—one of his book jackets calls him "arguably the most important intellectual alive"[15]—not only refers to Shahak as "an old friend" but has also given credit and praise to his ideas.[16] Indeed, much of the current anti-Israel rhetoric of the hard left—particularly, the Jewish hard left—can be traced to Shahak's drivel.[17] As recently as May 6, 2008, I was confronted at a speech in Greenwich, Connecticut, with an anti-Israeli leaflet that quoted extensively from Shahak's bizarre mischaracterizations of Judaism as a religion that believes that "all non-Jews are totally satanic creatures," and that Israel acts on that principle.[18]

In 1973, I engaged in an exchange of letters with Chomsky in the *Boston Globe* concerning Shahak's failed attempt to seize control over the Israel League for Human and Civil Rights and turn it into a hard-left organization that would defend only Shahak's ideological soul mates (as Chomsky himself does).[19] In his letters, Chomsky praised Shahak as "a man of honor and principle who needs no lessons from Alan Dershowitz or anyone else on what it means to be a civil libertarian."[20]

Chomsky's record of defending anti-Semites, Jewish and non-Jewish alike, does not stop with Shahak. He has made a career of defending—not as a matter of free speech, but on the *merits*— Israel-haters of every stripe, including out-and-out Holocaust deniers such as Robert Faurisson, who has called the Holocaust and the existence of Nazi gas chambers a "hoax" and a "fraud."[21] Chomsky has praised Faurisson, who, in addition to denying the real Holocaust, accuses Israel of inflicting a "Holocaust" on the Palestinians. Chomsky has characterized this anti-Semitic bigot as a "relatively apolitical liberal" who has done "extensive historical research" that supports his "findings" about the Holocaust not having occurred.[22] Chomsky's blindness to the bigotry of his ideological soul mates is perhaps best revealed by his linguistic opinion that there is not even a "hint of anti-Semitic implications" in Faurisson's claim that the so-called Holocaust was a fraud perpetrated by the Jewish people.[23] Chomsky, the linguist, assured his readers that "nobody believes there is an anti-Semitic connotation to the denial of the Holocaust . . . whether one believes it took place or not" (thus implying that reasonable people could believe that it did *not* take place).[24] Chomsky wrote a preface to Faurisson's book *Memoire on Defense*, lending this Holocaust denier his academic imprimatur, something no true civil libertarian would ever do.[25]

There is a difference between defending the *right* of Nazis to spew their hatred, which civil libertarians have done, and defending the *merits* of neo-Nazi "research" and "findings" denying the Holocaust, which Chomsky has done. Chomsky's favorite Holocaust denier attended Iran's 2006 Holocaust-denial hatefest as a featured speaker to discuss his "research" and "findings" on why the Holocaust never happened.[26] The event was sponsored by Mahmoud Ahmadinejad. Chomsky has also published his writings with a well-known neo-Nazi press.[27] Paul L. Berman, an accomplished essayist and Distinguished Writer in Residence at New York University, summarized Chomsky's record on these issues: "Chomsky's view of anti-Semitism is positively wild. His definition is so narrow, neither the *Protocols of the Elders of Zion* nor the no-Holocaust delusion fit into it. . . . I am afraid that his present remarks on anti-Semitism and Zionist lies disqualify him from ever being taken seriously on matters pertaining to Jews."[28]

Chomsky's own words on a range of subjects involving the United States and Israel raise questions about whether he should be taken seriously on any subject involving politics. Following the tragic events of September 11, 2001, Chomsky seemed to gloat, saying, "This is certainly a turning point: for the first time in history the victims are returning the blow to the motherland."[29] This was not surprising coming from a man who has insisted that what is needed in the United States today is not dissent but rather "denazification."[30] Chomsky has justified terrorism, not only against the United States and Israel, but also in Vietnam and Cambodia.[31] He has described Zionism as being based in part on "Hitler's conceptions"[32] and has accused the Jewish community in the United States of being "deeply totalitarian" and of rejecting both "democracy" and "freedom."[33] He has said this not about individual Jews but about "the Jewish community."[34]

But Chomsky continues to be taken seriously in hard-left academic circles. He has taught courses on the Middle East, despite his utter lack of qualifications on the subject, other than his extremist views.[35]

Since the 1970s, I have debated Chomsky on several occasions about the Israeli-Arab conflict. Our most recent encounter (which can be seen at www.democracynow.org/2005/12/23/noam_chomsky_v_alan_dershowitz), took place at the Harvard Kennedy School on November 29, 2005. I began my opening on a friendly, personal note indicating that it's an honor for me to be participating in a debate with a man who has been called "the world's top public intellectual." I then mentioned that my connections to Noam Chomsky go back to the 1940s when I was a camper and he a counselor in a Hebrew-speaking Zionist camp in the Pocono Mountains called Camp Massad. In the 1960s we both worked against the Vietnam War. In the 1970s, we had the first of our many debates about the Arab-Israeli conflict. I advocated ending the Israeli occupation in exchange for peace and recognition of Israel; he advocated a one-state solution, modeled on Lebanon and Yugoslavia.

I ended my remarks by proposing a "peace treaty" between Chomsky and me:

> I propose here today a peace treaty among academics who purport to favor peace between Israel and the Palestinians. I believe that by agreeing to this peace treaty and by implementing it, academics can actually contribute to encouraging a pragmatic peace. I call today for those who have supported the Palestinian cause to stop demonizing Israel, to stop de-legitimating Israel, to stop defaming Israel, to stop applying a double standard to Israel, to stop divestiture and boycotts of Israel, and most importantly, to stop being more Palestinian than the Palestinians themselves.

I also called on academics who support Israel to stop being more Israeli than the Israelis by demanding "a greater Israel" and to join "the vast majority of Israeli and American supporters of Israel who favor the two-state solution."

Rather than accept my olive branch, Chomsky began his opening by accusing me, in effect, of making "deceitful allegations about" him: "[I] congratulate Mr. Dershowitz on having made a true statement. I was a counselor at Massad. About the rest, there happens to be an ample record in print." Chomsky then proceeded to ignore virtually everything I said and to vilify Israel, making a series of misstatements that began with his claim that Israel's decision to leave Gaza was "in reality West Bank expansion." He then made up, out of whole cloth, the following fairy tale: "The official plan for disengagement stated that Israel will permanently take over major population centers, cities, towns and villages, security areas and other places of special interest to Israel in the West Bank. That was endorsed by the U.S. ambassador, as it had been by the President."

Israel, of course, left the major population centers in the 1990s and offered autonomy over them to the Palestinian Authority at Camp David and Taba; even Prime Minister Ariel Sharon indicated a willingness to end the occupation of these areas. Nowhere, except in Chomsky's mind, did Israel have a plan to "permanently take over" these Palestinian population centers.

Chomsky then provided his account of Camp David, which is totally contradicted by people who were there, including Dennis Ross. This is how Chomsky characterized it: "Maps of the U.S.-Israel proposals at Camp David show a salient, east of Jerusalem, bisecting the West Bank, and a northern salient virtually dividing the northern from the central canton. I have the maps if you want them. The current map considerably extends these salients and the isolation of East Jerusalem. . . . The crucial issue at Camp David was territorial, not the refugee issue, for which Arafat agreed to a pragmatic solution."

This is totally false. The crucial sticking point was the refugee issue, for which Arafat offered no solution, pragmatic or otherwise. He simply refused to compromise on the so-called right of return. The parties were very close on territorial issues.[36]

During the course of the debate, Chomsky and I disagreed about the relevant history of the conflict—including whether Israel accepted and the Arabs rejected Security Council Resolution 242, which called for Israel to return captured territories in return for full peace and recognition. As usual, Chomsky said that the issue was uncontroversial and that the diplomatic record was clear that Israel, "of course, rejected 242."[37] Chomsky was right about one thing: that the diplomatic record is clear. But he was wrong about what it showed: Israel "respond[ed] affirmatively" to 242, while the Palestinians and all the Arab states unanimously rejected it.[38] At a meeting in Khartoum, they issued their three infamous no's: "no peace with Israel, no recognition of Israel, no negotiations" with Israel.[39] Anyone is free to check the diplomatic record and see that Chomsky was simply making up the facts, but Chomsky's audience members rarely bother to check available sources. I urged my listeners to check the sources cited by Chomsky and decide for themselves whose rendition was correct.

When the debate ended, I extended my hand to Chomsky for a shake. He responded, "When will you finally stop lying?" Within days, I received e-mails from students who had checked the sources. They could not believe what they found: Chomsky had simply made up much of his history, including his reference to Resolution 242. I was not surprised, having debated him previously and checked his "sources."

Our debates continued on blogs, after Chomsky circulated a letter in August 2006 that he got two naive Nobel Prize winners—the playwright Harold Pinter and the poet José Saramago—to sign. The letter blamed the ongoing battle between terrorists and Israel on Israel alone.

It was vintage Chomsky, beginning with its first sentences: "The latest chapter of the conflict between Israel and Palestine began when Israeli forces abducted two civilians, a doctor and his brother, from Gaza. An incident scarcely reported anywhere, except in the Turkish press."[40]

Chomsky typically cites obscure news reports in languages relatively few can read. This time it's "the Turkish press." The problem with Chomsky's assertion is that a five-minute Google News check reveals that the incident he points to was widely reported by the English-language press, including the *Washington Post*, the *Chicago Tribune*, the *Boston Globe*, BBC, Reuters, and the Associated Press. (Lie number one.)

This is what the Associated Press reported:

> On Saturday, Israeli commandos seized two Palestinians suspected of being Hamas militants in the army's first arrest raid in the Gaza Strip since Israel's withdrawal nearly a year ago. An Israeli army spokesman said the two men, arrested at a house near Rafah in southern Gaza, were in the "final states of planning a large-scale terror attack" in coming days. The army did not provide details on the nature of the alleged plot. Hamas denied that the men, who were identified by neighbors as brothers, are members.[41]

This is quite a different account from the one provided by Chomsky, et al. (Lie number two.)

Chomsky said in interviews that "we don't know their names," referring to the arrested militants.[42] But a quick check of newspapers reveals that their names are Osama and Mostafa Muamar, whose father is Ali Muamar, a notorious Hamas leader. According to press reports, "local Hamas activists said the pair was . . . known to be members of [Hamas]."[43] (Lie number three.)

Nor was the arrest of these Hamas terrorists the origin of the crisis, as Chomsky asserts. Even Kofi Annan acknowledged that "Hezbollah's provocative attack on July 12 was the trigger of this particular crisis"; that Hezbollah is "deliberate[ly] targeting . . . Israeli population centers with hundreds of indiscriminate weapons"; and that Israel has the "right to defend itself under Article 51 of the UN Charter."[44] But on Planet Chomsky, Annan and the UN are dupes of Israel that suppress the real story, which only the Turkish press has the courage and honesty to report. (Lie number four.)

Even the *Turkish Daily News*—which simply reprinted a widely distributed international Reuters story, datelined June 25, Gaza—reported that the two arrested individuals were alleged Hamas militants, a fact that Chomsky conveniently omitted, even though he purported to rely on the Turkish press account.[45] (Lie number five.)

The lies continued. Chomsky claimed that Israeli missiles target areas "where the disinherited and crowded poor live, waiting for what was once called justice."[46] He never mentions that it is Hezbollah and Hamas that select those civilian areas from which they fire their antipersonnel rockets, precisely in order to make Israel choose to either allow the missiles to rain down on its own civilians or try to destroy the rocket launchers with smart bombs designed to minimize civilian casualties. (Lie number six.)

Finally, the Big Lie: "[Israel's] aim is nothing less than the liquidation of the Palestinian nation. This has to be said loud and clear for the practice, only half declared and often covert, is advancing fast these days, and, in our opinion, it must be unceasingly and eternally recognized for what it is and resisted."[47]

Again Chomsky ignores the historically indisputable facts that Israel (and the international community) offered the Palestinians a state in 1938, in 1948, and in 2001. The Palestinians responded with terrorism in each instance. The vast majority of Israelis and the Israeli government favor the two-state solution. It is Hamas and Hezbollah whose "aim is nothing less than the liquidation" of Israel. Just ask them. Just read their charter. Just look at what they're doing. But not on Planet Chomsky, where everything is the mirror image of reality, and where "facts" are made up, ignored, and distorted to serve a predetermined ideological end. (Lie number seven.)

Now look at the one truth in the Chomsky letter, the call for Israel's aims to be "resisted." This will surely be read by Hamas and Hezbollah as support for their terrorism against Israel and those who champion its existence.[48]

In a recent talk at Harvard, Chomsky suggested that Israel's possession of nuclear weapons (which it has never used) is more dangerous to the world than Ahmadinejad's nuclear weapons program for Iran (which it has threatened to use to wipe Israel off the map). This is what he said: "If a constellation of forces arose that forced the Israelis to accept the right of return, they would use their nuclear deterrent to destroy the world."[49] He has even claimed that Israel is threatening to impose "a final solution" upon the world: "Israel's 'secret weapon'. . . is that it may behave in the manner of what have sometimes been called 'crazy states' in the international affairs literature. . . eventuating in a final solution from which few will escape."[50] The implication is that the only way to stop Israel from imposing its "final solution" that will "destroy the world" is to attack its nuclear weapons first.

Chomsky's absurd worldview continues to have considerable influence, especially in Europe, where a 2003 poll showed that 59 percent of Europeans saw Israel as the greatest threat to world peace—ahead of Iran and North Korea.[51] So Chomsky's lies and his defense of the world's most dangerous and repressive regimes cannot simply be ignored.

Chomsky's most recent foray into the defense of falsehoods and those who live by them relates to Norman Finkelstein, a failed academic who by his own account has been fired by several universities, most recently DePaul. Since I played a role in the DePaul decision, Chomsky has attacked me viciously as a "maniac," "a liar," "a supporter of atrocities," and "a passionate opponent of civil rights," saying that I "launched a Jihad against Norman Finkelstein, simply to try to vilify and defame him, in the hope that maybe what he's writing will disappear."[52] The facts, as usual, are quite different from Chomsky's rendition. (For those interested in the details, a full account can be found in my book *The Case for Peace: How the Arab-Israeli Conflict Can Be Solved*, at pages 167–188.)[53]

As soon as my book *The Case for Israel* hit the best-seller lists, Finkelstein and Chomsky began to attack it, falsely claiming that I hadn't even written or read the book. The implication was that some Israeli intelligence agency wrote it and had me sign it—exactly as they had insisted was the situation with several earlier pro-Israel books. The problem for them is that I don't type or use a computer, so every word of the text was handwritten by me—and I still have the original, handwritten manuscript. Then they falsely claimed that I had plagiarized it.[54]

My first reaction was to ignore the attack, as I generally ignore the numerous made-up stories about me that are common on neo-Nazi and Holocaust-denial Web sites. But then I realized its underlying purpose: it was not so much directed at me as it was at young, untenured academics who might consider writing or speaking in support of Israel. Its goal was send a powerful message to such academics that if you write in support of Israel, you, too, will be accused of not having written your book, plagiarizing it, or concocting a fraud. Finkelstein and Chomsky knew they couldn't destroy me because I have the means to fight back, but they could deter others who lack such means. For an untenured assistant professor to be accused of academic dishonesty, it could be an academic death sentence, even if the accusation was baseless. As Churchill once quipped, "A lie makes its way halfway around the world before the truth can get its pants on." And Churchill said this before the advent of the Internet. Today a lie makes it all the way around the world, and the truth—which is often less interesting than the lie—makes it to the bottom of a Google search.

I decided that I had to fight back and send a countermessage: those who falsely accuse pro-Israel writers will be exposed as liars and they will have to pay a price for their defamations. Since I prefer the marketplace of ideas to the courtroom as the proper forum for answering defamations, I offered my contribution to the marketplace of ideas. In doing so, I followed the lead of Professor Deborah Lipstadt, who had exposed David Irving as a Holocaust-denying pseudohistorian by quoting his own words. (Irving sued Lipstadt for defamation and lost.)

I decided that the best weapon to use against Finkelstein was his own words. Accordingly, I compiled and circulated a list of Finkelstein's statements about Israel and the alleged "international Jewish conspiracy" that supports Israel. He claims that Israel's human rights record is worse than that of the Nazis: "[I] can't imagine why Israel's apologists would be offended by a comparison with the Gestapo."[55]

He also says that Israel's human rights record is "interchangeable with Iraq's" when it was ruled by Saddam Hussein.[56] He supports Hezbollah, an anti-Semitic terrorist group whose goal is to destroy Israel and commit genocide against the world's Jews: "The honorable thing now is to show solidarity with

Hezbollah as the US and Israel target it for liquidation. Indeed, looking back my chief regret is that I wasn't even more forceful in publicly defending Hezbollah against terrorist intimidation and attack."[57]

He supports Libya: "Libya had nothing to do with it [the blowing up of Pan Am 103, for which Libya has acknowledged responsibility] but they are playing along."[58] He seems to justify bin Laden's terrorism against the United States by saying, "We deserve the problem on our hands because some things Bin Laden says are true."[59]

Finkelstein believes that the international Jewish conspiracy includes Steven Spielberg's movie *Schindler's List*, Leon Uris's book *Exodus*, Andrew Lloyd Webber's musical *Cats*, and the NBC series *Holocaust*. In Finkelstein's own words:

> Give me a better reason! . . . Who profits [from the movie]? Basically, there are two beneficiaries from the dogmas [of *Schindler's List*]: American Jews and the American administration.[60]

> The name of the character [in Uris's novel *Exodus*] is Ari Ben Canaan because Ari is the diminutive for Aryan. It is the whole admiration for this blond haired, blue eyed type.[61]

> Some people [who support the thesis of a new anti-Semitism think that the musical] *Cats* is a codeword for K-A-T-Z, Katz.[62]

> In 1978, NBC produced the series *Holocaust*. Do you believe it was a coincidence, 1978? Just at this time, when peace negotiations between Israel and Egypt took place in Camp David?[63]

Finkelstein argues that Israel uses the Holocaust to justify its "Gestapo-like" tactics, and he demeans Holocaust survivors:

> I'm not exaggerating when I say that one out of three Jews you stop in the street in New York will claim to be a survivor.[64]

> "If everyone who claims to be a survivor actually is one," my mother used to exclaim, "who did Hitler kill then?"[65]

According to the *Guardian*, "Finkelstein says . . . that most 'survivors' are bogus."[66]

I then circulated a list of what other serious scholars had said about Finkelstein's writing, beginning with Michael Novick, the

University of Chicago historian who Finkelstein said had inspired him:

> As concerns particular assertions made by Finkelstein . . . , the appropriate response is not (exhilarating) "debate" but (tedious) examination of his footnotes. Such an examination reveals that many of those assertions are pure invention. . . . No facts alleged by Finkelstein should be assumed to be really facts, no quotation in his book should be assumed to be accurate, without taking the time to carefully compare his claims with the sources he cites.
>
> Finkelstein's book is trash.[67]

David Casarari, a leftist scholar, documented Finkelstein's "questionable use of sources," "selective quotations," and "misuse of evidence."[68]

The *New York Times* review of Finkelstein's book by the distinguished Brown University professor Omer Bartov characterized it as:

> a novel variation on the anti-Semitic forgery, "The Protocols of the Elders of Zion." There is also something indecent about it, something juvenile, self-righteous, arrogant and stupid.
>
> This book is, in a word, an ideological fanatic's view . . . by a writer so reckless and ruthless in his attacks. . . . [His theory is] both irrational and insidious. . . . An international Jewish conspiracy verges on paranoia and would serve anti-Semites.[69]

I followed the *Times* review with an assessment by Daniel Jonah Goldhagen, the author of *Hitler's Willing Executioners*: "Finkelstein's work is, from beginning to end, a tendentious series of inventions. It is worth noting that Finkelstein has never before written anything on the Holocaust or German history and cannot read German . . . which means that he cannot read many of the sources on which he is passing his 'expert' opinion."[70]

Finally, I showed how Finkelstein's work is relied on by neo-Nazis, citing the distinguished writer Gabriel Schoenfeld: "Crackpot ideas, some of them mirrored almost verbatim in the propaganda put out by neo-Nazis around the world."[71] To prove my point, I quoted a notorious neo-Nazi, Ingrid Rimland, the wife of neo-Nazi and Holocaust-denier Ernst Zuendel: "[Because of

Finkelstein's *The Holocaust Industry*] I feel like a kid in a candy store. . . . Finkelstein is a Jewish David Irving."[72]

As a result of my decision to fight back against Finkelstein's lies, I received a letter from one of Finkelstein's colleagues in the DePaul political science department, a man named Patrick Callahan, who had served as chairman of the department, which was then considering him for tenure. He invited me to submit a letter documenting "the clearest and most egregious instances of [intellectual] dishonesty on Finkelstein's part." This is part of what I wrote:

> I would like to point out from the outset that the ugly and false assertions that I will discuss below are not *incidental* to Finkelstein's purported scholarship; they *are* his purported scholarship. Finklestein's entire literary catalogue is one prepostcrous and discredited ad hominem attack after another. By his own admission, he has conducted no original research, has never been published in a reputable, scientific journal, and has made no contributions to our collective historical knowledge. . . . Although he claims to be a "forensic scholar," he limits his defamations to one ideological group and never applies his so-called "forensic" tools to his own work or to those who share his ideological perspective. . . . That is not forensic scholarship; it is propaganda.

After discussing his utter lack of any real scholarship, I focused on a particular article he had written about me titled "Should Alan Dershowitz Target Himself for Assassination?" Finkelstein had collaborated with an artist to create a pornographic cartoon of me, which accompanied the article. The cartoon aptly represented the content of Finkelstein's article, which accused me of being a "moral pervert." He called me a Nazi twice, first saying that I subscribe to "Nazi ideology" and then comparing me to Nazi propagandist Julius Streicher.[73]

I then proceeded to document a series of made-up quotations used by Finkelstein—quotes that simply didn't exist. These alone should have disqualified him from serious consideration at any U.S. university.[74] (On July 2, 2008, Finkelstein made up yet another quote and put it on his Web site. Referring to one of my clients, Finkelstein wrote, "Dershowitz predicts 'second Holocaust' if conviction is not overturned." I never said anything of the sort.)

While all of this was going on, Finkelstein received a letter from the Iranian government inviting him to participate in Mahmoud Ahmadinejad's Holocaust-denial hatefest. Only two Americans, to my knowledge, were honored by such an invitation. The other was David Duke.

Finkelstein apparently *accepted* the invitation, and his name appeared on the speakers' list published by a neo-Nazi hate site, along with an assortment of other nuts, neo-Nazis, Holocaust-deniers, Israel-bashers, and anti-Semites.[75] He ended up not going, apparently because of a disagreement about how much time he would be allocated for his speech.[76] In the end, DePaul denied him tenure and fired him.

Finkelstein now travels the world—paid in part by Arab sources—attacking Israel, Jews, the United States, DePaul University, and me. He recently visited Lebanon to show solidarity with Hezbollah, the terrorist group that killed hundreds of U.S. soldiers, Jewish children in Argentina, and Israeli civilians.[77] As a result of that trip, Israeli authorities prevented him from entering Israel in May 2008—a decision that I publicly criticized. Lacking the academic imprimatur of a university, his hateful message is fading in the marketplace of ideas, although he remains popular among left-wing extremists.

He has taken to mocking Jewish victims of terrorism, as he previously mocked Jewish survivors of the Holocaust. Following the bulldozer attack of July 2, 2008, in which three Israeli women were killed and more than forty others injured by a Palestinian terrorist, Finkelstein placed the following "news report" on his Web site:

> *Times* Exclusive: Deranged Arab in bulldozer attacks NY Times's Isabel Kershner at her pedicure. Reporting live from the scene still in her curlers and with her beautician at her side, Kershner gives a minute-by-minute account of the horrifying moment when the bulldozer crashed through the pedicure's windowfront crushing the nail on her little toe. "My friends in the Catskills just won't believe it," she said. "A smashed toe nail. How can Israelis live with so much anxiety?"

Yet there are those who continue to champion him. One of his staunchest supporters (in addition to Chomsky) is Rabbi Michael

Lerner, of *Tikkun* magazine, who is perhaps Israel's most rancorous hater among widely known rabbis (he was recently included in a *Newsweek* list of the fifty most influential American rabbis).[78]

Lerner personally circulated Finkelstein's article calling for me to be targeted for assassination—the one that was originally accompanied by the pornographic cartoon. I circulated my own response:

> This is from a rabbi who modestly purports to devote himself "to peace, justice, non-violence, generosity, caring, love and compassion." This is a rabbi who purports to observe the Jewish commandments against evil words (*"lashon harah"*) and bearing false witness. This is a man who ardently opposes Israel's targeted assassination of Hamas leaders, but who apparently has no qualms about the assassination of pro-Israel academics.

Nor was that the first time that Lerner had served as a megaphone for Finkelstein's hate speech. Lerner published an article-length version of one of Finkelstein's screeds in *Tikkun*, complete with Finkelstein's hateful thesis: "Alongside Israel [American Jewish elites] are the main fomenters of anti-Semitism in the world today. . . . They need to be stopped."[79] (Finkelstein had previously called American Jews "parasites.") In the same book that Lerner was promoting, Finkelstein invoked some of the most crass anti-Semitic caricatures found in contemporary America, "Should people like Abraham Foxman, Edgar Bronfman, and Rabbi Israel Singer [who are prominent Jewish leaders] get a free ride *because* they resemble stereotypes straight out of *Der Sturmer?*"[80] Can you imagine a professor issuing a similar description of a woman or a Muslim or describing the pope according to an anti-Catholic stereotype? Can you imagine *Tikkun* publishing an author who falsely described Rabbi Lerner as resembling a stereotype "straight out of *Der Sturmer*"?

Lerner tried to weasel out of what he had done by saying that he forwarded the Finkelstein attack against me in revenge because I had called him "an anti-Semitic rabbi."[81] (What I actually wrote is that "even a rabbi can support anti-Semitic actions"—as Lerner did when he advocated divestment from Israel and only Israel.)

Lerner himself has argued that the "Jewish establishment" intimidates critics of Israel into silence by falsely accusing them of anti-Semitism. In a 2007 article he wrote,

> Instead of seriously engaging with the issues raised (e.g. to what extent are Israel's current policies similar to those of apartheid and to what extent are they not?), the Jewish establishment and media responds by attacking the people who raise these or any other critiques—shifting the discourse to the legitimacy of the messenger and thus avoiding the substance of the criticisms. Knowing this, many people become fearful that they too will be labeled "anti-Semitic" if they question the wisdom of Israeli policies or if they seek to organize politically to challenge those policies.[82]

Lerner asserts that this "bubble of repression of dialogue" will engender a "'new' anti-Semitism."[83] By doing so, he undermines the seriousness of emergent anti-Semitism and deflects the blame for anti-Semitism from Israel's enemies to pro-Israel Jews. Indeed, Lerner portrays Zionist Jews as corrupters of Jewish identity, arguing that the Jewish establishment has "seriously lost sight of the Jewish values which early Zionists hoped would find realization" in Israel.[84] On the *Tikkun* Web site, the Israel section suggests that Zionism (at least of the kind he disagrees with) is a corruption of traditional Jewish values: "Perhaps the greatest victim of all these distortions has been Judaism itself."[85]

Lerner refuses to renounce terror against Israel without also suggesting a moral equivalence to Israeli self-defense actions. In a letter following the terrorist killings at Yeshivat Mercaz HaRav on March 7, 2008, Lerner qualified his unequivocal condemnation by criticizing the Israel army in the same breath. He wrote, "Just as last week we prayed for the speedy recovery of Israelis and Palestinians wounded in the fighting in Gaza and the bombings in Sderot, so today we pray for a speedy recovery for those who were injured in this ghastly attack."[86] Lerner was unwilling to blame the terrorists alone and hold them accountable; instead he excused the terrorist act as a reaction to prior Israeli violence and lamented the "seemingly endless cycle of violence" in the region.

Lerner has long equated the terrorists' intentional killing of innocent students with the military operations of the Israel Defense Force (IDF). He emphasized that those at *Tikkun*—he always presumptuously speaks in the plural for "the Tikkun community"—are "equally grieving" for the murdered students and the "victims of Israeli terror."[87] These statements draw a moral equivalence between the unintentional killing of civilians by the Israeli military and the purposeful targeting of Israeli innocents by terrorist groups. Yet Lerner disingenuously wrote, "Of course there is no 'moral equivalency' here, because as Talmud and other religious and spiritual traditions teach, every single life lost is a unique tragedy, and no life lost can be compared to or the loss justified in terms of the [lives] lost of others."[88]

Lerner's anti-Israel actions—singling out Israel for divestment, publishing and circulating anti-Semitic messages advocating violence, blaming Jews for anti-Semitism, equating terrorism with legitimate self-defense—would normally be relegated to the garbage bin of history, where it belongs. But because he is a rabbi who purports to speak for the "Tikkun Community"—a questionable claim at best, since many of his readers and several of his board members have told me that they disagree with many of his statements—his actions must be taken seriously and responded to in the marketplace of ideas.

Another hard-left academic—this one an Israeli—who blames Zionism for anti-Semitism is Avi Shlaim, a professor of international relations at St. Anthony's College in Oxford. Shlaim, who held "Israeli Apartheid Week" at Oxford University in 2007, identifies Zionism as the source of hatred toward the Jews.[89] In 2005 he wrote, "By Zionism today I mean the ideological, ultra-nationalist settlers and their supporters in the Likud-led government."[90] Recognizing that these radicals are "a tiny minority" within Israel, he nevertheless claimed that "they maintain a stranglehold over the Israeli political system" (and this only months before these settlers were forcibly removed from their homes in Gaza). "It is this brand of cruel Zionism," he wrote, "that is the real enemy of what remains of liberal Israel and of the Jews outside Israel. It is the enemy because it fuels the flames of virulent and sometimes violent anti-Semitism. Israel's policies are the cause; hatred of Israel and anti-Semitism are the consequences."[91]

As I have repeatedly demonstrated, anti-Semitism in fact bears no correlation to Israeli policy. Following Israel's unilateral withdrawal from Gaza, anti-Semitism continued to increase rather than decrease in response to favorable Israeli policy. Shlaim correctly observed that "Israel is increasingly perceived as a rogue state, as an international pariah, and as a threat to world peace." He also accurately identified "this perception of Israel [as] a major factor in the recent resurgence of anti-Semitism in Europe and in the rest of the world." Yet he falsely concludes, "In this sense, Zionism today is the real enemy of the Jews," failing to consider that international perceptions are misguided and driven by preexisting anti-Semitic dispositions, as well as by hateful comments of the kind in which he specializes.[92]

The anti-Semitic rhetoric of the hard left has recently been granted legitimacy by the United Nations Human Rights Council, which has appointed Richard Falk to investigate Israeli actions in the Palestinian territories. A professor emeritus at Princeton University and a member of the *Nation*'s editorial board, Falk has compared the Israeli army to Nazi Germany, recklessly using the language of the Holocaust to describe the Israeli-Palestinian conflict.[93] In a 2007 article titled "Slouching toward a Palestinian Holocaust," Falk wrote, "Is it an irresponsible overstatement to associate the treatment of Palestinians with this criminalized Nazi record of collective atrocity? I think not."[94]

Falk expresses his hateful rhetoric under the guise of fulfilling his moral responsibility as an American Jew with a conscience troubled by the actions of his people: "Against this background, it is especially painful for me, as an American Jew, to feel compelled to portray the ongoing and intensifying abuse of the Palestinian people by Israel through a reliance on such an inflammatory metaphor as 'holocaust.'" Lamenting that the UN has not acted sufficiently to prevent a Palestinian holocaust, Falk called on the international community "to act urgently to prevent these current genocidal tendencies from culminating in a collective tragedy." And yet he himself discredits his historically irresponsible analogy by acknowledging that no genocide has in fact occurred in Gaza. Comparing the situation in the territories to the genocides in Rwanda and Bosnia, Falk wrote, "But Gaza is morally far worse, although mass death has not yet resulted."[95] Falk, in keeping with existing patterns within the UN, belittles the tragedies of the Rwandan and Bosnian genocides in his effort to scapegoat Israel.

"Mass death," intentionally inflicted to eradicate a race, is, after all, the essence of genocide and was central to the Holocaust. Yet Falk abuses these terms to characterize a democracy's proportional response to terrorism directed against its civilians, just as Jimmy Carter abuses *apartheid,* despite the absence of its indispensible racial element.

Since his appointment, Falk has stood by his comments, prompting Israel to refuse him entry into the country. Rather than honor a responsibility to appoint fair-minded individuals to their investigative committee, the United Nations Human Rights Council has replaced John Dugard, who likens Israel to apartheid Africa, with Falk, who is an even more biased appointee. As Yitzhak Levanon, the Israeli ambassador to the United Nations in Geneva, explained, "Someone who has publicly and repeatedly stated such views cannot possibly be considered independent, impartial or objective."[96] Assessing the UN decision to appoint Falk, British journalist David Aaronovitch wrote in the *Times* (London):

> So, what did the 40-plus members of the Council see in the professor? As far as I can tell his attraction lies in the following. He is American; he is Jewish; and more deliciously in light of the first two, he blames Israel for just about everything—as opposed to those who (rightly, in my opinion) blame it for quite a lot. This, for example, is Falk in 2002, on the second intifada: "Palestinian resistance gradually ran out of military options, and suicide bombers appeared as the only means still available by which to inflict sufficient harm on Israel so that the struggle could go on."
>
> There are three problems with this analysis. The first is that suicide bombing began in Israel in 1994, when Hamas saw the Oslo peace process as threatening to succeed. Secondly, the suicide bombs were

obviously utterly counterproductive in terms of procuring peace, and indeed helped to destroy the Israeli peace movement. And thirdly, other "resistances" (Tibet, Darfur?) seem to have avoided the "only means" of suicide bombing aimed at civilians—family restaurants, buses, schools, discos, and groups of teenagers, to be more specific. . . .

It was transparently this political position that led to him being appointed to his job, not his expertise, nor his open-mindedness.[97]

A blog by Melanie Phillips on the *Spectator* Web site puts it well:

The UN has appointed a man to investigate Israel's behaviour who is incapable of telling the difference between genocide and the attempt to defend a people from becoming its victims. Professor Richard Falk, the UN Human Rights Council special rapporteur on the Palestinian territories (whose remit, however, will not include reporting on the Palestinians!), has compared Israel's behaviour in Gaza to the Nazis. He tells the BBC he is unrepentant about this comparison because he wanted to shake the American public from its torpor. Isn't it time the American public was shaken from its torpor over the fact that the UN now stands for the abandonment of free societies, the demonisation of their defenders and the extinction of truth and justice, and the endorsement, justification and incitement of terror, tyranny and hatred? The virulent malice towards Israel openly displayed by both the terms of Falk's appointment and the prejudice of the man himself is but the latest illustration of the UN's true character as a club of tyranny.[98]

Falk is also an enthusiastic promoter of conspiracy theories alleging that the U.S. government is covering up the "truth" of the attacks by al-Qaeda on the World Trade Center and the Pentagon on September 11, 2001. In a foreword to a book widely cited by conspiracy theorists, Falk argues for "the possibility that the terrible events of 9/11 were from the outset, or before, obscured by deliberately woven networks of falsehoods." Earlier in his career, he praised the Ayatollah Khomeini and whitewashed human rights abuses in the Iranian revolution, writing, "[The Iranian Revolution] is amazingly non-violent in its tactics and orientation, despite extraordinary levels of provocation and incitement designed to induce violence. . . . One of the stereotypes that has been definitely fostered by the US government to create confusion and resistance to the movement is that anything Islamic is necessarily reactionary. It is very important to clarify its real identity, which I think is progressive."[99]

This is the person the UN has chosen to investigate the human rights situation in the West Bank and Gaza—a man who has declared that "Palestinian resistance to the occupation [presumably including the targeting of children and other civilians] is a legally protected right."[100]

Another prominent Jew from the hard left who maligns Israel is the award-winning American playwright Tony Kushner. At a conference hosted by *Tikkun* in 2002, Kushner stated that it "would have been better" if Israel had never come into existence.[101] He described the establishment of the state of Israel as a "historical, moral, political calamity," blamed the existence of Israel for putting the entire world in "peril," and condemned "American Jews" for the "shame" of failing to denounce Israel.[102]

Ignoring the Jewish presence in Palestine prior to the founding of Israel and the Arab rejection of the 1947 UN Partition Plan, Kushner claims that the forceful expulsion of the Palestinians was a precondition of Israel's founding. In an introduction to their compilation of essays *Wrestling with Zion,* Tony Kushner and Alisa Solomon wrote, "Tracking through a forest of competing identities and histories of persecution and oppression, one must adhere to this simple fact or else one's moral compass loses its true north and ceases to function: The founding of the state of Israel required the dispossession of a sizable indigenous population." This initial dispossession, according to Kushner and Solomon, is to blame for all subsequent acts of Palestinian terror and violence. They wrote, "One hardly justifies suicide bombings by pointing out that there's also no 'equivalence' between a dispossessed people resisting a thirty-six-year-old occupation and a massive military machine enforcing that repressive occupation, nor by noting that IDF attacks on civilians are themselves sometimes far less than careful or innocent."[103]

Kushner repeatedly redirects blame for terrorism onto the Israelis. Elsewhere, he and Solomon wrote, "Encountering new, desperate, and deadly Palestinian resistance, failing utterly to comprehend realities of Palestinian life, or cynically exploiting those realities to provoke a state of crisis as cover for settlement building and unending occupation, the current government has brought its country to a time in which Israelis die in far greater numbers from Palestinian attacks than under any previous government." According to this logic (which has little basis in reality), it is the Israeli government that has "brought" Israel to a time of death and violence, and not the Palestinian suicide bombers stealing across the border. As they explain, "Justified in the name of security, the wall, on the contrary, will more likely provoke more animosity and violence as its building results in the expropriation of yet more Palestinian land and as it cuts off entire communities from external connection and livelihood."[104] This has proved not to be true.

Another hard-left Israel-basher is Ilan Pappé, now a professor at the University of Exeter in England. He was once a professor at Haifa University. In 2005, Pappé, while still teaching at Haifa, led the campaign by the Association of University Teachers to boycott Haifa and Bar-Ilan universities. As a result, Haifa University president Aharon Ben-Ze'ev called for Pappé's resignation. Refusing to take disciplinary action against Pappé on the principle of academic freedom, Ben-Ze'ev explained that, nonetheless, "It is fitting for someone who calls for a boycott of his university to apply the boycott himself."[105]

Now entrenched at Exeter, Pappé frequently writes articles accusing Israel of genocidal policies against the Palestinians and of ethnic cleansing. Rewriting the history of Israel's establishment, Pappé claims that "the Zionist leadership became convinced that only through a total expulsion of the Palestinians would they be able to create a state of their own."[106] As a result, says Pappé, "From [Israel's] early inception and up to the 1930s, Zionist thinkers propagated the need to ethnically cleanse the indigenous population of Palestine if the dream of a Jewish state were to come true."[107] These assertions obviously ignore the Zionist acceptance of the 1938 and 1947 partition plans and a two-state solution, but Pappé dismisses the Partition Plan as "a pro-Zionist solution, and a very unjust and impractical one at that."[108]

Constructing his own Zionist conspiracy theory and his own selective history, Pappé alleges a carefully prepared Zionist scheme to expel all Palestinians from Israel, making no mention of the 1948 Israeli-Arab war initiated by the Arab countries that rejected the two-state solution. In another article, Pappé wrote, "The take-over of Palestine in 1948 produced the inevitable local resistance that in turn allowed the implementation of an ethnic cleansing policy, preplanned already in the 1930s."[109] By Pappé's account, Israeli acceptance of UN partition—which allocated more than half of the arable land to a Palestinian state—was a "takeover of Palestine." The invasion of Israel by five Arab armies that vastly outnumbered the Zionists was merely an "inevitable local resistance" that provided a pretext for ethnic cleansing.

According to Pappé, the conspiracy continues, with Israel's current solution of "imprisoning large numbers of Palestinians in enclaves in the West Bank and the Gaza Strip" and oppressing the Palestinians living within Israel by means of "an apartheid system."[110] More recently, he stated, "A creeping transfer in the West Bank and a measured genocidal policy in the Gaza strip are the two strategies Israel employs today."[111] An advocate of the one-state solution (a solution that means the demographic destruction of Israel), Pappé is also a supporter of Hamas. In March 2007, he wrote, "I support Hamas in its resistance against the Israeli occupation though I disagree with their political ideology."[112] In other words, he supports their terrorism against Jewish children but not their religious motivation.

As outlined in these pages, Marx's anti-Semitic rhetoric has persisted in the ideas espoused by Jews seeking entry into today's hard left. Yet in many respects, their portrayal of Jews and Israel is more threatening to the Jewish position than was Marx's writing in his own time. For while Marx sought to distance himself entirely from religion and from Judaism, current academics on the hard left, professing to denounce "real" anti-Semitism, seek to justify their ideas on the basis of their own claim to authentic Jewishness and to align Jewish identity with a rejection of Jewish nationalism. As political scientist Emanuele Ottolenghi wrote,

"They have much in common: They denounce Israel as evil; they accuse Israel and Zionism of having betrayed Judaism's authentic voice; they embrace a narrative of victimization, where the authors present themselves as victims of a Jewish establishment that tries to silence them; and, in describing Israel and its policies, they frequently use vocabulary, imagery, and stereotypes that are dangerously close to the old repertoire of classical anti-Semitism."[113]

The Hard Right

Many conservative supporters of Israel, both Jewish and non-Jewish, seem to be under the impression that all of Israel's enemies are on the left. They acknowledge that in the past, most of the opposition to Israel came from the right: from oil interests, conservative diplomats, and other "classic" right-wing anti-Semites. They also acknowledge that much of Israel's early support came from the left: from American liberals, labor unions, and even the Soviet Union and European socialist and communist parties. But everything has now changed, they say. Today, "the right" supports Israel, and "the left" does not. Yet in making this claim, they are comparing apples and oranges. Yes, "the right" supports Israel—but only if "the right" is limited to the centrist right and the religious right. Yes, "the left" opposes Israel—but only if "the left" is limited to the hard left and the religious left. The centrist left—the real liberals, as contrasted with the extremist radicals—generally supports Israel, though sometimes critically (as I do). The centrist right, as contrasted with the radical right, also supports Israel, along with many on the religious right, often less critically.

The condemnation of Israel from the hard left has received far more attention than the condemnation from the hard right, in part because (1) there are many more hard-leftists in academia and in the media than there are hard-rightists, and (2) the proportion of highly vocal members is far greater in the hard left as compared to the hard right. These facts notwithstanding, the far-right Israel-bashers may have as much, or even more, influence on governmental policies than do people on the hard left because they are more likely to serve in government (as Patrick Buchanan and James Baker did) or be influential in government circles (as Robert Novak has long been). We therefore shift our focus from the hard left to the equally (if not more) dangerous hard right.

Just as the hard left has received inspiration from an intellectual who is widely respected (as well as reviled) by many—namely, Karl Marx—so, too, has the hard right received inspiration from a widely respected literary figure, the great Russian writer Fyodor Mikhailovich Dostoyevsky, who in 1877 wrote a notorious article, "The Jewish Question." Like other anti-Semites of both the right and the left, he blamed anti-Semitism on the Jews. Dostoyevsky argued that "this universal hatred [of Jews] does mean something." And instead of looking for the sources within the haters, he looked to the actions of the hated and declared that "the Jew himself is guilty." "The Jew, wherever he has settled, has . . . humiliated and debauched the people." It was the Jews who "ruined" the Lithuanians "with vodka." He believed that it was the Jews who would re-enslave the "millions of liberated Negroes" in the American South: "The negroes have now been liberated from their slave owners, but . . . that will not last because the Jews, of whom there are so many in the world, will jump at this new little victim."[114]

Dostoyevsky's views of the worldwide Jewish conspiracy are not much different from the views expressed in Hitler's *Mein Kampf* or the infamous czarist forgery *The Protocols of the Elders of Zion*. In Dostoyevsky's anti-Semitic world "the Jews are reigning everywhere over stock exchanges," "they control capital," "they are masters of credit," "they are also the masters of international politics," and "what is going to happen in the future is known to the Jews themselves." He predicted that "their reign, their complete reign is approaching!" He believed that "Judaism and the *Jewish idea*" are "clasping the whole world instead of Christianity." (Emphasis in original.) Like Marx, he believed that "the overwhelming majority of Jews have a predilection for but one profession—the trade in gold." When the messiah comes, according to Dostoyevsky, "it will be easier [for the Jews] to carry [the gold] away."[115] (It is quite remarkable that a man as brilliant and insightful as Dostoyevsky could believe such nonsense!)

Today's right-wing anti-Semites—especially those whose bigotry stems from religious convictions, as Dostoyevsky's did—are more politically sophisticated than the great Russian novelist, but their irrational hatred runs just as deep. The guru of the U.S. hard right is Patrick Buchanan, who, in addition to being a classic theological anti-Semite, is a vicious hater of Israel, which he accuses of acting in an "un-Christian manner."[116] Normally, one would expect a strident cold war anticommunist like Buchanan to admire Israel for standing up to the Soviet Union, for giving cold war assistance to the United States, and for representing the Judeo-Christian civilization in the conflict with a rabidly anti-Christian enemy.

But in Buchanan's case, his anti-Jewish bigotry trumps his political leanings. On this issue and this issue alone, he sides with the enemies of the United States, of Christianity, of capitalism, and of Western morality. If Israel were not the Jewish state, he would be its most vocal supporter. If the Palestinians were not the enemies of the Jewish state, he would be their most vocal detractor. There is no theory or policy that explains Buchanan's upside-down view on this issue except simple anti-Semitism. As far as Buchanan is concerned, anything Jewish, including the Jewish religion and the Jewish state, is morally, theologically, and politically damned.

Indeed, Buchanan started out as a supporter of Israel but turned against the Jewish state when his theological anti-Semitism was exposed.[117] He now claims that the accusations of anti-Semitism that have long been made against him are in revenge for his anti-Zionism, but the record proves that his anti-Semitism preceded his anti-Zionism.

Even the late William F. Buckley, the intellectual godfather of modern American conservatism, could not understand Buchanan's views on Israel, which he characterized as "amount[ing] to anti-Semitism."[118] Indeed, how else could any objective person characterize the following statements:

- "To orthodox Catholics, the demand that we be more 'sensitive' to Jewish concerns is becoming a joke. . . . The slumbering giant of Catholicism may be about to awaken" and target "those who so evidently despise our Church"—namely, "the Jews."[119]

- Regarding the infamous John Demjanjuk, who was convicted of being Ivan the Terrible of Treblinka, a death camp in Poland where some 870,000 Jews perished, Buchanan publicly declared Demjanjuk to be "the victim of an American Dreyfus case."[120] Although the Supreme Court of Israel eventually reversed his conviction on the basis of newly discovered evidence, there was absolutely no doubt that Demjanjuk was a Nazi death camp guard who taunted, abused, and murdered Jewish prisoners. But to Buchanan, he was as commendable as the absolutely innocent Alfred Dreyfus, who had been framed by anti-Semitic French military officials. (There is little doubt that had Buchanan lived at the time of the Dreyfus affair he would have sided with the Catholic hierarchy in condemning Dreyfus.)

- Buchanan warns the Jews not to count on the bridge-building efforts of U.S. cardinals. He regards their conciliatory statements, obviously blessed by the Vatican, as "the clucking appeasement of the Catholic cardinalate." He warns these princes of reconciliation to "step aside" and make room for "bishops and priests ready to assume the role of defender of the faith."[121]

- Buchanan has expressed doubts about whether Jews were gassed at Treblinka, citing as his evidence, "In 1988, 97 youths, trapped 400 feet underground in a D.C. tunnel while two locomotives spewed diesel exhaust into the car emerged unharmed after 45 minutes." Asked by the *New Republic* where he got his misinformation about Treblinka—Jews were killed by a variety of gases, including Zyklon B pumped into airtight chambers—Buchanan responded, "Somebody sent it to me."[122] The *New Republic*, after investigating Buchanan's sources, concluded that "much of the material on which Buchanan bases his columns is sent to him by pro-Nazi, anti-Semitic cranks."[123]

- While Buchanan acknowledges that Hitler was "racist," he also has referred admiringly to that genocidal mass murderer as "an individual of great courage, a soldier's soldier in the Great War, a political organizer of the first rank," and "a leader steeped in the history of Europe."[124]

- Like other anti-Semites, Buchanan has shown unswerving support for every Nazi war criminal, regardless of the evidence of that person's complicity in the Holocaust. He has spoken out in defense of Klaus Barbie ("the Butcher of Lyon"), John Demjanjuk, and Karl Linnas (a confessed death-camp guard who was found responsible by U.S. courts for the murder of twelve thousand Estonians and Jews).[125] Furthermore, Buchanan used to attack Kurt Waldheim when the latter was the UN secretary-general but suddenly began to defend Waldheim when Waldheim's Nazi past was disclosed.[126]

  As Allan Ryan, a former Justice Department official with long experience in prosecuting war criminals, put it, "Great numbers of people are asking themselves: why is Pat Buchanan so in love with Nazi war criminals?"[127] The most plausible answer was provided by Buchanan himself when he acknowledged to the *New York Times* that "he had frequently been accused of antisemitism."[128]

- Like most anti-Semites, Buchanan refuses to treat Jewish people as individuals. Instead, he inveighs against "U.S. Jewry" and "the Jews."[129]

- Like other anti-Semites, Buchanan seems incapable of discussing any subject—whether it be abortion, gay rights, mercy killing, or organized crime—without bringing in "the Jews."[130]

- Buchanan uses ethnically identifiable names to foment bigotry. When compiling a list of the type of people who, in his opinion, favored the original war in Iraq, Buchanan selected only those with identifiably Jewish names from a list that included many non-Jews. But when describing those who would fight in a war against Iraq, he goes out of his way to include only "kids with names like McAllister, Murphy, Gonzales and Leroy Brown."[131]

- Like other anti-Semites, Buchanan applies a double standard to the Jewish state. He supports every repressive action of every despotic regime that purports to be fighting in favor of American values. But when Israel overreacts in its efforts to defend itself against one of the most anti-American terrorist groups in the world, Buchanan becomes indignant about "gratuitous brutality against Palestinian women, teenagers and children."[132] Notably absent is any similar indignation from Buchanan for the victims of apartheid South Africa, El Salvador, Chile, or the contras.

- Buchanan has called Capitol Hill "Israeli occupied territory" and has said, "There are only two groups that are beating the drums for war in the Middle East—the Israeli Defense Ministry and its *amen corner* in the United States."[133]

- Buchanan has called for a McCarthy-like investigation (McCarthy and Franco were his heroes) of "whether there is a nest of Pollardites [Pollard is an American Jew who pleaded guilty of spying for Israel] in the Pentagon who have been transmitting American secrets through AIPAC, the Israeli lobby, over to Reno Road, the Israeli embassy, to be transferred to Mr. Sharon. If this has been going on . . . we are getting dangerously close to the T-word."[134]

- In his article "Whose War?" published in Buchanan's own *American Conservative* magazine (which he founded), Buchanan wrote,

> We charge that a cabal of polemicists and public officials seek to ensnare our country in a series of wars that are not in America's interests. We charge them with colluding with Israel to ignite those wars and destroy the Oslo Accords. We charge them with deliberately damaging U.S. relations with every state in the Arab world that defies Israel or supports the Palestinian people's right to a homeland of their own. We charge that they

have alienated friends and allies all over the Islamic and Western world through their arrogance, hubris, and bellicosity.[135]

Buchanan then easily morphs from his role as the self-righteous accuser to the self-righteous victim:

> They charge us with anti-Semitism—i.e., a hatred of Jews for their faith, heritage, or ancestry. False. The truth is, those hurling these charges harbor a "passionate attachment" to a nation not our own that causes them to subordinate the interests of their own country and to act on an assumption that, somehow, what's good for Israel is good for America.[136]

Buchanan concludes the article by launching into a vicious ad hominem attack against those whom he puts in the category of "neoconservatives" (by which he means Jewish Republicans). According to Buchanan, what these people have in common is that "All are interventionists who regard Stakhanovite support of Israel as a defining characteristic of their breed."[137] "To the neocons . . . Zionism is second nature. . . . *They are dangerously close to imbibing the poisonous brew that drove Jonathan Pollard to treason*: If it is good for Israel, it cannot be bad for America."[138]

- Buchanan has blamed the U.S. attack on Iraq on "one nation, one leader, one party. Israel, Sharon, Likud."[139] Buchanan, like Stephen Walt and John Mearsheimer, conveniently ignores the fact that Sharon actually *opposed* the war against Iraq.

- When Israel was defending its civilians against rocket attacks by Hezbollah, Buchanan said, "What Israel is doing is imposing deliberate suffering on civilians, collective punishment on innocent people, to force them to do something they are powerless to do: disarm the gunmen among them. Such a policy violates international law and comports neither with our values nor our interests. *It is un-American and un-Christian*."[140] (Emphasis added.)

While Buchanan may be the most well known of the anti-Israel hard-rightists, he is far from the only member of that wing. In fact, Buchanan has the company of a number of well-regarded and highly influential right-wing personalities, all of whom have gone on record with statements just as hateful and bigoted as those listed here.

One such figure is the journalist and writer Taki Theodoracopulos, better known as "Taki." Taki's conservative credentials are impeccable—he's spent the last twenty-five years writing a column for the British magazine the *Spectator,* a robustly conservative pub lication, and has also published pieces in America's own *National Review,* which is about as far to the right in the United States as the *Spectator* is in England. The crown jewel of Taki's conservative résumé, however, is his deep involvement with the *American Conservative,* a biweekly political magazine that he cofounded with Buchanan, which bills itself as (not surprisingly) "a considerable part Buchananite."[141] So what does Taki, a widely published author and journalist and a card-carrying member of the hard right, have to say about Israel and Jews?

Taki has done much to take the guesswork out of any attempt to characterize his views on Judaism and Israel, proudly identifying himself as a *"soi-disant* anti-Semite," in the same article where he wrote, "The way to Uncle Sam's heart runs through Tel Aviv and Israeli-occupied territory."[142]

In a February 2001 column for the *Spectator,* Taki presents as indisputable fact a conspiracy theory that—at least to the ears of the rational among us—evokes a sense of deep paranoia normally associated with claims of a faked moon landing or downed UFOs in the New Mexico desert.[143] Taki relates that Marc Rich, flying in a private jet above Switzerland, was warned by the Mossad that U.S. fighter jets were heading for him in an attempt to "grab him." Taki explains that the Mossad, which "knew that the snatch was on by listening in on the Americans," was willing to warn Rich of this impending attack since Rich had given "lotsa moolah to Israel." According to Taki, Rich's donations to Israel resulted in his "being fed information by the Mossad that even the top brass of the Pentagon weren't getting."

An acquaintance of mine who is a close personal friend of Taki's has told me that Taki is "obsessed with Jews" and hates Israel because "it is Jewish." He has characterized Taki as an "old fashioned European anti-Semite" (pronouncing the first syllable of the second word as "see" in the manner of elite British Jew haters). My acquaintance, who is not Jewish, told me that Taki's views are not that uncommon among his "clubby" conservative friends.

A frequent contributor to Buchanan and Taki's *American Conservative* magazine is the well-known journalist and television personality Robert "Bob" Novak. Novak was born Jewish and converted to Catholicism, but he has long been belligerently anti-Israel. Like Buchanan and Taki, Novak has never been shy about using his considerable media exposure to polemicize against Israel at every opportunity.

In an op-ed piece that appeared in the *New York Post* in November 2007, Novak voiced his support for Jimmy Carter's characterization of Israeli behavior toward Palestinians in the West Bank as "apartheid."[144] Regarding a documentary film about Carter titled *Jimmy Carter: Man from Plains*, Novak wrote,

> In the film, Carter repeatedly and unequivocally states what Palestinian and Israeli peace advocates view as undeniable: To achieve Israeli-Palestinian peace with all its benefits for the world, Israel must end its illegal and oppressive occupation of the West Bank. That is a prerequisite that neither President Bush nor congressional leaders of both parties can approach for fear of being labeled anti-Israeli or even anti-Semitic (as Carter has been).[145]

Novak agrees with Carter on virtually no other issue except Israel. (The same can probably be said about Buchanan and Chomsky.)

Novak's anti-Israel bias was also on exhibition in a series of April 2007 editorials published in several major national newspapers. The title of one was "Worse Than Apartheid?"—referring to Israel's treatment of the Palestinians living in the West Bank.

Novak wasted no time answering in the affirmative. He wrote of his recent visit to Bethlehem, noting that while "Jimmy Carter raised hackles by titling his book about the Palestinian question *Peace Not Apartheid*," the Palestinians with whom Novak spoke "allege [that Israeli treatment] is worse than the former South African racial separation."[146] Novak, like Buchanan, was far less critical of apartheid South Africa (and other right-wing tyrannies) than of democratic Israel.

Not content to attack Israel for its alleged mistreatment of Palestinians, Novak suggested that Israel oppresses Christians as well:

> Republican Rep. Chris Smith of New Jersey . . . an active Catholic layman, was drawn here because of the rapid emigration of the Holy Land's Christian minority. They leave more quickly than Muslims because contacts on the outside make them more mobile. Peter Corlano, a Catholic member of the Bethlehem University faculty, told Smith and me: "We live the same life as Muslims. We are Palestinians." Concerned by the disappearance of Christians in the land of Christianity's birthplace, Smith could also become (as I did) concerned by the plight of all Palestinians. If so, he will find precious little company in Congress.[147]

Conveniently, Novak ignored or dismissed the impact on Christian emigration of radical Islam in general and Hamas in particular, never mentioning the intolerance of radical Muslims for other religions, including Christianity.

In another editorial, Novak stridently portrayed Hamas— recognized as a terrorist organization by the United States and many European nations—as a "victim," which was snubbed by the United States despite its valiant attempts to bring an end to violence in the Middle East: "On Saturday, April 7, ending a seven-day visit to Israel, I finally got an interview I had sought for a year. I sat down in a Palestinian National Authority office in Ramallah with a leader of Hamas, the extremist organization that won last year's elections. He pushed a two-state Israeli-Palestinian solution and deplored suicide bombers. *But officials in Washington seemingly do not want to hear Hamas calling for peace.*"[148] (Emphasis added.)

While acknowledging that Hamas's official position regarding Israel continues to be insistence that Israel has no right to exist, Novak nonetheless claims that "[the current Hamas] regime recognizes Israel's right to exist and forgoes violence."[149] This is a total falsehood! Novak laments the fact that the United States and Israel are ignoring the sincere efforts of this "new regime" to achieve peace. Conspicuously absent is a disclosure from Novak that his information about this "new regime" is wholly based on a conversation with a *single member* of Hamas, who, in the words of Novak, *"signaled"* that the current Hamas regime supports Israel's existence. Novak apparently got his "signals" crossed because the leader of Hamas has repeatedly made it clear that any temporary peace or truce with Israel would merely be a tactic on the road to military destruction of the Zionist entity.

If any further evidence is needed of Novak's anti-Israel bias, it can be found in the fact that Novak has become such a good friend to the anti-Israel community that it features his columns on its Web sites. The American-Arab Anti Discrimination Committee (ADC), whose 2007 resolutions include a "deep concern" about the situation in "the occupied Palestinian territories, due to the flagrant and persistent violations of International Humanitarian Law by the State of Israel," proudly reproduces a Novak column from July 2006 in which he wrote, "[Israel's use of] military force to achieve the 'new paradigm' wins either enthusiastic or tacit support across America's ideological spectrum. Apart from hesitant pleas for Israeli restraint from President Bush and his administration's officials, the U.S. political community has been cheering on the punishment of Hezbollah."[150] Remember that Novak is a mainstream Republican, widely respected by many in the Bush administration and previous Republican administrations.

Another member of Buchanan's hard-right anti-Israel club is the journalist and writer Joseph Sobran. Sobran, currently a syndicated columnist, wrote for the esteemed conservative publication *National Review* until 1993, when he was fired for a series of openly anti-Semitic columns. Since his ignominious termination, Sobran has not hesitated to freely express anti-Israel and anti-Jewish perspectives in his writings.

In an article available on Sobran's official Web site titled "Chutzpah and Hubris," Sobran explicitly labels Israelis as terrorists: "You know the excellent but now tired old joke about 'chutzpah': that it's best exemplified by the guy who kills both his parents, then begs the court to have mercy on him as an orphan. Well, that orphan has been topped by the state of Israel. It used a missile fired from a helicopter to take out an old, half-blind quadriplegic in a wheelchair—and claimed self-defense."[151]

Just to be clear, the "target" Sobran is writing about was the head of Hamas, who ordered terrorist attacks against thousands of civilians, and was in the process of ordering more. Sobran continues, *"It's often said that the Israelis have had long experience fighting terrorism. Well, they also have had long experience committing it.* What they don't have much experience of is defeating it. In cracking down on it, they kill more innocent people than their enemies do, which makes the problem worse." (Emphasis added.) Sobran has made similar attacks on Israel in other columns, even going so far as to compare Israeli treatment of Palestinians with the antebellum enslavement of blacks in the American South.[152]

Sobran seems to question the historical occurrence of the Holocaust, in this 2002 piece titled "For Fear of the Jews":

> Even if the Holocaust had really happened . . . maybe it should be studied with a critical rationality most of its believers obviously lacked. After all, even Stalin's crimes might be exaggerated, quite understandably, by his victims. . . .
>
> Why on earth is it "anti-Jewish" to conclude from the evidence that the standard numbers of Jews murdered are inaccurate, or that the Hitler regime, bad as it was in many ways, was not, in fact, intent on racial extermination? Surely these are controversial conclusions; but if so, let the controversy rage.[153]

While in the spirit of questioning historical facts, Sobran also takes the opportunity to question the existence of anti-Semitism:

> An *anti-Semite* used to mean a man who hated Jews. Now it means a man who is hated *by* Jews. . . .
>
> Suppose the Holocaust had never occurred, had never been alleged, had never been *called* "the Holocaust." . . . In that case, Israel's treatment of its Arab minorities would appear to the world in a very different light. Its denial of equal or even basic rights to those minorities would lack the excuse of a past or prospective "Holocaust." . . . In short, the Holocaust has become a device for exempting Jews from normal human obligations. It has authorized them to bully and blackmail, to extort and oppress.
>
> Benjamin Netanyahu has written that Israel is "an integral part of the West." I think it would be truer to say that Israel has become a deformed limb of the West.[154]

And finally, in a piece that reveals Sobran to be little more than a parrot of the old *Protocols of the Elders of Zion* rhetoric, he blames the Jews not only for everyone else's problems, but even for their own. He asks the world to face "the possibility that Jewish problems are sometimes due to Jewish attitudes and Jewish behavior." He accuses the "Jewish faction," which he calls "the Tribe" (with a capital T), of deliberately provoking Christian enmity:

> *The organized Jewish faction is what I call the Tribe.* What is striking about the Tribe is not that its positions on such matters [as abortion and gay rights] are necessarily wrong, but that they are anti-Christian . . . [It] adopts them chiefly *because* they are repugnant to Christians.[155] [Emphasis added.]

In other words, according to Sobran, Jews support a woman's right to choose not because they support women's rights, but because they hate Christians![156] This is pure and simple anti-Semitism, missing even the "fig-leaf" excuse of anti-Zionism.

Another hard-rightist who is no stranger to unadorned hatred of the Jews is David Duke. Duke is, of course, different from the right-wing pundits quoted earlier since he has been delegitimized by mainstream conservatives, while most of those quoted previously are largely accepted by the hard right. It must be remembered, however, that Duke received the Republican nomination for the governor of Louisiana and made a credible showing (39 percent of the vote), despite having been the Grand Wizard of the Ku Klux Klan and the leader of the American Nazi Party. So we must face the scary fact that even if Duke is outside of the mainstream, he isn't outside by much—at least, in some parts of our nation.

In one essay, titled "Israeli Terrorism and Sept. 11," Duke wrote, "If you agree that those who commit terrorist acts against America should be punished, then America should put Israel at the top of our hit list; for . . . Israel has committed deliberate acts of murderous terrorism and treachery against America."[157]

He calls Israel the "worst terrorist rogue state on earth," saying that Israel was aware of, if not responsible for, 9/11:

> There can be little doubt the Mossad has deeply penetrated one of the oldest, largest and what is considered the most dangerous Arabic terrorist organizations on earth: bin Laden's al-Quaida. . . . Could Mossad agents in al-Quaida . . . not have known about the most extensive and ambitious Arabic terrorist operation in history? . . .
>
> As monstrous as it may seem, Sharon and the extremists of Israel needed the 9–11 attacks to mobilize Americans against their enemies and give Israel a free hand in dealing with the Palestinians. It was an easy operation for Israel's top agents inside al-Qaida to propose and plan this terrorist operation for the fanatical Muslims yearned [*sic*] to strike back at America for supporting the crimes of Israel.[158]

Duke then presents a disturbing array of mistranslated and out-of-context quotes from the Talmud, which according to Duke undeniably demonstrate that "Judaism is intrinsically and viciously anti-Christian." (Shahak would surely have nodded his head in agreement.) Then he seamlessly moves from an attack on Judaism back to an assault on Israel:

> Some Christians might think that these [i.e., Duke's "misquotes" from the Talmud] are simply old beliefs of the Jewish religion, and that Judaism might have softened its attitude toward Jesus Christ and Christians. In actual fact, these are the formal policies of the Israeli state. . . . In Jewish schools in Israel it is forbidden to even

read from the New Testament gospels or even mention the name of Jesus Christ. It is even a criminal offense in Israel for a Christian to preach the salvation of Jesus Christ to a Jew. Israel so hates the Christian cross that they have specified that elementary schools use a "T" instead of a plus sign because it so resembles the hated Christian cross! The Israeli government has even supported public burnings of the New Testament![159]

All of these allegations are made up out of whole cloth.

Duke then resorts to a "moral" argument of sorts, charging that "by supporting anti-Christian Israel," evangelical leaders such as Jerry Falwell and Pat Robertson "are directly supporting the murder, torture and oppression of thousands of our fellow Christians in the Mideast." Duke continues, "What kind of Christian chooses to support murderous anti-Christian extremist Jews rather then [*sic*] their own Christian brethren. It is no wonder that Christianity is losing ground in the Mideast, when major Christian leaders will support the killing of Palestinian Christians by anti-Christian, Israeli Jews. When Israel indiscriminately sends bombs and missiles and bullets into Palestinian neighborhoods, many of the children and adults murdered are, in fact, Christians."

Referencing the beliefs of evangelicals that Israel must be supported so as to hasten the "End of Days," Duke argues,

> The fact that the New Testament in Revelation suggests that a small number of Jews will repent and accept Christ at the end of times does not change the fact that Jews who embrace anti-Christian Judaism have become the enemies of God and the allies of Satan.
>
> To support anti-Christian Jews in their evil actions against Christians and Christianity is a betrayal of Jesus Christ Himself! Arguing that we should support a man's evil deeds because the man doing it may someday repent is insane. . . .
>
> *If indeed the Anti-Christ is Jewish and is from modern Israel, are we not actually supporting him by supporting Israel and anti-Christian Judaism?* [Emphasis added.]

Duke also parrots Buchanan's reference to Capitol Hill as Israeli-occupied territory: "We must understand that it is not only the Palestinians who are occupied by Jewish power, it is America, too. Until we stand up to their power, there will be no freedom for the occupied West Bank of the Jordan River or the Jewish-occupied East Bank of the Potomac, the heart of the federal government."

These, then, are the hard-right extremists who match their ideological opposites on the far left in their hatred for Israel and sometimes for "the Jews." Even more dangerous, however, are some "centrist" right-wing political figures whose views, while less extreme, may carry far more weight as a result of their proximity to power.

Consider, for example, James Baker, the former secretary of state and an influential Republican power broker who helped George W. Bush become president. During Baker's time in office, he developed a reputation for being "tough" on Israel, but many defended his harsh dealings with Israel as evidence of an earnest desire to bring peace, rather than a personal bias against Israel or the Jews. Baker's own words, however, seem to tell a different story:

- According to former New York mayor Ed Koch, after "Baker was criticized . . . at a meeting of high-level White House advisers for his belligerent attitude toward Israel," he said, "Fuck the Jews. They didn't vote for us anyway."[160]

- Baker also reportedly said, "Jews remember the Holocaust, but they forget insults as soon as they smell cash."[161]

- A *Los Angeles Times* article, reporting on the "strong language" that Baker has used "about Israel's political supporters" in U.S. politics, quoted him as calling pro-Israel members of Congress "the little Knesset."[162]

Baker also offensively (not to mention bizarrely) likened Israel to turkeys during an interview for a 1989 profile in *Time* magazine.[163] According to an article in the *Jerusalem Post*, Baker was being interviewed by a *Time* magazine reporter while on a turkey hunt. During the hunt, Baker turned to the reporter and said, "The trick is in getting them where you want them, on your terms. . . . Then you control the situation, not them. You have the options. Pull the trigger or don't. It doesn't matter once you've got them where you want them. The important thing is knowing that it's in your hands, that you can do whatever you determine is in your interest to do."

When the reporter sought to confirm that Baker's words were referring to turkeys, Baker replied, "No . . . I mean Israel."[164]

Baker now apparently supports the so-called Palestinian right of return, which many regard as a code word for destroying the Jewish state by demographic, rather than military, means.[165]

To be sure, none of the comments listed here compare to some of the language used by those on the hard right and the hard left, but at the same time they do reflect an undeniably deep-seated antagonism for Israel by an extremely influential Republican political figure, who is not alone among Republicans in this regard. The point to be taken is that it is naive to think that anti-Israel attitudes are the province of the left alone. They appear in both sides of the political spectrum and on both sides of the aisle.

We can certainly take heart in the fact that for the most part, the hard-core, unadulterated hatred of Jews and Israel comes from people on the extremes and not from those who occupy the socio-political mainstream—at least, not in the United States and not at the moment. We would, however, be shortsighted if we didn't feel uneasy about how quickly the status quo could change if the extreme views on either the right or the left gravitate toward, or begin to influence, the mainstream, as they have in many other parts of the world.

5 The Case against Israel's Suicidal Enemies

It is far more difficult to fight against enemies who want to die than against enemies who want to live. The cold war between the United States and the Soviet Union did not become a hot war because both sides wanted to live, and each realized that a nuclear attack on the other would result in massive retaliation and mutual death. The acronym MAD stands for "mutual assured destruction," and it served as a powerful deterrent to a first strike. That is why the Soviet Union was far more fearful of U.S. *defensive* technology than it was of increased U.S. *offensive* weaponry. If we developed a "Star Wars" defensive shield, we could—at least, in theory—attack the Soviets and still survive the inevitable counterattack.

A nation with suicidal leaders—with people who really believe that being killed by their enemies will *improve* their situation by assuring them eternal paradise instead of the earthly misery they are now enduring—is not easily deterred by the threat of mutual annihilation. Extremists in that type of nation welcome it because by annihilating their heathen enemies and dying in the process, they assure themselves a place in paradise.

Thomas Jefferson confronted this phenomenon as far back as 1786, when he and John Adams met with the ambassador from the Barbary Coast to discuss the attacks on American ships in the Mediterranean by the first Islamic terrorists to do battle with the United States: namely, the Barbary pirates. This is what Jefferson wrote to Secretary of State John Jay following the meeting: "The ambassador answered us that [the right to kill non-Muslims] was founded on the Laws of the Prophet, that it was written in their Koran, that all nations who should not have answered their authority were sinners, that it was their right and duty to make war upon them wherever they could be found, and to make slaves of all they could take as prisoners, and that every Mussulman who should be slain in battle was sure to go to Paradise."[1]

Very little has changed, as evidenced by Zahra Maladan. Maladan is an educated woman who edits a women's magazine in Lebanon. She is also a mother, who undoubtedly loves her son. She has ambitions for him, but they are different from those of most mothers in the West. She wants her son to become a suicide bomber. At the funeral for the assassinated Hezbollah terrorist Imad Mugniyah—the mass murderer responsible for killing 241 marines in 1983 and more than 100 women, children, and men in Buenos Aires in 1992 and 1994—Ms. Maladan was quoted in the *New York Times* offering the following admonition to her son: "If you're not going to follow the steps of the Islamic resistance martyrs, then I don't want you."[2]

Nor is Ms. Maladan alone in urging her children to become suicide murderers. Umm Nidal, who ran for the Palestinian Legislative Council, "prepared all of her sons" for martyrdom. She has ten sons, one of whom already engaged in a suicide operation, which she considered "a blessing, not a tragedy." She is now preparing to "sacrifice them all."[3]

Even during Israel's War of Independence in 1948, some Jordanian mothers demanded martyrdom from their sons. The historian Benny Morris recounts what the mother of Ma'an Abu Nowar, a young Jordanian officer, shouted at him as he left to battle the Israelis: "Don't come back. Martyrdom my son."[4]

Zahra Maladan and Umm Nidal represent a shift (or a return to what Jefferson was told) in the way we must fight to protect our citizens against enemies who are sworn to kill their foes by killing themselves. The traditional paradigm was that mothers who love their children want them to live in peace, marry, and produce grandchildren. Women in general, and mothers in particular, were seen as a counterweight to male belligerence. The picture of the mother weeping as her son is led off to battle—even a just battle—has been a constant and powerful image.

Now there is a new image of mothers urging their children to die and then celebrating the martyrdom of their suicidal sons and daughters by distributing sweets and singing wedding songs. More and more young women—some married with infant children—are strapping bombs to their (sometimes pregnant) bellies because they have been taught to love death rather than life. Look at what is being preached by certain influential Islamic leaders.

"We are going to win, because they love life and we love death," said Hassan Nasrallah, the leader of Hezbollah. He has also said: "Each of us lives his days and nights hoping more than anything to be killed for the sake of Allah." Shortly after 9/11, Osama bin Laden told a reporter: "We love death. The U.S. loves life. That is the big difference between us."

"The Americans love Pepsi-Cola, we love death," explained Afghan al-Qaeda operative Maulana Inyadullah. Sheik Feiz Mohammed, leader of the Global Islamic Youth Center in Sydney, Australia, preached: "We want to have children and offer them as soldiers defending Islam. Teach them this: There is nothing more beloved to me than wanting to die as a mujahid." Ayatollah Ali Khamenei said in a speech: "It is the zenith of honor for a man, a young person, boy or girl, to be prepared to sacrifice his life in order to serve the interests of his nation and his religion."

Sheikh Ibrahim Madhi, a popular imam in the Palestinian Authority, related a discussion he had with a child:

A young man said to me: "I am 14 years old, and I have four years left before I blow myself up." . . . We, the Muslims on this good and blessed land, are all—each one of us—seekers of Martyrdom. . . . The Koran is very clear on this: The greatest enemies of the Islamic nation are the Jews, may Allah fight them. . . . Blessings for whoever assaulted a soldier. . . . Blessings for whoever has raised his sons on the education of *Jihad* and Martyrdom. . . . Shame and remorse on whoever refrained from raising his children on *Jihad*. . . . Blessings to whoever put a belt of explosives on his body or on his sons' and plunged into the midst of the Jews, crying "Allahu Akbar, Allah, we strive for martyrdom for your sake."[5]

How should Western democracies fight against an enemy whose leaders preach a preference for death?

The two basic premises of conventional warfare have long been that soldiers and civilians prefer living to dying and can thus be deterred from killing by the fear of being killed; and that combatants (soldiers) can easily be distinguished from noncombatants (women, children, the elderly, the infirm, and other ordinary citizens). These premises are being challenged by women like Zahra Maladan. Neither she nor her son—if he listens to his mother—can be deterred from killing by the fear of being killed. Clearly, they must be prevented from succeeding in their ghoulish quest for martyrdom. Prevention, however, carries a high risk of error. The pregnant woman walking in a suspicious manner toward the group of soldiers or civilians might well be an innocent civilian. A moment's hesitation may cost innocent lives. But a failure to hesitate may also have a price. These are the sorts of tragic choices imposed on democracies by the increasing use of women (some made to appear pregnant) and children (some as young as twelve) as suicide terrorists.

In February 2008, a young female bomber was shot as she approached some shops in central Baghdad. The Iraqi soldier who drew his gun hesitated as the bomber, hands raised, insisted that she wasn't armed. The soldier and a shop owner finally opened fire as she dashed for the stores; she was knocked to the ground but still managed to detonate the bomb, killing three and wounding eight. Had the soldier and the other bystanders not called out a warning to others—and had they not shot the woman before she could enter the shops—the death toll certainly would have been higher. Had the soldier not hesitated, the number of dead might have been lower.[6] On June 29, 2008, another woman wearing an explosive belt was shot in Baghdad. According to the Associated Press, she was "the latest of more than 20 suicide missions by women this year."

In a British trial of eight terrorists who planned to blow up seven planes flying to the United States, it was revealed that some of them wanted to bring their wives and children on the targeted planes to help them get through security. It is unclear whether these terrorists intended to tell their wives that they were going to be "martyred," along with their children, in the explosions.[7]

As more women and children are recruited by their mothers, fathers, and religious leaders to become suicide bombers, more women and children will be shot at—some mistakenly. That, too, is part of the grand plan of democracy's enemies. They want us to kill their civilians, whom they also consider martyrs, because when we accidentally kill a civilian, they win in the court of public opinion. Democracies lose, both politically and emotionally, when they kill civilians, even inadvertently. As Golda Meir once put it, "We can perhaps someday forgive you for killing our children, but we cannot forgive you for making us kill your children."

Civilian casualties also increase when terrorists operate from within civilian enclaves and hide behind human shields. This relatively new phenomenon undercuts the second basic premise of conventional warfare: combatants can easily be distinguished from noncombatants. Has Zahra Maladan become a combatant by urging her son to blow himself up? Have the religious leaders who preach a culture of death lost their status as noncombatants? What about "civilians" who willingly allow themselves to be used as human shields? Or their homes as launching pads for terrorist rockets?

The traditional sharp distinction between soldiers in uniform and civilians in nonmilitary garb has given way to a continuum.

We need a new vocabulary to reflect the realities of modern warfare. A new phrase should be introduced into the reporting and the analysis of current events in the Middle East: "the continuum of civilianality." Though cumbersome, this concept aptly captures the reality and the nuance of warfare today and provides a fairer and more precise way to describe those who are killed, wounded, and punished.

There is a vast difference—both moral and legal—between a two-year-old who is killed by an enemy rocket and a thirty-year-old civilian who has allowed his house to be used to store Katyusha rockets. Both are technically civilians, but the former is far more innocent than the latter. There is also a difference between a civilian who merely favors or even votes for a terrorist group and one who provides financial or other material support for terrorism. Finally, there is a difference between civilians who are held hostage against their will by terrorists who use them as involuntary human shields and civilians who voluntarily place themselves in harm's way in order to protect terrorists from enemy fire.

These differences and others are conflated within the increasingly meaningless word *civilian*—a word that carried great significance when uniformed armies fought other uniformed armies on battlefields far from civilian population centers. Today this same word equates the truly innocent with guilty accessories to terrorism.

The domestic law of crime, in virtually every nation, reflects this continuum of culpability. For example, in the infamous Fall River rape case (fictionalized in the film *The Accused*), there were several categories of morally and legally complicit individuals: those who actually raped the woman; those who held her down; those who blocked her escape route; those who cheered and encouraged the rapists; and those who could have called the police but did not.[8] No rational person would suggest that any of these people were entirely free of moral guilt, although reasonable people might disagree about the legal guilt of those in the last two categories. Their accountability for rape is surely a matter of degree, as is the accountability for terrorism of those who work with the terrorists.

It will, of course, be difficult for international law—and for the media—to draw the lines of subtle distinction routinely drawn by domestic criminal law. This is because domestic law operates on a retail basis: one person and one case at a time. International law and media reporting about terrorism tend to operate on more of a wholesale basis: with body counts, civilian neighborhoods, and claims of collective punishment.

But the recognition that "civilianality" is often a matter of degree, rather than a bright line, should still inform the assessment of casualty figures in wars involving terrorists, paramilitary groups, and others who fight without uniforms—or help those who fight without uniforms.

Turning specifically to the fighting between Israel and Hezbollah and Hamas, the line between Israeli soldiers and civilians is relatively clear. Hezbollah missiles and Hamas rockets target and hit Israeli restaurants, apartment buildings, and schools. They are loaded with antipersonnel ball bearings and shrapnel designed specifically to maximize civilian casualties.

Hezbollah and Hamas combatants, on the other hand, are difficult to distinguish from the "civilians" who recruit, finance, harbor, and facilitate their terrorism. Nor can women and children always be counted as civilians, as some organizations do, since terrorists are increasingly using women and teenagers to play important roles in their attacks.

In an effort to reduce civilian casualties, the Israeli army gave well-publicized notice to civilians to leave the areas of southern Lebanon that had been turned into war zones.[9] Those who voluntarily remain behind become complicit. Others—those who cannot leave on their own—should be counted among the innocent victims.

If the media were to adopt this "continuum," it would be informative to learn how many of the "civilian casualties" fall closer to the line of complicity and how many are nearer to the line of innocence. Every civilian death is a tragedy, but some are more tragic than others.

We need new rules, strategies, and tactics to deal effectively and fairly with these dangerous new realities. We cannot simply wait until the son of Zahra Maladan—and the sons and the daughters of hundreds of others like her—decides to follow his mother's demand. We must stop them before they export their sick and dangerous culture of death to our shores, and Israel must stop them before or when they cross the borders into Israel's population centers, intent on blowing themselves up on crowded buses and in theaters, restaurants, and synagogues. This is what Israel succeeded in doing on the eve of Yom Kippur in 2006, when security officials confronted a ticking-bomb situation. Several days before Yom Kippur, they had received credible information that a suicide bomber was planning to blow himself up in a crowded synagogue on the holiest day of the Jewish year. After a gun battle in which an Israeli soldier was killed, the commander of the terrorist cell in Nablus was captured. Interrogation led to the location of the bomb in a Tel Aviv apartment.[10]

A phenomenon that is similar in some ways to the use of civilians as suicide bombers operates when rockets are fired at Israeli civilians by terrorists who hide behind civilians in densely populated residential areas, as they do from the Gaza Strip and did from Lebanon.

On the night of March 20, 2008, my wife and I visited the Israeli town of Sderot, which is only a few miles from Gaza. Over the last four years, Palestinian terrorists—in particular, Hamas and Islamic Jihad—have fired two thousand rockets at this civilian area, which is home to mostly poor and working-class people, many of them recent immigrants from the former Soviet bloc and Africa.[11] The rockets are designed exclusively to maximize civilian deaths, and some have barely missed schoolyards, kindergartens, hospitals, and school buses. But others hit their targets, killing nine civilians since 2001, including in February 2008 a father of four who had been studying at the local university. These anticivilian rockets have also injured and traumatized countless children.

We arrived in Sderot on the Jewish holiday of Purim, which commemorates the Jewish victory over the evil Persian Haman, who had plotted to kill all the Jews of Persia. Despite the threat of rocket attacks, the Purim festivities, headed by my cousin David Fendel, were in full swing at the yeshiva. The students were dancing and singing so loudly that the person in charge of security was worried that they would not hear the "red alert" siren that signals an incoming Kassam rocket. The residents of Sderot have fifteen seconds from the launch of the rocket to run into a shelter. The rule is that everyone must always be within fifteen seconds of a shelter, regardless of what they are doing. Shelters are everywhere, but the aged and the physically challenged often have difficulty making it to safety. On the night I was in Sderot, a rocket landed nearby, but there had been no "red alert." The warning system is far from foolproof.

In most parts of the world, the first words learned by toddlers are "mommy" and "daddy." In Sderot, they are "red alert." I was in Sderot to show solidarity with its residents, who are on the front line in the war against terrorism. I made a speech to the residents (and others who watched by videoconference) from the police station, standing in front of hundreds of rocket fragments that had been recovered. Many bore the name of the terrorist group that had fired the deadly missiles. Although firing deliberately to kill civilians is a war crime, the terrorists who fired at the civilians of Sderot were proud enough of their crimes to "sign" their murderous weapons. They know that in the real world in which we live, they will never be prosecuted for their murders and attempted murders.

As I spoke, I stood beside a teenage boy who had been seriously injured by a rocket that blew off his younger brother's leg. I also stood near a grieving mother whose four-year-old daughter had been killed by a rocket and a man whose wife and two children had been murdered by terrorists. The tension was palpable as a car alarm sounded, frightening only those of us who could not distinguish it from a red alert.

This is some of what I said to the victims of terrorism:

> Hamas is playing one of the most despicably immoral and dangerous games of Russian roulette with the lives of Jewish children.
>
> 8,000 rockets aimed at civilians . . . not a single one of them has a legitimate military purpose. Every one of them is an unlawful, antipersonnel, terrorist bomb. Where is the United Nations? Where are the human rights organizations? Where are those that claim to speak out on behalf of human rights and against international war crimes? These are war crimes against Jewish people, against the people of

Israel, against children, against women. . . . We hear [that] . . . only 9 people have died, as if 9 people dying is not enough. Every single person who dies is a generation missing. Children and grandchildren and great grandchildren. And what about the people so traumatized and so injured and so wounded. . . . The world is waiting for one of those rockets to hit a school bus . . . an ambulance . . . a hospital. Then the world will say [it is] okay for Israel to respond. . . .

What other democracy in the world would wait . . . wait until that horrible disaster occurs? It's inevitable. It's the law of averages. It is absolutely amazing that greater catastrophes have not befallen this city. This brave city. This embattled city. . . .

Sderot is an important symbol . . . for resisting terrorism around the world. If Sderot is allowed to be victimized today, it will be Tel Aviv tomorrow. It will be Haifa the day after tomorrow. And it will be Toronto next year. Because terrorism doesn't stop at national borders. It is not directed only against Israel. It is directed against all people who don't agree with the philosophy [of radical Islam].

We need strength and power. You are here tonight to help provide that power. You have an obligation to speak to your neighbors, to call your representatives, to petition your newspapers, to call into every talk show, to write letters to the editor, to write op ed pieces, to contribute, to do whatever it takes. . . . Every one of you in this room can satisfy that Talmudic precept of saving a human life.

We are with you. We are you. And you are us. We will never, ever abandon you.

It is impossible to justify the actions of Hamas in firing antipersonnel rockets at the civilians of Sderot. Yet the *New York Times* radio station, WQXR-FM, refused to run a paid advertisement from the American Jewish Committee condemning the Hamas action. The station manager complained that "the description of the missiles as arriving 'day or night' and 'daily' is also subject to challenge as being misleading, at least to the degree that reasonable people might be troubled by the absence of any acknowledgment of reciprocal Israeli military actions."[12] In other words, in order for the paid ad to be acceptable, the advertiser must acknowledge the moral equivalence between Hamas targeting civilians and Israel targeting those who fire the rockets.

The firing of rockets at civilians from densely populated civilian areas is the newest tactic in the war between terrorists who love death and democracies that love life. The terrorists have learned how to exploit the morality of democracies against those who do not want to kill civilians, even enemy civilians. In one recent incident, Israeli intelligence learned that a particular house was being used to manufacture and store rockets. It was a clear military target since their rockets were being fired at Israeli civilians. But the house was also being lived in by a family. So the Israeli military phoned the house, informed the owner that it was a military target, and gave him thirty minutes to leave with his family before the house was attacked. The owner called Hamas, which immediately sent dozens of mothers carrying babies to stand on the roof of the house. Hamas knew that Israel would never fire at a home with civilians in it. They also knew that if, by some fluke, the Israeli authorities did not learn that there were civilians in the house, and fired on it, Hamas would win a public relations victory by displaying the dead civilians to the media. In this case, Israel did learn of the civilians and withheld its fire. The rockets that were spared destruction by the human shields were then used against Israeli civilians. In another recent incident, captured on video, a terrorist can be seen moving a rocket launcher adjacent to a Palestinian elementary school run by the United Nations Relief Agency and then firing it at Israeli civilians. The head of the Israeli air force asked, "Are we going to hit the terrorist" and risk killing children? "We decided not to hit the terrorist," he said, "but you can see how they behave."

This, in a nutshell, is the dilemma faced by democracies with a high level of morality. The Hamas tactic would not have worked against the Russians in Chechnya. When the Russians were fired upon, they fired against civilians without hesitation. Nor would it work in Darfur, where *janjaweed* militias have killed thousands of civilians and displaced 2.5 million in order to get the rebels who were hiding among them.[13]

Certain tactics work only against moral enemies. I'm reminded of an exchange between Mohandas Gandhi and Martin Buber following Kristallnacht. Gandhi recommended that the Jews of Europe employ the tactics of civil disobedience (*"satyagraha"*) that had proved successful when used by Gandhi against the British. Buber reminded Gandhi that his tactic worked because the British were a moral people, whereas the Nazis were not.[14]

Gandhi then urged the Jews of Europe to commit collective suicide to demonstrate their moral superiority over the Nazis. He did not himself threaten to commit suicide in protest against the world's worst barbarity, even when he learned of the Nazi genocide. Instead, he railed against Zionism, supporting the British decision to exclude the Jews of Europe from Palestine, where many could have been saved.[15]

I was not surprised to learn, therefore, that more than half a century later, Gandhi's grandson—who regards himself as his grandfather's spiritual heir—accused the Jews of "overplay[ing]" the Holocaust "to the point that it begins to repulse friends."[16] He also blamed the Jews for creating a worldwide "culture of violence," of which "Israel and the Jews are the biggest players."[17] He predicts that this Jewish culture of violence "is eventually going to destroy humanity."[18] Not a word about Islamic or Arab violence, about Iran's threatened genocide against Israel by nuclear weapons, or about North Korea, Darfur, Rwanda, Cambodia, China, or other threats to world peace. No, it's the Jews who are the "biggest players" in this culture of violence and the Jews who threaten to "destroy humanity." This "blame the Jews" mentality is classic anti-Semitism, barely distinguishable from the rantings of *Der Sturmer* and the Hamas charter. Although such bigotry may be motivated by anti-Israel hate, it quickly morphs into anti-Jewish hate.

Comments such as those made by Arun Gandhi encourage terrorists to hide behind civilians and use them as human shields to increase civilian casualties on both sides. What rights does a democracy have when faced with such a tactic?

Article 51 of the United Nations Charter guarantees its members "the inherent right to . . . individual self defense" against "an armed attack."[19] In January 2006, Hamas was elected to govern the Palestinian territories. After Israel ended its occupation of

Gaza and removed all of its settlers, Hamas threw the Palestinian Authority out of Gaza and assumed de facto as well as de jure control over the entire Gaza Strip. Its leaders then instructed its military wing to direct rockets at civilian targets in southern Israel. At first, these rockets were Qassams with a relatively short range. Now they include Katyushas, which can reach Israel's large cities, including Ashkelon, with its population of 120,000 civilians. Hamas has officially declared that its policy is to develop or smuggle even longer-range missiles capable of reaching Israel's largest city, Tel Aviv, and its lifeblood, Ben-Gurion Airport. It has promised to keep aiming its missiles at civilian targets until the Jewish state is finally destroyed.

If this is not an "armed attack" under Article 51, then I don't know what is. The only argument against it being an armed attack is that firing rockets at civilian population centers, as Hamas is doing, is a war crime. International law prohibits, even during a declared war, the deliberate targeting of civilians or the bombing of areas of civilian population centers with absolutely no military significance. But war crimes may also constitute an armed attack: Hitler's invasion of Poland was both, as the Nuremberg Tribunal determined. If anything, an armed attack that is also a war crime justifies the right of self-defense even more than a mere armed attack does.

Nor can it be said that these attacks on Israeli towns and cities are merely the work of individual terrorists or terrorist groups. The military wing of Hamas is in fact a terrorist organization, as the United States and the European community have recognized. But since Hamas is in political and military control of the liberated Gaza Strip, the military wing of Hamas is also the official army of that government, as Hamas itself has proclaimed.

What, then, are Israel's rights under international law, under the law of war, under historical precedents, and under various treaties and human rights concepts? What would other nations do if their cities and towns were attacked by enemy rockets, and what have they done in the past? Israel certainly has the right to counterattack its enemy, destroy its capacity to fire rockets, and engage in "belligerent reprisal."[20] The only constraint on Israeli action, according to international law, is "proportionality."[21] Israel's military actions must be proportional. But proportional to what? Certainly not to the actual number of people who have thus far been killed or injured by rocket attacks. Israel has spent an enormous amount of money building shelters to protect against rockets. Thousands of rockets have been aimed at southern Israel in recent years.[22] Each one of them had the capacity to kill dozens, if not hundreds, of civilians. The fact that no Hamas rocket has yet hit a school bus, a kindergarten, an ambulance, a synagogue, or a school yard is simply happenstance. It is only a matter of time until this happens. No nation has to wait until the goals of its enemy are fulfilled before it engages in a proportional response. Proportion must be defined by reference to the *threat* posed by the enemy and not by the *harm* it has thus far produced.

Israel has tried several options, each of which has been condemned by vocal members of the international community, human rights groups, and religious organizations—some of whom have been silent about the Hamas war crimes that precipitated the Israeli actions. Israel has tried economic sanctions, border controls, targeted attacks on terrorists, and ground incursions. Each of these generally acceptable war measures carries with it the risk of some civilian casualties. In whatever manner Israel responds, Hamas wins. If Israel does nothing, Hamas taunts it for being impotent. If it does something, Hamas accuses it of a "disproportionate" response. Hamas leader Khaled Meshal characterized Israel's military actions in Gaza as "the real Holocaust."[23] Even Mahmoud Abbas, the so-called moderate Palestinian leader in the West Bank, said that Israel's military efforts to stop the rockets were "more than a Holocaust."[24] Then the international community pounced on Israel. This chorus of condemnation actually encourages the terrorists to operate from civilian areas. This is a point that must be emphasized because it actually affects the tactics on the ground selected by terrorists.

Moreover, even Israel's efforts to provide fuel and food to the residents of Gaza are frequently thwarted by Hamas's rocket and terrorist attacks on the fuel depots and the food transit points.[25] Hamas is seeking to create a humanitarian crisis in order to have Israel condemned by the international community. How else can anyone explain Hamas's attack on the fuel depot in which two Israeli civilians who work to provide fuel to Gaza were shot and killed? What choice did Israel have at that point but to temporarily shut down the depot because Israelis were reluctant to endanger their lives to provide fuel to Hamas-controlled Gaza? I have not heard of Israel's critics volunteering to serve in these depots or crossing points.

The time has come for Israel's critics to tell Israel what it should do in the face of these escalating rocket attacks on its civilian population centers. If economic sanctions, border controls, targeting terrorists, and ground incursions should not be employed, what are the alternatives?

The answer to this question is important, not only to Israel, but to the United States and other democratic nations that will surely face the prospect of having to take actions to prevent terrorist attacks by enemies who deliberately hide among civilians. The barrage of unconstructive criticism directed against Israeli self-defense actions will only encourage more terrorism of this kind.

The tactic of terrorists hiding behind civilians reached its zenith (or nadir) in Lebanon during the summer of 2006, when Hezbollah fired 4,228 rockets, mostly short-range Katyushas, at Israeli civilian targets in Haifa (a mixed Israeli city of 240,000 Jews and 26,000 Arabs) and other residential areas.[26] The goal of Hezbollah was revealed in an apology issued by its leader.

Hassan Nasrallah apologized to the families of two Israeli children who were killed by a Hezbollah rocket that hit the Christian holy city of Nazareth.[27] He called them *shahids*, martyrs, even though they did not choose to die at the hands of Hezbollah terrorists. The apology was issued not because they were children or innocent bystanders, but because they were Israeli Arabs and not Jews. Hezbollah's rockets are aimed at Jews and earn cheers whenever they kill a Jewish baby or a grandmother. No apologies there.

The so-called Arab-Israeli conflict represents the first instance since the Holocaust that Jews, as Jews, are being specifically targeted by an international organization that seeks recognition as a legitimate power. Hezbollah has threatened to attack Jewish targets outside of Israel as well. And it has proved its willingness to do so, as evidenced by its attack on a Jewish community center in Buenos Aires in 1994, in which Hezbollah collaborated with Argentine neo-Nazis to murder many Jews, including children. The collaboration between neo-Nazis and Islamic terrorists should come as no surprise to anyone familiar with the history of the collaboration between the Palestinian leadership and Hitler during World War II. The grand mufti of Jerusalem, Haj Amin al-Husseini, who was recognized as the official leader of the Palestinians during this period, was a virulent anti-Semite whose hatred of Jews was both religious and racial. (More on him in the next chapter.)

Husseini rejected the two-state solution, arguing that Palestine was part of Syria. He objected to any Jewish state, even one the "size of a postage stamp," on Islamic holy land. He wanted all of the Middle East to become *judenrein* (free of Jews). Husseini's heir was Yasser Arafat, a cousin who also targeted Jews, through his surrogate terrorist groups. When a young student at the Hebrew University was gunned down while jogging through a mixed neighborhood of Jews and Arabs in north Jerusalem in 2004, the Al-Aqsa Martyrs Brigade, a wholly owned subsidiary of Arafat's Fatah movement, joyously claimed credit for killing yet another innocent Jew.[28] When it was later learned that the jogger was a Jerusalem Arab and not a Jew, Al-Aqsa quickly apologized to the family, calling it an accident.[29]

This is anti-Semitism, pure and simple. And despite efforts by supporters of Palestinian terrorism to justify the murder of innocent civilians as national liberation or by any other euphemism, these selective apologies prove that Islamic terrorists' targeting of Jews is little different in intent from other forms of exterminatory anti-Jewish murders.

And yet Kofi Annan, the former UN secretary-general; Louise Arbour, the former high commissioner of human rights at the UN; and many within the European Union have condemned Israel for its reasonable military actions to prevent these racist murders. They insist that equal blame falls on the anti-Semitic targeting of Jews by Hezbollah and on the defensive actions that Israel directs at military targets.

Hezbollah's goal is not the "liberation" of Palestine. Its members are not Palestinian. They are Islamic extremists who want to "liberate" all Islamic land, which includes all of Israel proper, including Tel Aviv, from the "crusaders," a term that includes Jews and Christians (even though Jews were among the victims of the Crusades). They seek to liberate Lebanon from Christians as well. The fight against Hezbollah is a fight against anti-Jewish, anti-Christian, and antihumanistic values.

Nasrallah has called for revenge against Israelis and Jews around the world for the assassination of Imad Mugniyah in 2007, which he claims was done by Israel.[30] It does not matter, of course, who actually pulled off the assassination. Israel and the Jews would be blamed by Hezbollah even if Syria had been responsible. Hezbollah always blames Israel and the Jews for everything. In the past, Hezbollah has taken revenge against what it claimed to be Israeli actions by murdering Jewish schoolchildren. Once again, it is threatening to attack innocent Jews around the world.

Yet some in the media describe this targeting of Jews as part of a cycle of violence, thus suggesting that the military targeting of a terrorist combatant who is responsible for the deaths of hundreds of innocent civilians is the same, morally, as the random murders of men, women, and children who had absolutely nothing to do with killing Imad Mugniyah but just happen to be Jewish. Sheik Hassan Nasrallah's call for the killing of Jews around the world is nothing short of incitement to genocide, or at least to mass murder. Until the media understand the crucial distinction between these very different actions, we will all be vulnerable to the revenge tactics of Hezbollah and other terrorist organizations.

While I had reservations about the wisdom of Israeli counterattacks against Hezbollah's rockets, I had no doubt about their legality or morality. No democracy in the world would or should tolerate missiles being fired at its cities without taking every reasonable step to stop the attacks. The big question raised by Israel's military actions in Lebanon is what is "reasonable." The answer, according to the laws of war, is that it is reasonable to attack military targets, so long as every effort is made to reduce civilian casualties. To reiterate the point made earlier, if the objectives cannot be achieved without some civilian casualties, these must be "proportional" to the civilian casualties that would be prevented by the military action.

This is all well and good for democratic nations that deliberately locate their military bases away from civilian population centers. Israel has its air force, nuclear facilities, and large army bases in locations as remote as anything can be in that country. It is possible for an enemy to attack Israeli military targets without inflicting "collateral damage" on its civilian population. Hezbollah and Hamas, by contrast, deliberately operate military wings out of densely populated areas.

While Israel does everything reasonable to minimize civilian casualties—not always with success—Hezbollah and Hamas do everything they can to maximize civilian casualties on both sides. Islamic terrorists, a diplomat commented years ago, "have mastered the harsh arithmetic of pain. . . . Palestinian casualties play in their favor and Israeli casualties play in their favor."[31] These are groups that send children to die as suicide bombers, sometimes without the child knowing that he is being sacrificed. In March 2004, an eleven-year-old was paid to take a parcel through Israeli security. Unbeknownst to him, it contained a bomb that was to be detonated remotely. (Fortunately, the plot was foiled.)[32]

This misuse of civilians as shields and swords requires a reassessment of the laws of war. Making the distinction between combatants and civilians was easy when combatants were uniformed members of armies that fought on battlefields distant from civilian centers. It becomes blurred in the present context. Now, there is the continuum of "civilianality," about which I have written.[33]

The laws of war and the rules of morality must adapt to this reality. An analogy to domestic criminal law is instructive: a bank robber who takes a teller hostage and fires at police from behind his human shield is guilty of murder if they, in an effort to stop the robber from shooting, accidentally kill the hostage. The same should be true of terrorists who use civilians as shields from behind whom they fire their rockets. The terrorists must be held legally and morally responsible for the deaths of the civilians, even if the direct physical cause was an Israeli rocket aimed at those who targeted Israeli citizens.

A democracy is entitled to prefer saving the lives of its own innocents over the lives of the civilians of an aggressor, especially if the latter group contains many who are complicit in terrorism.[34] Israel will—and should—take every precaution to minimize civilian casualties on the other side. Indeed, the Israeli military works closely with renowned academic experts in moral philosophy, international law, and other disciplines to articulate and enforce "principles of the military ethics of fighting terror."[35]

Nor is the answer the simple-minded one offered by some of Israel's critics: end the occupation and the terrorism and the rockets will go away. Israel left Lebanon in 2000 and Gaza in 2005. These are not "occupied" territories. Yet they serve as launching-pads for attacks on Israeli civilians. Occupation does not cause terrorism, but terrorism seems to cause occupation. If Israel is not to reoccupy to prevent terrorism, the Lebanese government and the Palestinian Authority must ensure that these regions cease to be terrorist safe havens. Until that happens, human rights organizations must place the blame for civilian casualties among human shields on those who unlawfully use the shields, rather than on those who lawfully seek to defend their civilians from attack.

When I was in Israel in March 2008, I was shown military videos that clearly proved that rockets had been launched from densely populated civilian areas, despite the willfully false claims of Human Rights Watch (HRW) and other so-called neutral human rights NGOs (nongovernmental organizations). One video was particularly telling. It showed the rocket launcher mounted on a truck. The mobile launching pad had deliberately been placed among civilian homes. As soon as the rockets were launched, the large truck maneuvered through the congested traffic and entered a preselected "safe house" in whose below-ground garage it sought sanctuary, knowing that Israel would not fire at a residence with people in it. This time, it didn't work. The Israeli air force watched the house until the truck emerged, loaded with rockets, and then it fired a laser-guided missile at the truck. The result was multiple explosions, visible on the video, as the Katyushas exploded one at a time. There were no civilian casualties, only some broken windows.

But sometimes, there are civilian casualties, as in Qana, where Hezbollah chose a location near a building filled with refugees to launch rockets at Israeli civilians. This induced Israel to make a terrible misjudgment. Its defensive rocket missed the Hezbollah launchers and hit the civilian building. That was Hezbollah's plan all along. As Israelis wept in grief over the deaths of the Lebanese civilians, Hezbollah leaders celebrated its propaganda victory.

Yes, Hezbollah was happy that an Israeli rocket had killed Lebanese children. It had deliberately prevented families from leaving the war zone in order to place children in harm's way. The children were now in paradise, martyrs to Hezbollah's cause. Israel was condemned throughout the world for killing children—*massacre* was the most common word used in the Arab media. The Israelis apologized, but that was not enough to put out the flames of anger or to quiet the shrill calls for revenge.

Israel produced evidence proving that it was largely Hezbollah's fault.[36] Hezbollah was using Lebanese children as involuntary human shields—surely, a war crime. Hezbollah was preventing civilians, who had been repeatedly warned by Israel to leave the battle zone, from leaving. Hezbollah sympathizers were shown on TV defiantly tearing up the Israeli leaflets, as if to say "we're staying." Hezbollah had refused to build bomb shelters for ordinary civilians—only for their own leaders and their rocket launchers. Hezbollah knew (and Israel didn't) that children were in the so-called safe house.[37] That is why it deliberately used the safe house as a shield behind which to fire rockets at Israel. Hezbollah used its rocket launchers as "bait" to induce Israel to fire at them in order to increase the chances that Israel's rocket would misfire and hit the "safe house." It was a perfect plan. Leaders of Hezbollah knew they could count on the international community to finish their dirty work by condemning Israel, rather than Hezbollah, for the deaths intentionally caused by Hezbollah.

While Israel has rightly apologized for the deaths caused by its rocket, Hezbollah never apologizes for causing civilian deaths, except when the deaths are of Arab children, as was the case in Nazareth.

Even some UN officials, who are usually quick to condemn Israel, understood the dangerous game Hezbollah was playing with the lives of civilians. Just days before Hezbollah orchestrated the tragedy at Qana, Jan Egeland, the UN undersecretary general for humanitarian affairs, had essentially predicted it. He chided Hezbollah for being "a bunch of cowards hiding behind women and children." He said that he "cannot understand how someone could be proud that there were more women and children hurt than armed militants." And he "call[ed] for the Hezbollah to immediately stop mixing with the civilian population."[38] But Hezbollah leaders did not listen to Egeland. Instead, they again fired their Katyusha from behind the building in Qana, knowing that it was filled with civilians.

The Arab world, the Islamic world, and the rest of the Israel-haters rallied behind Hezbollah. Hatred of Israel has even managed to heal the millennium-long divisions between Shias and Sunnis.

Every day more Arabs and Muslims kill other Arabs and Muslims in Sudan, Iraq, Afghanistan, and other parts of the world than the Israelis have killed in years of combat. But the international community—and the Arab world—turns a blind eye. Indeed, in Sudan, where hundreds of thousands have died, many Arab governments actually support the Sudanese government and its genocidal policies. Even "peaceful" nations, such as Egypt and Jordan, have killed more Muslim and Arab dissidents, extremists, and terrorists than Israel has—and without much protest.

There are Israeli actions deserving of criticism, such as its excessive use of cluster bombs toward the end of the war, which left unexploded droplets in civilian areas. Many Israelis and American Jews were justly critical of Israel (and other nations) for misusing cluster bombs. But Hezbollah benefited from Israel's mistakes, as it benefits whenever Israel kills civilians.

The real victory for Hezbollah is that it caused enormous grief and dissent in Israel over the deaths of the children, causing Israel to show more "restraint," as it did by declaring a forty-eight-hour cessation of air attacks following the mistake in Qana. This gave the terrorists a freer hand at launching rockets. The end result is more Israel civilian casualties. The sad truth is that the Israelis care more about the lives of innocent Lebanese children than Hezbollah does.

This cruel and unlawful terrorist tactic employed by Hezbollah in Lebanon (and by Hamas in Gaza), of inducing Israel to cause civilian casualties by firing rockets at Israeli citizens from densely populated civilian areas, could not succeed without the help of so-called human rights groups, such as Amnesty International and Human Rights Watch. Within days of the Hezbollah attack against Israel, Amnesty International announced that Israel was guilty of a slew of war crimes for "widespread attacks against public civilian infrastructure, including power plants, bridges, main roads, seaports, and Beirut's international airport."[39]

There were two problems with the Amnesty International report and conclusion. First, Amnesty International is wrong about the law. Israel committed no war crimes by attacking parts of the civilian infrastructure in Lebanon. Second, it was wrong about the facts on the ground.

In actuality, through restraint, Israel was able to minimize the number of civilian casualties in Lebanon, despite Hezbollah's best efforts to embed itself in population centers and to use civilians as human shields. The total number of Muslim civilians killed by Israeli weapons during a month of ferocious defensive warfare was a fraction of the number of innocent Muslims killed by other Muslims during that same period in Iraq, Sudan, Afghanistan, Algeria, and other areas of Muslim-on-Muslim civil strife. Yet the deaths caused by Muslims received a fraction of the attention devoted to alleged Israeli "crimes." This lack of concern for Muslims killed by other Muslims—and the lack of focus by so-called human rights organizations on these deaths—is bigotry, pure and simple.

Amnesty International's evidence that Israel's attacks on infrastructure constitute war crimes comes from its own idiosyncratic interpretation of the already vague word *disproportionate.* Unfortunately for Amnesty International, no other country in any sort of armed conflict has ever adopted such a narrow definition of the term. Indeed, among the very first military objectives of most modern wars is precisely what Israel did: to disable portions of the opponent's electrical grid and communication network, to destroy bridges and roads, and to do whatever else is necessary to interfere with those parts of the civilian infrastructure that support the military capability of the enemy.

That's how the U.S. and British militaries fought World War II. (In fact, Israel shows far more restraint than Britain did during World War II. Prime Minister Winston Churchill directed the Royal Air Force to bomb the centers of towns with the express purpose of killing as many civilians as possible.)[40] Had the Allies been required to fight World War II under the rules of engagement selectively applied by Amnesty International to Israel, our "greatest generation" might have lost that war.

The strategy of destroying some infrastructure was particularly appropriate against Hezbollah. Israel first had try to ensure that its kidnapped soldiers would not be smuggled out of the country (as other soldiers had been and were never returned); then it had to prevent Hezbollah from being rearmed, especially given that Hezbollah damaged a ship while using advanced radar technology provided by the Lebanese army and rockets provided by Iran.[41]

Hezbollah was being armed by Syria and Iran—as those countries admitted—and the president, the government, and the population of Lebanon were overwhelmingly in favor of the militia's indiscriminate rocket attacks against Israeli civilian population centers. The Lebanese army actively supported Hezbollah's military actions. Israel was, in a very real sense, at war with Lebanon itself and not simply with a renegade faction of militants.

Here's how law professor David Bernstein answered Amnesty International's charge: "The idea that a country at war can't attack the enemy's resupply routes (at least until it has direct evidence that there is a particular military shipment arriving) has nothing to do with human rights or war crimes, and a lot to do with a pacifist attitude that seeks to make war, regardless of the justification for it or the restraint in prosecuting it [at least if it's a Western country doing it], an international 'crime.'"[42]

In other words, if attacking the civilian infrastructure is a war crime, then modern warfare is entirely impermissible, and terrorists have a free hand in attacking democracies and hiding from retaliation among civilians. Terrorists become de facto immune from any consequences for their atrocities.

The more troubling aspect of Amnesty International's report was its relative inattention to Hezbollah, especially during the early days of the war. If Israel is guilty of war crimes for targeting civilian infrastructure, imagine how much greater is Hezbollah's moral responsibility for targeting civilians! But Amnesty International showed little interest in condemning the terrorist organization that started the conflict, indiscriminately killed both Israeli civilians (directly) and Lebanese civilians (by using them as human shields), and has announced its intention to kill Jews world-wide (already having started by blowing up a Jewish community center in Argentina). When the war was over, Amnesty finally released a report characterizing Hezbollah's targeting of civilians as "amounting to war crimes," but its condemnations of Israel were more strident and received more attention.[43]

Even Al-Jazeera expressed surprise at the imbalance in the Amnesty International report:

> During the four-week war Hezbollah fired 3,900 rockets at Israeli towns and cities with the aim of inflicting maximum civilian casualties.
>
> The Israeli government says that 44 Israeli civilians were killed in the bombardments and 1,400 wounded.
>
> AI has not issued a report accusing Hezbollah of war crimes.[44]

Amnesty International does not even seem to understand the charges it is making. Take, for example, this paragraph from its report: "Israeli government spokespeople have insisted that they were targeting Hizbullah positions and support facilities, and that damage to civilian infrastructure was incidental or resulted from Hizbullah using the civilian population as a 'human shield.' However, the pattern and scope of the attacks, as well as the number of civilian casualties and the amount of damage sustained, makes the justification ring hollow."[45]

But the issues of human shields and infrastructure are different. The first relates to civilian casualties; the second concerns property damage. Of course, Israel intentionally targeted bridges and roads. It would have been militarily negligent not to have done so under the circumstances. But it did not target innocent civilians. It would have given Israel no military benefit to do so.

The allegations become even more tenuous, as when Amnesty International wrote, "A road that can be used for military transport is still primarily civilian in nature."[46] By this reasoning, terrorists could commandeer any structure or road initially constructed for civilian use, and Israel could not touch those bridges or buildings because they were once, and still could be, used by civilians. This is not, and should not be, the law.

Consider another example: "While the use of civilians to shield a combatant from attack is a war crime, under international humanitarian law such use does not release the opposing party from its obligations towards the protection of the civilian population."[47] Well, that certainly sounds nice. But what does it mean? What would Amnesty International suggest a country do in the face of daily rocket attacks launched from civilian populations? Nothing, apparently. The clear implication of Amnesty International's arguments is that the only way Israel could have avoided committing "war crimes" would have been if it had taken only such military action that carried with it no risk to civilian shields—that is, to do absolutely nothing.

The real problem with Amnesty International's paper is that its blanket condemnations do not consider the consequences of its arguments. (It doesn't have to; it would never advance these arguments against any country but Israel.)

Amnesty International's conclusions are not based on sound legal arguments. They're certainly not based on compelling moral arguments. They're simply anti-Israel arguments. Amnesty International reached a predetermined conclusion—that Israel committed war crimes—and it is marshaling whatever sound-bites it can to support that conclusion.

Amnesty International is not only sacrificing its own credibility when it misstates the law and omits relevant facts in its obsession over Israel. It also harms progressive causes that Amnesty International should be championing.

In 2005, for example, Amnesty International blamed Palestinian rapes and "honor killings" on—you guessed it—the Israeli occupation.[48] When I pointed out that there was absolutely no statistical evidence to show that domestic violence increased during the occupation and that Amnesty International's report relied exclusively on the conclusory and anecdotal reports of Palestinian NGOs, Amnesty International stubbornly repeated that "Israel is implicated in this violence by Palestinian men against Palestinian women."[49]

This episode only underscored Amnesty International's predisposition to blame everything on Israel. Even when presented with an ideal opportunity to promote gender equality and feminism in the Arab world, it preferred to take wholly unrelated and absurd shots at Israel. Amnesty International just can't seem to help itself when it comes to blaming Israel for the evils of the world, but rational observers must not credit the predetermined conclusions of a once-reputable organization that has destroyed its own credibility by repeatedly applying a double standard to Israel.

Human Rights Watch (HRW) was even more biased in its reporting of the facts on the ground. This was its conclusion, allegedly reached after extensive "investigations": "Human Rights Watch found no cases in which Hezbollah deliberately used civilians as shields to protect them from retaliatory IDF attack." After investigating a handful of cases, HRW found that in "none of the cases of civilian deaths documented in this report [Qana, Srifa, Tyre, and southern Beirut] is there evidence to suggest that

Hezbollah forces or weapons were in or near the area that the IDF targeted during or just prior to the attack."[50] No cases!

Anyone who watched even a smattering of TV during the war saw direct evidence of rockets being launched from civilian areas. But not Human Rights Watch. "Who are you going to believe, me or your lying eyes?" as Groucho Marx once asked. The lying eyes belonged to the pro-Hezbollah witnesses whom HRW's investigators chose to interview—and claimed to believe. But the mendacious pens belonged to Kenneth Roth, HRW's executive director, and his minions in New York City, who know how to be skeptical when it serves their interests not to believe certain witnesses. How could an organization, which claims to be objective, have been so demonstrably wrong about so central a point in so important a war? Could it have been an honest mistake? I don't think so. Despite its boast that "Human Rights Watch has interviewed victims and witnesses of attacks in one-on-one settings, conducted on-site inspections . . . and collected information for hospitals, humanitarian groups, and government agencies," it didn't find one instance in which Hezbollah failed to segregate its fighters from civilians.[51]

Nor, apparently, did HRW even ask the Israelis for proof of their claim that Hezbollah rockets were being fired from behind civilians, and that Hezbollah fighters were hiding among civilians. Its investigators interviewed Arab "eyewitnesses" and monitored "information from public sources including the Israeli government statements." But it conducted no interviews with Israeli officials or witnesses. It also apparently ignored credible news sources, such as the *New York Times* and the *New Yorker.* Here are some of the reports that were available before HRW published its conclusion that Hezbollah forces did not operate "in or near" civilian areas.

Sabrina Tavernise, writing for the *New York Times,* reported,

"Hezbollah came to Ain Ebel to shoot its rockets," said Fayad Hanna Amar, a young Christian man, referring to his village. "They are shooting from between our houses."

"Please," he added, "write that in your newspaper.". . .

One woman, who would not give her name because she had a government job and feared retribution, said Hezbollah fighters had killed a man who was trying to leave Bint Jbail.

"This is what's happening, but no one wants to say it" for fear of Hezbollah, she said.[52]

John Lee Anderson wrote in the *New Yorker*,

Near the hospital, a mosque lay in ruins.

A younger man came up to me and, when we were out of earshot of others, said that Hezbollah had kept bombs in the basement of the mosque, but that two days earlier a truck had taken the cache away. It was common knowledge in Sidon, he said, and everyone was expecting the mosque to be hit.[53]

Reported Sonia Verma of Canada's *National Post*,

The surgeon led a group of journalists over what remained: mangled debris, shredded walls and a roof punched through by an Israeli shell.

"Look what they did to this place," Dr. Fatah said, shaking his head. "Why in the world would the Israelis target a hospital?"

The probable answer was found a few hours later in a field nearby. Hidden in the tall grass were the burned remnants of a rocket-launcher.

Confronted with the evidence, Dr. Fatah admitted his hospital could have been used as a site from which to fire rockets into Israel.[54]

In addition to the numerous reports of Hezbollah using Lebanese civilians as shields, there were also reports they were using UN peacekeepers as shields.

Charlie Gillis of *Maclean's* reported,

the possibility that Hezbollah fighters used [a UN outpost] as a shield from which to unleash fire. They've done so in the past says Maj.-Gen. Lewis MacKenzie (ret'd.), who witnessed the technique while on peacekeeping assignments in the area. "It's the same as if you set up your weapons systems beside a mosque or a church or a hospital."[55]

Steven Edwards of the CanWest News Service wrote,

> But far from saying there was no Hezbollah activity in the area to jus-
> tify Israeli interest, Hess-von Kruedener's e-mail, written July 19 and
> posted on the website of CTV, recounts numerous incidents.
>
> He also said of Israeli counter-fire to that date: "This has not been
> deliberate targeting, but has rather been due to tactical necessity.". . .
>
> "What that means is, in plain English, 'We've got Hezbollah
> fighters running around in our positions, taking our positions here
> and then using us for shields and then engaging the (Israeli Defence
> Forces),'" said MacKenzie, who led Canadian peacekeepers in
> Bosnia.[56]

The United Nations Interim Force in Lebanon (UNIFIL) said,
"It was also reported that Hezbollah fired from the vicinity of five
UN positions at Alma Ash Shab, AtTiri, Bayt Yahoun, Brashit, and
Tibnin."[57]

And Chris Tinkler of the *Sunday Mail* wrote,

> While these pictures have escaped the ravaged country, images taken
> by local newspaper and television teams are routinely seized by armed
> Hezbollah fighters at roadblocks.
>
> In one image a group of terrorists, including youths, are preparing
> to fire an anti-aircraft gun just metres from an apartment block with
> sheets hanging on a balcony to dry.
>
> Others show a Hezbollah thug armed with a nickel-plated AK47
> rifle guarding no-go zones after Israeli blitzes.
>
> Another depicts the remnants of a Hezbollah Katyusha rocket in
> the middle of a residential block, blown up in an Israeli air attack.
>
> The Melbourne man who smuggled the shots out of Beirut told
> yesterday how he was less than 400m from the residential block when
> it was obliterated.
>
> "Hezbollah came in to launch their rockets, then within minutes
> the area was blasted by Israeli jets," he said.
>
> "Until the Hezbollah fighters arrived, it had not been touched by
> the Israelis. Then it was totally devastated.
>
> "After the attacks Hezbollah didn't even allow the ambulances
> or the Lebanese Army to come in until they had cleaned the area,
> removing their rockets and hiding other evidence.

"It was carnage. Two innocent people died in that incident, but it was so lucky it was not more.

"The people there were horrified and disgusted at what Hezbollah were doing."

The extremist fighters used trucks, driven into residential areas, as launching pads for the rockets, he said.[58]

How could HRW have ignored—or more likely suppressed—this evidence from so many different sources? The only reasonable explanation is that HRW wanted there to be no proof of Hezbollah's tactic of hiding behind civilians, so they cooked the books to make it come out that way. Even after the fighting ended and all the reports of Hezbollah hiding among civilians were published, Kenneth Roth essentially repeated the demonstrably false conclusions that "in none of those cases was Hizbullah anywhere around at the time of the attack."[59] So committed is HRW to its predetermined conclusions that it refused to let the facts, as reported by objective sources, get in its way.

After the war, I learned that the Israeli air force had tapes and other documentation proving beyond any doubt that Hezbollah had systematically and deliberately fired its rockets from behind human shields in heavily populated civilian areas. This evidence was still classified and was being studied by the military. I worked with Danny Grossman, a former U.S. and Israeli air force navigator, to urge the Israeli government to declassify this important material in order to put the lie to the accusations of HRW, Amnesty International, and other so-called objective human rights groups. Finally, in the late fall of 2006, the evidence was declassified and given to the *New York Times,* which reviewed it carefully. The *Times* also reviewed a research report produced by the Intelligence and Terrorism Information Center that had been conducted by a retired colonel in military intelligence. That report concluded that "Hezbollah stored weapons in mosques, battled Israelis from inside empty schools, flew white flags while transporting missiles and launched rockets near United Nations monitoring posts."[60]

On December 5, 2006, the *New York Times* reported on the newly declassified videos in a front-page story that gave an entirely different account of what took place in Lebanon than the one being peddled by HRW. This is what the *Times* reported:

> In video from July 23, a truck with a multi-barreled missile launcher, presumably from Hezbollah, is parked in a street, sandwiched between residential buildings. . . .
>
> In another video, from a Lebanese village, rockets are seen being fired from a launcher on the back of a truck. The truck then drives a short distance and disappears inside a building. . . .
>
> The report says that there were many such examples, and that Hezbollah has been preparing for such an engagement for years, embedding its fighters and their weapons in the Shiite villages of southern Lebanon. When Hezbollah fired its rockets from those areas, Israel faced a choice of attacking, and possibly causing civilian casualties, or refraining from shooting because of the risk, the report said.
>
> Elias Hanna, a retired Lebanese Army general, said of the Israeli allegations, "Of course there are hidden invisible tunnels, bunkers of missile launchers, bunkers of explosive charges amongst civilians." . . .
>
> Asked whether Hezbollah should be seen as responsible for the deaths of Lebanese civilians in the war, he replied: "Of course Hezbollah is responsible. But these people are ready to sacrifice their lives for Hezbollah. If you tell them, 'Your relative died,' they will tell you 'No, he was a martyr.' The party's military preparations from 2000 till 2006 took place in their areas. They were of course done with complete secrecy, but in accordance with the civilians."
>
> During the war, Israel dropped leaflets urging villagers to leave southern Lebanon and also to evacuate from Hezbollah strongholds in southern Beirut. Many did flee, but some remained and among them were hundreds who were killed.[61]

The *Times* also reported on a video of three Hezbollah prisoners admitting that they had used civilian homes: "Hezbollah operated freely from homes in the village, with the permission of residents who had fled. The departing residents either left their doors unlocked or gave their keys to Hezbollah." The prisoners acknowledged that "homes used by Hezbollah were more likely to draw fire." One of them said he had posed as a civilian carrying "a white flag" while "transporting missiles." Another explained "how he had set up a rocket-firing position on the front porch of a house on the outskirts of Aita al Shaab." Yet another told how "group members had worn civilian clothes, tried never to show their weapons, and traveled in ordinary civilian cars."[62]

Even after the release of three videos and the *New York Times* report, HRW refused to withdraw its original report stating that there were no cases of Hezbollah operating from civilian areas or using human shields. (Amnesty International had "acknowledged the presence of Hezbollah fighters in civilian areas" but insisted that "this was not conclusive evidence of intent to use civilians as human shields."[63] The evidence of "intent" that Amnesty International requires to level charges against Israel is significantly lower than it is to make charges against Hezbollah.)

The Intelligence and Terrorism Information Center Report concluded that "the construction of a broad military infrastructure, positioned and hidden in populated areas, was intended to minimize Hezbollah's vulnerability. Hezbollah would also gain a propaganda advantage if it could represent Israel as attacking innocent civilians."[64]

Many former supporters of HRW have become alienated from the organization because of, in the words of one early supporter, "their obsessive focus on Israel." Roth and his organization's willful blindness when it comes to Israel and its enemies have undermined the credibility of a once-important human rights organization. HRW no longer deserves the support of real human rights advocates. Nor should its so-called reporting be credited by objective news organizations. The same must be said about Amnesty International.

The so-called human rights organizations that constantly side with the terrorists are actually guilty of encouraging the tactic of using human shields and firing rockets from civilian neighborhoods. The terrorists themselves acknowledge that they are counting on these biased organizations to make their case for them, and the organizations are succeeding. That's why terrorists persist in this doubly criminal tactic and civilians continue to be killed. And that is also why Israel did not win a more decisive victory in its battle against Hezbollah in the summer of 2006.

Israel compromised its military effectiveness in the interest of sparing Lebanese civilians who had deliberately been placed in harm's way by Hezbollah. It is possible, of course, that the Israeli military could have been more successful against Hezbollah, while at the same time killing fewer civilians. This is a technical military question that warrants serious consideration by a military commission of inquiry. If it is possible for Israel to strike more military targets with less collateral damage, it should, of course, do so. No moral issue is raised by improving military accuracy.[65] But the larger question of morality is anything but technical. It involves a classic conundrum about a choice of evils. How many innocent Lebanese civilians can be endangered to prevent the deaths of how many Israeli civilians? Moral societies have been debating variations of this dilemma since Abraham argued with God over the destruction of Sodom. And this choice will increasingly face democracies as they combat terrorists in proxy wars against state sponsors of Islamic fascism and fanaticism.[66]

The Islamic radicals, by hiding behind their own civilians, issue a challenge to democracies: either violate your own morality by coming after us and inevitably killing some innocent civilians, or maintain your scruples and leave us with a free hand to target your civilians. This challenge presents democracies such as Israel with a lose-lose option and terrorists with a win-win option.

Sadly, the world has yet to recognize the true moral culprits behind civilian (and not-so-civilian) deaths, when noncombatants are used to shield terrorists. That is why using human shields, although a clear violation of the international rules of armed conflict, is a win-win game for the terrorists.

One variable could change this dynamic and present democracies with a viable option that could make terrorism less attractive as a tactic: the international community, large segments of the media, and human rights organizations should stop falling for this gambit and acknowledge that they are being used to promote the terrorist agenda. Whenever a democracy is presented with the lose-lose option and chooses to defend its citizens by going after the terrorists who are hiding among civilians, this trio of predictable condemners can be counted on by the terrorists to accuse the democracy of "overreaction," "disproportionality," and "violations of human rights." In doing so, they play into the hands of the terrorists and cause more terrorism and more civilian casualties on both sides.

If instead this trio could, for once, be counted on to blame the terrorists for the civilian deaths on both sides, this tactic would no longer be a win-win situation for the terrorists. It should be obvious by now that Hezbollah and Hamas actually want the Israeli military to kill as many Lebanese and Palestinian civilians as possible.

Israel has every self-interest in minimizing civilian casualties, whereas the terrorists have every self-interest in maximizing them—on both sides. Israel should not be condemned for doing what every democracy would and should do: taking every reasonably military step to stop the killing of its own civilians. The idea that terrorists shed crocodile tears over the deaths of civilians whom they deliberately put in harm's way gives new meaning to hypocrisy. These same terrorists use women and children as suicide bombers against other women and children. We all know that hypocrisy is a terrorist tactic, but it is shocking that others fall for it and become complicit with the terrorists. Let the blame fall where it belongs: on the terrorists who seek to kill enemy civilians and give their democratic enemies little choice but to kill some civilians whom the terrorists hide behind.

Those who condemn Israel cause more civilian deaths and make it harder for Israel to withdraw from the West Bank. How the world reacts to Israel's military efforts to protect its citizens will have a considerable impact on future Israeli steps toward peace.

Prior to the recent kidnappings and the rocket attacks, the Israeli government announced its intention to engage in further withdrawals—this time from large portions of the West Bank. Israelis think of it as "land for peace." But how can Israel be expected to move forward with any withdrawal plan if all that it can expect in return is more terrorism—what the terrorists regard as "land for rocket launchings"—and more condemnation when it seeks to protect its civilians? This is a challenge that transcends Israel. The world must recognize the new way in which terrorists are fighting democracies, and it must devise counterweapons that are consistent with both morality and efficiency.

Hezbollah has announced that it has new surprises in store for Israel that may include chemical and biological weapons. What would Israel's critics regard as "proportional" to a chemical or biological attack? What would they say if Israel tried to preempt such an attack and, in the process, killed some civilians? Must a democracy absorb a first strike from a weapon of mass destruction before it fights back, as Amnesty International seems to advise in its reports on Israel's "war crimes"? (More on this in chapter 6.)

Israel's enemies therefore include some so-called human rights groups that care only about the rights of those with whose politics they agree.

Israel's enemies are also the elements of the media that report only on Israel's imperfections and never on its successes. When Israel was engaged in a campaign of targeted killings against Gaza terrorists during the height of the Palestinian intifada, for example, the press eagerly detailed every civilian casualty. Human rights organizations had a field day criticizing Israel for its failure to pinpoint legitimate military targets and for the large number of collateral deaths that its campaign of targeted killings was producing. In those days, especially in 2002–2003, approximately half of the people killed by Israeli missiles were civilians. The other half were terrorists who were engaged in trying to kill as many civilians as possible. Sometimes the civilian casualties exceeded the legitimate military killings. The most notorious such case was the Israeli military's assassination of Salah Shehadeh, a terrorist commander who was responsible for hundreds of Israeli deaths and who was actively involved in planning hundreds, perhaps thousands, more. After several failed attempts, a rocket managed to kill him, and few tears were shed over his well-deserved demise. But in the rocket attack, his wife and daughter were also killed, along with thirteen other civilians.[67] This caused an enormous outcry, not only in the international press, but among Israelis as well. Even though Shehadeh's death may well have prevented the deaths of many more Israeli civilians, the cost in Palestinian civilian casualties was still too high for most Israelis to accept and for the international media to tolerate.

Since the Shehadeh tragedy, the Israeli air force has undertaken a major effort to reduce civilian casualties, while continuing to go after enemy combatants who are planning terrorist attacks against Israeli citizens. By using smaller bombs, the Israeli air force kills fewer civilians but also misses many legitimate military targets. For example, it used a small bomb and failed to kill several Hamas terrorist leaders who were assembled in one place.[68]

Under the leadership of Eliezer Shkedi, the former head of the Israeli air force, Israel dramatically reduced the number of civilian deaths, by developing greater technical proficiency and by forgoing attacks when the risk of civilian deaths is too high. This is how the improvement was reported in *Haaretz*, an Israeli newspaper known for its criticism of targeted killings:

> Lately, the thwartings have indeed become more worthy of the title "pinpointed." In all the attacks of recent weeks, only gunmen were hurt, as confirmed by Palestinians. The rate of civilians hurt in these attacks in 2007 was 2–3 percent. The IDF has come a long way since the dark days of 2002–2003, when half the casualties in air assaults on the Gaza Strip were innocent bystanders. The attacks fall into three main categories: targeting specific known terrorists; targeting Qassam rocket-launching cells en-route or in action; and punitive bombardments of Hamas outposts, in response to rocket or mortar fire into Israel.
>
> Reducing the number of civilian casualties in the attacks on Gaza was one of the first tasks . . . IAF chief, Eliezer Shkedi, marked out for himself. The data improved commensurately. From a 1:1 ratio between killed terrorists and civilians in 2003 to a 1:28 ratio in late 2005. Several IAF mishaps in 2006 [raised] the ratio to 1:10, but the current ratio [as of the beginning of 2008] is at its lowest ever—more than 1:30.[69]

In other words, for every thirty legitimate combatants killed by the Israeli air force's campaign of targeted killings, only one civilian is killed. Even this figure may be misleading, because some of the civilians are anything but innocent bystanders, while others, such as young children, surely are. Every death of a civilian is a tragedy to be avoided whenever possible, but civilian deaths are an inevitable consequence of warfare, especially the immoral tactics employed by terrorist groups such as Hamas and Islamic Jihad.

No army in history has ever had a better ratio of combatants to civilians killed in a comparable setting. Israel's ratio is far better than that of the United States, Great Britain, Russia, or any other country combating terrorism. Yet this remarkable improvement has hardly been reported by the international press. Neither have human rights organizations taken appropriate note of it, especially considering the extraordinary and disproportionate criticism directed against Israel when the ratio was worse. Nor have these organizations noted that the selective employment of targeted killings in 2007, coupled with other defensive actions, has resulted in the lowest number of Israeli civilian deaths *and* the lowest number of Palestinian civilian deaths in recent times.[70]

It is true, as the media always note, that more Palestinians have been killed than Israelis overall. That is largely because Israel has successfully thwarted thousands of attacks against its civilians, which were intended to kill many more Israelis than the total number of Palestinians who have been killed. Moreover, some Palestinian spokespersons count among the Palestinian dead some or all of the following: the suicide bombers themselves; armed Palestinian fighters; leaders of terrorist groups; terrorists who were shot in self-defense while they were planting or throwing bombs; bomb makers (and their neighbors) who have been killed when the bombs they were making accidentally blew up; collaborators who have been killed by other Palestinians; and even people who have died as a result of the absurd and dangerous practice of shooting live ammunition in the air at Palestinian funerals and protests.[71]

The improvements in the ratio of terrorists to innocents who have been killed by the IDF should be widely reported and carefully analyzed. Silence in the face of this fact misleads many to believe that there has been no progress since the dark days of the intifada. Misleading by silence is as grievous a journalistic sin as misleading by mistake. The time has come to correct this sin and set the record straight.

Indeed, the time is long overdue for a reasoned, comparative assessment of how Israel, and other nations faced with comparable or lesser threats, have responded to such dangers. Such an assessment will show that no other such nation has tried harder to comply with the rule of law or has achieved a higher standard of human rights and civil liberties than embattled Israel.

These biased media and nongovernmental organizations, as well as the official organs of the United Nations, devote more attention to Israel than to any other nation, despite the reality that Israel has a vibrant self-critical press and a judicial system that is responsive to the claims of Palestinians and others. The real human rights violators of the world, which receive scant attention from the press and NGOs, do not have freedom of the press or judicial review. They really need the attention that outside groups can bring to abuses that are chronic, systematic, and without any security justifications. Yet criticism of these injustices is drowned out by the cacophony of condemnation directed against Israel. Consider, for example, the Vatican's one-sided approach to the conflict.

In 2005, Pope Benedict XVI condemned terrorist attacks against civilians in Great Britain, Egypt, Iraq, and Turkey. In a pregnant omission—very pregnant, in light of the Vatican's long history of silence in the face of attacks against Jews—the pope omitted any mention of the country that has suffered the largest number of terrorist attacks against civilians since 9/11, namely, Israel.[72] When the Israeli government understandably protested the omission, the Vatican's position became even more troubling. It singled out Israel for criticism, saying that that beleaguered nation's responses to attacks against its civilians were "not always compatible with the rules of international law."[73] The Vatican then went on to say that it could not protest every Palestinian attack against Jewish civilians if Israel did not always follow international law.

Let's try to understand what this means. Unless a country is absolutely flawless in its response to terrorism, the Vatican will not condemn terrorism against its civilian citizens. This seems to justify the killing of civilians as a protest against violation of international law. If that "moral" position is not bizarre enough, let us turn to the actual facts. Egypt's response to terrorism violates international law far more than Israel's does. Egypt routinely tortures—actually tortures *to death*—suspected terrorists, to say nothing of mere dissidents.[74] Turkey's record is not all that much better.[75] The United States and Great Britain have killed many more civilians in responding to terrorism in Iraq than Israel has done. So even if the Vatican's statement of principle were morally acceptable—which it surely is not—that principle would in no way justify leaving Israel off a list that includes many worse violators of international law.

Why, then, did the Vatican deliberately refuse to condemn terrorist attacks against Jewish civilians in Israel? I fear it is for the same reason that the Vatican took too long and did too little in protesting against the mass extermination of Jews by Nazi Germany. I suspect that it also has something to do with the Vatican's close relationship with the godfather of international terrorism, Yasser Arafat. Pope Benedict XVI's good and decent predecessor met with Arafat more often than with almost any other world leader and certainly more often than with Israeli leaders.

The truth is that the Vatican has always had something of a Jewish problem. Today that problem focuses more on the Jewish state than on the Jewish religion. But the Vatican's refusal to condemn attacks against Jewish civilians in Israel raises even broader questions of discrimination.

Listen to its recent statement about Israel's mild criticism: "The Holy See cannot take lessons or instructions from any other authority on the tone and content of its own statements."[76] The days are long past, however, when any other religious group is exempt from outside criticism, especially when it makes political pronouncements that can have the effect of encouraging terrorism.

For centuries, Catholic teaching has properly distinguished between the willful targeting of innocent civilians, on the one hand, and the inadvertent killing of civilians while pursuing appropriate military targets, on the other. The former is always morally prohibited, whereas the latter is permitted under the principle of double effect, unless the number of civilians killed is out of proportion to the military benefits obtained. Under this very Catholic principle, the pope should always condemn all suicide bombings and should condemn only disproportionate reprisals. If those principles were applied fairly to all nations, then the Vatican would have to include all terrorist attacks that target Israeli civilians.

A recent fatwa issued by U.S. Muslim leaders might serve as an example to the Vatican. It condemned all suicide bombings as a violation of Islamic law. Certainly, Catholic morality demands no less.

At the heart of the one-sided criticism directed at the Jewish state is the oft-reported mantra that "occupation causes terrorism"— a claim that has been disproved over and over again by history and contemporary experience.

The old myth was once again undercut by the arrest and trial in Britain of two dozen suspects in a plot to blow up ten commercial airliners.[77] The British do not occupy Arab land. Britain, of course, is one of the freest countries on earth. The suspects do not live—and apparently have not lived—under occupation (unless they consider the entire Christian world to be occupied by "crusaders"). And yet the same slogan—that occupation causes terrorism—persists.

Consider some of these examples as well:

1. Palestinian terrorism began well before there was any occupation. It began in 1929 when the grand mufti of Jerusalem ordered a terrorist attack against Jewish residents of Hebron, whose families had lived in that Jewish holy city for generations.[78]

2. Other occupied people—for example, the Tibetans—have never resorted to terrorism against innocent Chinese civilians, although they have never been offerred independence, and their occupation has been longer and more brutal than anything experienced by the Palestinians.

3. Terrorism against Israel got worse after Israel ended its occupation of southern Lebanon and Gaza, as these unoccupied lands became launching pads for rockets and missiles and grew rife with kidnappings.

4. While it may be that a brutal occupation might increase the number of people who are willing to become suicide bombers, it is also true that suicide bombers do not send themselves to die. They are sent by well-educated, affluent leaders such as Osama bin Laden, who do not live in occupied areas but who have terrorized the United States, Australia, Great Britain, and Spain, which do not occupy any Arab lands.

5. Islamic terrorists have sworn to continue terrorism even if Israel were to end its occupation of the West Bank, as it did of the Gaza Strip and southern Lebanon. Terrorists regard all of Israel as occupied. Even if there were no Israel, terrorism would persist as long as any part of the world is not under Islamic control.

Accordingly, occupation does not cause terrorism. Terrorism is caused by the culture of death preached by radical Islamic clerics and by the world's reaction to it: namely, making concessions and blaming the victims of terrorism who fight back. Terrorism persists because it is rewarded—because it works.[79] Occupation does not cause terrorism, but terrorism does cause occupation and reoccupation. Israel would have left Gaza and much of the West Bank long ago if not for the fear of terrorism from that area. It never would have gone into southern Lebanon in 1982 were that area not being used as a base for terrorism. In 2006, Israel once again entered southern Lebanon to stop rocket attacks and try to retrieve its kidnapped soldiers.

If the international community cannot or will not protect Israeli citizens from cross-border rocket attacks, kidnappings, and suicide bombings, Israel will have no choice other than some limited and hopefully temporary form of reoccupation to protect itself. Nor will it leave the West Bank unless it can be assured that the areas it leaves will not become outposts for increased terrorism. Israel is willing to give land for peace, but it is not willing to give land for terrorism. No nation would be so suicidal.

When Israeli forces left Gaza after a two-day occupation in July 2006, a rocket from Gaza hit an Israeli kindergarten, sending two children to the hospital.[80] This occurred despite leaflets left behind by departing Israeli soldiers that warned of dire consequences if rockets were fired from the areas they left. What should Israel do in this situation?

Imagine what the United States would have done if Germany or Japan, which it occupied after World War II, persisted in attacking the United States from occupied or recently unoccupied areas. And Germany and Japan do not adjoin our country the way that Gaza, the West Bank, and Lebanon adjoin Israel.

There is, of course, a difference between civilian settlements and a military presence in a hostile war zone. Regardless of what happens in Lebanon, Israel should begin to dismantle civilian settlements deep in the West Bank that have no military purpose—indeed, that divert military resources from areas where they are really needed. But it will be difficult to completely end the military presence—the checkpoints, the teams that search out terrorists, the network of electronic protections—without some assurance of an international presence that will be at least as effective in controlling terrorism as the Israeli army has been.

There has been far less terrorism from the occupied West Bank than from unoccupied south Lebanon and Gaza. Yet human rights groups persist in blaming terrorism on the occupation.

Some who lay claim to the honorable title of human rights advocates (such as the National Lawyers Guild) are simply hard-left groups that seek to hide their partisan agenda in neutral-sounding terms.[81] These groups rarely condemn human rights abuses committed in the name of left-wing regimes, such as Zimbabwe, China, Venezuela, Cuba, the former Soviet Union, and Cambodia. Indeed, they often seek to justify grievous assaults on human rights as necessary to "the revolution." But it is hard to see how Islamic extremists, such as Hezbollah, Hamas, Islamic Jihad, or the Iranian mullahs can be considered on the left. They oppress women, gays, racial minorities, religious dissidents, and real human rights advocates. They torture and murder civilians, use human shields, and advocate nuclear proliferation, environmental destruction, and everything else that is generally anathema to real human rights groups. And they grew out of a close alliance with Nazism, as we will see in the next chapter. Yet the hard left gets in bed with them against Israel and the United States. A group of hard-left professors said they were traveling to Iran to apologize to Ahmadinejad following the critical introduction he received from Columbia University president Lee Bollinger. Would the same professors have traveled to Nazi Germany to apologize to Hitler or to apartheid South Africa to apologize to its leaders, if a university president had made a critical introduction of those racist tyrants?

Why is Ahmadinejad different? He, too, is a bigoted tyrant who has incited genocide and whose government has murdered innocent Jewish children, women, and other civilians in Argentina. It is to Ahmadinejad and his Iranian government that we now turn.

6 The Case against Mahmoud Ahmadinejad and Iran's Genocidal Nuclear Weapons Program

The greatest danger Israel faces in the years to come is from Iran's nuclear weapons. Iran's leaders have threatened to "wipe Israel off the map," and they have said that it is a religious obligation to develop and use weapons of mass destruction to do so. The world ignored similar threats from an anti-Semitic dictator three-quarters of a century ago, and the result was the genocide of European Jewry. Now, nearly the same number of Jews are gathered in one small nation, and the leader of Iran's surrogate in Lebanon—Hezbollah—has been crystal clear that its target is not only Israelis, but Jews throughout the world. Listen to Hassan Nasrallah: "If they [Jews] all gather in Israel, it will save us the trouble of going after them worldwide."[1]

Nasrallah has also said, "If we search the entire world for a person more cowardly, despicable, weak and feeble in psyche, mind, ideology and religion, we would not find anyone like the Jew."[2] To be certain that no one could accuse him of merely being anti-Zionist, as distinguished from anti-Semitic, Nasrallah made it clear that he was characterizing "the Jew." He added for emphasis, "Notice, I do not say the Israeli."[3] (We should also notice that it was Nasrallah and his anti-Semitic organization Hezbollah that Norman Finkelstein praised and regretted not having supported more forcefully.)

Nor have the Iranian leaders and their surrogates limited themselves to talk alone. They have already murdered hundreds of Jewish children, women, and men in Argentina and in Israel. In July 1994, a bomb attack on the Argentine Jewish Mutual Association, a Jewish community center in Buenos Aires, killed eighty-five people and wounded hundreds. In 2006, Argentina's chief prosecutor, Alberto Nisman, announced, "We deem it proven that the decision to carry out an attack . . . was made by the highest authorities of the Islamic Republic of Iran which directed Hezbollah to carry out the attack."[4] Prosecutors sought warrants for the arrest of several Iranian officials, which the Iranian government vehemently protested. Iran was also responsible for the bombing of the Israeli Embassy in Buenos Aires in 1992, in which 29 were killed and 242 injured.[5] (This constituted an armed attack against Israel, fully justifying an Israeli reprisal under international law.)

In addition, the Iranian government has provided unlawful weapons to Hezbollah and Hamas—weapons that have no military value and can only be used against civilians.[6] In doing so, the Iranian government has committed a casus belli (an act of war) against Israel. It has also committed war crimes by inciting genocide, deliberately bombing civilian buildings filled with children and other noncombatants, and providing weapons to terrorists that are designed for use against civilian targets.

These war crimes were not committed by Mahmoud Ahmadinejad alone. They were begun under the more "moderate" and "liberal" administration of Mohammed Khatami, but the hate-filled incitements to genocide and the war crimes against Israel (and the United States) have increased under Ahmadinejad, to whom we now turn.

It is instructive to see how so extremist a figure as Mahmoud Ahmadinejad rose to power in a nation with as much of a secular tradition as Iran. Ahmadinejad was born in 1956 in the Iranian city of Garmaar; his family moved to Tehran a year later, where he completed his primary and secondary education and subsequently his university studies in civil engineering at the Science and Technology University in Tehran. He earned his master's degree there in 1986 and joined the faculty in 1989. In 1997, he received his PhD in transportation engineering and planning from that university.[7]

Ahmadinejad rose to political prominence at the end of the 1990s, supported by a neoconservative groundswell that developed against the reformist policies of then president Mohammed Khatami. In 2003, partly due to extremely low voter turnout (15 percent), the neoconservatives swept the city council elections in Tehran; Ahmadinejad was elected mayor. At that time, according to Professor Ali Ansari, the director of the Iranian Institute at the University of St. Andrews, he was widely regarded as "a political lightweight with strangely unorthodox religious ideas." His "obsession with the Twelfth ['Hidden'] Imam" seemed "unhealthy," even to many conservatives.[8] (That he was largely dismissed as a joke and an eccentric, in light of his stunning rise to power, suggests some interesting parallels to Germany in the 1920s.)

Reportedly, the only official who was concerned about Ahmadinejad was the president himself, Khatami. He "summarily refused to accord [Ahmadinejad] the customary seat in the cabinet [awarded to the mayor of Tehran]" and "considered [Ahmadinejad] to be dangerous for the country."[9]

Ahmadinejad surprised his detractors, however, and, according to Ansari, soon "proved to be an adept public relations man . . . quick to present himself as a man of the people, and, importantly, a straight-talking, simple veteran, with simple if firm beliefs." (In this respect, he reminds some people of London's bizarre former mayor "Red Ken" Livingstone, who was regarded as a bad joke by many serious British politicians but who remained popular with the disaffected among London's lower classes.)[10] Despite Ahmadinejad's "deft personal touch," he lacked managerial skills and accomplished little in his tenure as mayor. Still, his popularity grew, especially as the reformists (Khatami, in particular) lost favor with the public. This was due in part to his efforts to woo disaffected conservatives by burying martyrs in public places and claiming to know where the "imminent" return of the Twelfth Imam would take place: "in the small town of Jamkaran . . . [making] it a policy priority to keep the shrine there well supplied with refreshments and amenities to encourage pilgrimages." While his "Jamkaran cult" was laughable to the political and intellectual elite, it appears to have been part of a clever millennialist political strategy to rouse his conservative base.[11]

The reformist establishment, as well as the conservative establishment, did not recognize Ahmadinejad's appeal and continued to give him little credit. The hard-liners maneuvered to take over the Majlis (parliament) in the 2004 election and succeeded, largely because they were able to bar "un-Islamic" candidates (reform candidates) through their control of the Guardian Council.[12] The reformists were caught off guard, and the neoconservatives swept the elections in what amounted to a "parliamentary coup." When they then set their sights on the presidency in the 2005 elections, few regarded Ahmadinejad as anything more than a "marginal" figure.[13]

Still, Ahmadinejad ran and won, as the result of several factors. First, the reformist candidate was "a clumsy prospective successor, uncomfortable in public and unable to engage with the electorate," in sharp contrast to the predecessor, Khatami. Second, the crowded conservative field of five candidates, redundant, aloof, and prone to gaffes, split the vote and opened the way for Ahmadinejad and his "loyal if small following." Third, Ahmadinejad ran a populist campaign that emphasized oil-wealth redistribution and combating corruption, which spoke to domestic discontent. Finally, the hard-line establishment threw its logistical support behind Ahmadinejad at the eleventh hour, judging the other hard-line candidates unelectable. Ahmadinejad finished a close second in the first round, just after former president and relative moderate Hashemi Rafsanjani. This led to a flurry of attacks from the media elite against Ahmadinejad, which only served to solidify and widen his support among the disaffected in the runoff.[14]

In 2005, Ahmadinejad won the presidency with 62 percent of the vote to Rafsanjani's 36 percent, despite the fact that the "country is almost evenly split along ideological lines and . . . many younger people—more than 50 percent of the population—want liberalization."[15] The result produced "a rather bitter atmosphere in the country, as . . . many people who had voted for Ahmadinejad viewed the president their protest votes had let in with some discomfort."[16] Accounts cite a general sense of embarrassment and even fear at the outcome. Others viewed Ahmadinejad as the lesser of two evils. "I know a government by Ahmadinejad will mean regressing to the fiery days of the revolution," said one Iranian, "but I couldn't bring myself to go and vote for Rafsanjani."[17]

Iranians' fears about their eccentric president quickly proved to be well founded, as a catalogue of his absurd statements and dangerous actions makes clear. Ahmadinejad began to incite violence against Israel immediately upon taking office. Within months of his election he announced that "As the imam [referring to Ayatollah Khomeini] said, Israel must be wiped off the map." At the same speech—to about four thousand students at a program called "The World without Zionism," in preparation for an annual anti-Israel demonstration held on the last Friday of the holy month of Ramadan—he said, "The establishment of a Zionist regime was a move by the world oppressor against the Islamic world. . . . The skirmishes in the occupied land are part of the war of destiny. The outcome of hundreds of years of war will be defined in Palestinian land."[18] He went on to say, "There is no doubt that the new wave in Palestine will soon wipe off this disgraceful blot from the face of the Islamic world," and "Anybody who recognizes Israel will burn in the fire of the Islamic nation's fury."[19] He also said, "Many have tried to disperse disappointment in this struggle between the Islamic world and the infidels. . . . They say it is not possible to have a world without the United States and Zionism. But you know that this is a possible goal and slogan."[20]

Although most Arab governments were silent, the Palestinian negotiator Saeb Erekat, to his credit, said, "We have recognized the state of Israel and we are pursuing a peace process with Israel. . . . We do not accept the statements of the president of Iran." Other leaders swiftly and strongly condemned Ahmadinejad's remarks. Still, according to the *New York Times,* some noted that "He said it more loudly, more directly, more forcefully and more offensively than anyone has said it for a long time . . . but he is essentially stating what is known to be Iranian policy."[21]

Days later, Ahmadinejad reiterated and confirmed the remarks, saying, "My words are the Iranian nation's words. . . . Westerners are free to comment, but their reaction is invalid." Members of the Expediency Council tried to soften Ahmadinejad's words, saying, "What the president meant was that we favor a fair and long-lasting peace in Palestine."[22] (Good thing they cleared that up!) Some people blamed ineptitude for the president's words, which the UN Security Council "condemned" and which led Secretary General Kofi Annan to cancel a trip to Iran a few weeks later.[23]

A month later, in early December 2005, Ahmadinejad began to question the Holocaust, saying at a news conference in Mecca,

> Some European countries insist on saying that Hitler killed millions of innocent Jews in furnaces, and they insist on it to the extent that if anyone proves something contrary to that, they condemn that person and throw them in jail. . . . Although we don't accept this claim, if we suppose it is true, our question for the Europeans is: Is the killing of innocent Jewish people by Hitler the reason for their support to the occupiers of Jerusalem? If the Europeans are honest, they should give some of their provinces in Europe—like in Germany, Austria or other countries—to the Zionists, and the Zionists can establish their state in Europe.[24]

Again, there was international condemnation, with "swift rebukes from Israel and Washington. . . . The White House spokesman, Scott McClellan, said, 'It just further underscores our concerns about the regime in Iran, and it's all the more reason why it's so important that the regime not have the ability to develop nuclear weapons.'"[25]

A week later, Ahmadinejad struck again, this time in south-eastern Iran: "Today they have created a myth in the name of Holocaust and consider it to be above God, religion and the prophets. . . . If you committed this big crime, then why should the oppressed Palestinian nation pay the price? . . . This is our proposal: If you committed the crime, then give a part of your own land in Europe, the United States, Canada or Alaska to them so that the Jews can establish their country."[26]

The reaction to these statements was even more widespread; the Associated Press reported that the "remarks drew swift condemnations from the White House, Israel, Germany, France, and the European Commission." The German foreign minister called Ahmadinejad's statements "shocking and unacceptable," saying they would have an impact on nuclear negotiations. The Israeli Foreign Ministry spokesman said, "The repeated outrageous remarks of the Iranian president show clearly the mind-set of the ruling clique in Tehran and indicate clearly the extremist policy goals of the regime. . . . The combination of fanatical ideology, a warped sense of reality and nuclear weapons is a combination that no one in the international community can accept." The Bush administration also linked Ahmadinejad's hate-filled rhetoric to his quest for nuclear weapons. As McClellan put it, "All responsible leaders in the international community recognize how outrageous [the statements are]. . . . [They] only underscore why it is so important that the international community continue to work together to keep Iran from developing nuclear weapons."[27]

On January 1, 2006, Ahmadinejad asked in a speech, "Don't you think that continuation of genocide by expelling Jews from Europe was one of their aims in creating a regime of occupiers of Al Quds [Jerusalem]? Isn't that an important question?" According to the Associated Press report, "Mr. Ahmadinejad said Europeans had decided to create a 'Jewish camp' as the best means for ridding the continent of Jews. He said the camp, Israel, now enjoyed support from the United States and Europe in the slaughter of Muslims."[28]

In mid-January, Ahmadinejad said at a news conference that "No excuse could deprive the country from this right" to nuclear weapons. He went on, "Now it is time for the Western countries to build confidence and prove to us that they will allow our people to achieve scientific progress. Despite their own scientific and technological development, these countries have a medieval mind set. They tell us that we do not have the right to scientific progress."[29] This, from the leader of a country where petty thieves lose their hands and victims of rape are stoned to death.

In April, he returned to the Israel-Holocaust theme at a three-day conference for Palestinian militants and their sympathizers. "The Zionist regime is an injustice and by its very nature a permanent threat. . . . Whether you like it or not, the Zionist regime is on the road to being eliminated." He compared Israel to a "'rotten tree' that would collapse in 'one storm.'"[30]

In May 2006, Ahmadinejad wrote a letter directly to President Bush, in which he questioned whether U.S. policy on a host of subjects was consistent with Christian values (which, he stressed, are honored in the Koran). Following are some highlights:

> Is support for this regime [Israel] in line with the teachings of Jesus Christ (Peace Be Upon Him) or Moses (Peace Be Upon Him) or liberal values? . . .
>
> September eleven was not a simple operation. Could it be planned and executed without coordination with intelligence and security services—or their extensive infiltration? Of course this is just an educated guess. . . .
>
> We increasingly see that people around the world are flocking towards . . . the Almighty God. . . . My question for you is: "Do you not want to join them?"[31]

At a news conference in September 2006, Ahmadinejad was asked about Iran's nuclear program and said, "Iran considers the nuclear issue a political one. . . . They're not concerned about the bomb, they want to stop the development of our country." Regarding his comments about wiping Israel off the map, he said, "These Zionists are not Jews. This is the biggest deception we have faced. They are a power group, a power party. We oppose any group that seeks raw power. . . . [Iran] loves everyone around the world, Jews, Christians, Muslims."[32]

In December 2006, Iranian officials announced their plans for an international conference on the Holocaust, which they hoped would "provide the opportunity for scholars from both sides to give their papers in freedom and without preconceived ideas." They noted that Iran does not "[deny] the crimes of Hitler" and added, "'Since we are not accused and responsible for the Holocaust, we are an impartial judge."[33] Among those invited were two American scholars: "Dr." David Duke, who had just been awarded a "PhD" in "history" by a "university" in the Ukraine, and Norman Finkelstein, who has been fired by several universities.

At the conference, Ahmadinejad welcomed the participants: "The Zionist regime will disappear soon, the same way the Soviet Union disappeared. . . . Humanity will [thus] achieve freedom."[34] He also railed against European countries that have imprisoned academics "because they attempted to write about the Holocaust or research it from a different perspective, questioning certain aspects of it." This was a clear reference to David Irving, who was imprisoned in Austria for Holocaust denial—a suppression of free speech that I and many other pro-Israel civil libertarians have criticized. Ahmadinejad and his regime, on the other hand, have demanded the imprisonment or the execution of Europeans who publish cartoons depicting Mohammed, who insult Islam, or who write books or make films questioning certain aspects of the Islamic religion.[35] Free speech for me, but not for thee!

Ahmadinejad didn't make major headlines again until his visit to New York City in September 2007, where he addressed the United Nations and students at Columbia University. At Columbia, President Lee C. Bollinger delivered a cutting introduction that enabled Ahmadinejad to assume his favorite role: the embattled but unflappable underdog. He began by saying, "In Iran, tradition requires when you invite a person to be a speaker, we actually respect our students enough to allow them to make their own judgment, and don't think it's necessary before the speech is even given to come in with a series of complaints to provide vaccination to the students and faculty." Ahmadinejad went on to deny that there were any homosexuals in Iran, to claim that "Women in Iran enjoy the highest levels of freedom," to say that the Holocaust was a "theory," to suggest that the United States and Israel were "really involved" in 9/11, and to say that Iran wouldn't recognize Israel "because it is based on ethnic discrimination, occupation and usurpation and it consistently threatens its neighbors."[36] He emphasized the theme that the Palestinian people played "no role" in the Holocaust: "If [the Holocaust] is a reality, we need to still question whether the Palestinian people should be paying for it or not. After all, it happened in Europe. The Palestinian people had no role to play in it. So why is it that the Palestinian people are paying the price of an event they had nothing to do with? . . . The Palestinian people didn't commit any crime. They had no role to play in World War II. They were living with the Jewish communities and the Christian communities in peace at the time."

Following Ahmadinejad's speech at Columbia, I decided that I had to respond to his repeated claim that the Palestinian people and their leadership had absolutely nothing to do with the Holocaust. The conclusion that is supposed to follow from this "fact" is that the establishment of Israel in the wake of the Nazi genocide of the Jewish people was unfair to the Palestinians. Central to this claim is that neither the Palestinian people nor their leadership bore any responsibility for the Holocaust, and if any reparations are owed the Jewish people, it is from Germany and not from the Palestinians. The propounders of this historical argument suggest that the West created the Jewish state out of guilt over the Holocaust. It might have been understandable if a portion of Germany (or Poland, Lithuania, Latvia, France, Austria, or other collaborator nations) had been allocated for a Jewish homeland—but why Palestine? Palestine, according to this claim, was as much a "victim" as were the Jews.

I hear this argument on university campuses around the United States, and even more so in Europe. Sometimes, when offered by Islamic extremists, it is coupled with the caveat "if the Holocaust occurred at all." When offered by hard-leftists who do not deny the Holocaust (because it was perpetrated by the Nazi right, which was defeated by the Stalinist left), it is often accompanied by the claim that "Israel and its Jewish supporters *exploit* the Holocaust to justify Israel's own 'Holocaust' against the Palestinian people." Ahmadinejad's point, which is often repeated on university campuses by anti-Israel speakers, seems to resonate with many students, but it is as false as his claim that there are no gays in Iran.

The truth is that the Palestinian leadership, supported by the Palestinian masses, played a significant role in Hitler's Holocaust. The Palestinian leader at the time was Haj Amin al-Husseini, the grand mufti of Jerusalem. As Professor Edward Said, who was the most articulate proponent of Palestinian rights, has acknowledged, "Hajj Amin al-Husseini represented the Palestinian Arab national consensus, had the backing of the Palestinian political parties that functioned in Palestine, and was recognized in some form by Arab governments as the voice of the Palestinian people." A biographer—who is generally favorable to the grand mufti—characterized Husseini as "the principal leader of the Palestinian national movement and a popular personality in the Arab world during most of the years of British rule over Palestine (1917–1948)."[37] Another said he was "more than the leader of the Muslims of Palestine; he was also the defender of Jerusalem . . . the most revered defender of Muslim honor in the world."[38]

Husseini was not only the highest-ranking religious and political figure in Palestine, he was among the most revered and respected leaders in the entire Arab world. He was selected as president of the Arab Higher Committee and the first president of the "new government" of all of Palestine.[39] Husseini was "Palestine's national leader," and it was in his capacity as "the voice of the Palestinian people" that he made his notorious alliance with Hitler and played an active role in promoting the Holocaust. Here is the true story that Ahmadinejad and so many other enemies of Israel have tried to suppress or mythologize.

Shortly after Hitler came to power, the grand mufti decided to emulate him. He informed the German consul in Jerusalem that "The Muslims inside and outside Palestine welcome the new regime of Germany and hope for the extension of the fascist anti-democratic, governmental system to other countries."[40] In an effort to bring it to his own country, Husseini organized the "Nazi Scouts," based on the "Hitler Youth."[41] The swastika became a welcome symbol among many Palestinians.[42]

The mid- to late 1930s were marked by Arab efforts to curtail immigration and Jewish efforts to rescue as many Jews as possible from Hitler's Europe.[43] These years were also characterized by escalating Muslim violence orchestrated by Husseini and other Muslim leaders.[44] In 1936, Arab terrorism took on a new dimension. In the beginning, the targets were once again defenseless Jewish civilians in hospitals, movie theaters, homes, and stores. This was followed by strikes and shop closures, and then by the bombing of British offices.[45] The Nazi regime in Germany and the Italian fascists supported the violence, sending "millions" to the mufti.[46] The SS, under the leadership of Heinrich Himmler, provided both financial and logistical support for anti-Semitic pogroms in Palestine.[47] Adolf Eichmann visited Husseini in Palestine and subsequently maintained regular contact with him.[48]

The support was mutual, as one Arab commentator put it: "Feeling the whip of Jewish pressure and influence, the Arabs sympathized with the Nazis and Fascists in their agony and trials at the hands of Jewish intrigues and international financial pressures."[49]

The Palestinians and their Arab allies were anything but neutral about the fate of European Jewry. The official leader of the Palestinians, Haj Amin al-Husseini, spent the war years in Berlin with Hitler, serving as a consultant on the Jewish question.[50] He was taken on a tour of Auschwitz by Himmler and expressed support for the mass murder of European Jews. He also sought to "solve the problems of the Jewish element in Palestine and other Arab countries" by employing "the same method" being used "in the Axis countries."[51] He would not be satisfied with the Jewish residents of Palestine—many of whom were descendants of Sephardic Jews who had lived there for hundreds, even thousands, of years—remaining as a minority in a Muslim state. Like Hitler, he wanted to be rid of "every last Jew."[52] As Husseini wrote in his memoirs, "Our fundamental condition for cooperating with Germany was a free hand to eradicate every last Jew from Palestine and the Arab world. I asked Hitler for an explicit undertaking to allow us to solve the Jewish problem in a manner befitting our national and racial aspirations and according to the scientific methods innovated by Germany in the handling of its Jews. The answer I got was: 'The Jews are yours.'"[53]

The mufti was apparently planning to return to Palestine in the event of a German victory and to construct a death camp, modeled after Auschwitz, near Nablus.[54] Husseini incited his pro-Nazi followers with the words "Arise, o sons of Arabia. Fight for your sacred rights. Slaughter Jews wherever you find them. Their spilled blood pleases Allah, our history and religion. That will save our honor."[55] During the war, he had been recruited by Joseph Goebbels, the Nazi propaganda minister, to broadcast daily pro-Nazi, anti-Semitic harangues from Berlin. According to one of his biographers, "in these exhortations, the mufti frequently reiterated to his Muslim listeners that they could achieve eternal salvation by rising up and killing the Jewish infidels living in their countries."[56] His speeches were anti-Semitic to the core: "Kill the Jews wherever you find them—this pleases God, history and religion."[57] He frequently applied Nazi terminology to Koranic references, such as in the following: "[The Jews] cannot mix with any other nation but live as parasites among the nations, suck out their blood, embezzle their property, corrupt their morals. . . . The divine anger and curse that the Holy Koran mentioned with reference to the Jews is because of this unique character of the Jews."[58]

In his broadcasts, the mufti explicitly supported Hitler's goal of exterminating the Jews, praising the Nazis for having "definitively solved the Jewish problem."[59] As his biographer concluded,

> His broadcasts were irrefutable evidence that he knew about the extermination of the Jews. In a radio broadcast from Berlin on September 21, 1944, al-Husseini spoke of "the eleven million Jews

of the world." The mufti knew that in 1939 there were seventeen million Jews in the world. The Israeli historian Moshe Pearlman, a contemporary of the mufti living in Jerusalem, concluded that the numbers used in this broadcast revealed the full extent of the mufti's knowledge. "Why 'eleven million'? No one outside Germany knew at the time the scale of Jewish extermination. It was known that before the war the Jewish population numbered nearly seventeen million. The ex-Mufti's figure was written off at the time as a slip of the tongue, or an error in the script. But now the facts are known. It was no arithmetic error. Haj Amin knew then what only Hitler, Himmler and Eichmann knew: that more than five million Jews had been liquidated."[60]

Not only did Husseini exhort his followers to murder the Jews; he also took an active role in trying to bring about that result. For example, in 1944, a German-Arab commando unit, under Husseini's command, parachuted into Palestine and tried to poison Tel Aviv's wells.[61]

Husseini also helped to inspire a pro-Nazi coup in Iraq and helped to organize thousands of Muslims in the Balkans into military units known as Handselar divisions, which carried out atrocities against Yugoslav Jews, Serbs, and Gypsies.[62] After a meeting with Hitler, he recorded the following in his diary:

The Mufti: "The Arabs were Germany's natural friends. . . . They were therefore prepared to cooperate with Germany with all their hearts and stood ready to participate in a war, not only negatively by the commission of acts of sabotage and the instigation of revolutions, but also positively by the formation of an Arab Legion. In this struggle, the Arabs were striving for the independence and the unity of Palestine, Syria and Iraq. . . .

Hitler: "Germany was resolved, step by step, to ask one European nation after the other to solve its Jewish problem, and at the proper time direct a similar appeal to non-European nations as well. Germany's objective would then be solely the destruction of the Jewish element residing in the Arab sphere under the protection of British power. The moment that Germany's tank divisions and air squadrons had made their appearance south of the Caucasus, the public appeal requested by the Grand Mufti could go out to the Arab world."[63]

Hitler assured Husseini about how he would be regarded following a Nazi victory and "the destruction of the Jewish element residing in the Arab sphere." In that hour the mufti would be the most authoritative spokesman for the Arab world. It would then be his task to set off the Arab operations that he had secretly prepared.[64]

Husseini's significant contributions to the Holocaust were multifold: first, he pleaded with Hitler to exterminate European Jewry and advised the Nazis on how to do so[65]; second, he visited Auschwitz with Eichmann and urged Eichmann and Himmler to accelerate the pace of the mass murder[66]; third, he personally stopped 4,000 children, accompanied by 500 adults, from leaving Europe and had them sent to Auschwitz and gassed[67]; fourth, he prevented another two thousand Jews from leaving Romania for Palestine and one thousand from leaving Hungary for Palestine who were subsequently sent to death camps[68]; fifth, he organized the killing of thousands of Bosnian Jews by Muslims, whom he recruited to the Waffen-SS Nazi-Bosnian division.[69] He was also one of the few non-Germans who was made privy to the Nazi extermination while it was taking place. It was in his official capacity as the leader of the Palestinian people and its official representative that he made his pact with Hitler, spent the war years in Berlin, and worked actively with Eichmann, Himmler, von Ribbentrop, and Hitler himself to "accelerate" the final solution by exterminating the Jews of Europe and laying plans to exterminate the Jews of Palestine.[70]

Husseini personally has the blood of more than twenty thousand Jewish children and adults on his hands. As David G. Dalin and John F. Rothmann summarized it in their well-documented account of Husseini's role in the Holocaust: "In recruiting the Bosnian Waffen-SS, Husseini played an important role in Hitler's extermination of Europe's Jews. It was not, however, his only direct contribution." This conclusion was confirmed by the testimony of Eichmann's deputy at the Nuremberg Trials: "The Mufti was one of the initiators of the systematic extermination of European Jewry and had been a collaborator and adviser of Eichmann and Himmler in the execution of the plan." He was "convinced the mufti had 'played a role in the decision to exterminate the European Jews.'"[71]

It is fair to conclude that the official leader of the Muslims in Palestine, Haj Amin al-Husseini, was a full-fledged Nazi war criminal, and he was so declared and sought by Yugoslavia as a war criminal after the war.[72] He escaped to Egypt, where he was given asylum. There, he helped to organize many former Nazis and Nazi sympathizers against Israel.[73]

Not only did the grand mufti play a significant role in the murder of European Jewry, he sought to replicate the genocide against the Jews in Israel during the war that produced a so-called Nakba. The war started by the Palestinians against the Jews in 1947 and the war started by the Arab states in 1948 against the new state of Israel were both genocidal wars. Their goal was not merely the ethnic cleansing of the Jews from the area but their total annihilation. The leaders said so, and the actions of their subordinates reflected this genocidal goal. They were aided in their efforts by Nazi soldiers—former SS and Gestapo members—who had been given asylum from war crime prosecution in Egypt and who had been recruited by the grand mufti to complete Hitler's work. They were joined by deserters from the British Army who openly expressed anti-Semitism and worked together with their Nazi ideological allies to complete Hitler's work.[74]

The Palestinian warriors attacked primarily Jewish civilians. When Jews surrendered, they were massacred, their bodies mutilated, and the women were often raped. Children were murdered along with the elderly. Had the Palestinians and Arabs won the war, which they came close to doing during the early phases, there would have been no Jewish refugee problem: the Jews would have been murdered.[75]

It is also fair to say that Husseini's pro-Nazi sympathies and support were widespread among his Palestinian followers, many of whom regarded him as a hero even after the war and the disclosure of his role in Nazi atrocities.[76] The notorious photograph of Husseini and Hitler, together in Berlin, was proudly displayed in many Palestinian homes, even after Husseini's activities in the Holocaust became widely known and praised among Palestinians.

Husseini is still regarded by many as "the George Washington" of the Palestinian people, and if the Palestinians were to get a state of their own, he would be honored in the way our founding father is.[77] He was their hero, despite—more likely, because—his active role in the genocide against the Jewish people, which he openly supported and assisted. According to Husseini's biographer, "Large parts of the Arab world shared [Husseini's] sympathy with Nazi Germany during the Second World War. . . . Haj Amin's popularity among the Palestinian Arabs and within the Arab states actually increased more than ever during his period with the Nazis."[78]

Nor was it merely a hatred of Zionism that animated this support for Nazi ideology. The grand mufti's "hatred of Jews . . . was fathomless, and he gave full vent to it during his period of activity alongside the Nazis (October 1941 to May 1945)."[79] In 1948, the National Palestinian Council elected Husseini as its president, even though he was a wanted war criminal living in exile in Egypt.[80] Indeed, Husseini is still revered today among many Palestinians as a national hero. Yasser Arafat, in an interview conducted in 2002 and reprinted in the Palestinian daily *Al-Quds* on August 2, 2002, called Husseini "our hero," referring to the Palestinian people. Arafat also boasted of being "one of his troops," even though he knew Husseini was "considered an ally of Nazis." (If a German today were to call Hitler "our hero," he would appropriately be labeled a neo-Nazi.)

Dalin and Rothmann summarized Husseini's legacy as follows:

> Haj Amin al-Husseini has been, and remains, the inspiration for the leaders of the PLO, Hamas, Hezbollah, Islamic Jihad, al-Qaeda, and other radical Islamic groups to continue their campaigns of violence and terror against Israel, the United States, and their allies and friends. The terrorism, fanaticism, and ruthlessness of the Palestine National Movement reflect the mufti's enduring legacy and influence. Today, more than thirty years after his death, Haj Amin al-Husseini deserves recognition as the icon of evil that he was, as the father of radical Islamic anti-Semitism and political terrorism as we know it today. Al-Husseini's notorious *fatwas*, calling for the defeat and destruction of Israel, Great Britain, and the United States, like the religious rulings

of Sheik Omar Abd al-Rahman, Osama bin Laden, and other terrorists who would follow him, became new warrants for genocide in the clash of civilizations between radical Islam and the West and in the ongoing war of the mufti and his followers who sought to carry out, posthumously, Hitler's war against the Jews.[81]

It is a myth, therefore—another myth perpetrated by Iran's myth-maker-in-chief—that the Palestinians played "no role" in the Holocaust. Considering the active support by the Palestinian leadership and masses for the losing side of a genocidal war, it was more than fair for the United Nations to offer them a state of their own on more than half of the arable land of the British mandate. The Sudeten Germans received a lot less.

Indeed the analogy between the Palestinian refugees—who Ahmadinejad claims are faultless victims of the Israeli-inflicted "Nakba," or catastrophe—and the Germans who were expelled from the Sudetenland following World War II, is far more compelling than the false analogy Ahmadinejad and his ilk sometimes try to make between the Nakba and the Holocaust.

The eminent historian Benny Morris, whose original archival research has often been cited by Israel's enemies as totally "objective" and "unbiased," blames the Nakba largely on the Palestinians themselves and their Arab allies who started the 1948 war. In his book *1948*, Morris quotes Israel's first foreign minister, Moshe Shertok:

> There are those who say that we uprooted Arabs from their places. But even they will not deny that the source of the problem was the war: had there been no war, the Arabs would not have abandoned their villages, and we would not have expelled them. Had the Arabs from the start accepted the [U.N. decision,] the State of Israel would have arisen with a large Arab minority, which would have . . . constituted an organic part of the state.

Morris concluded that Shertok, "of course, was right." He agrees that

> the refugee problem was created by the war—which the Arabs had launched. . . . And it was that war that propelled most of those displaced out of their houses and into refugeedom. Most fled when their villages

and towns came under Jewish attack or out of fear of future attack. They wished to move out of harm's way. At first, during 1947–March 1948, it was the middle and upper-class families who fled, abandoning the towns; later, from April on, after the Yishuv shifted to the offensive, it was the urban and rural masses who fled, in a sense emulating their betters. Most of the displaced likely expected to return to their homes within weeks or months, on the coattails of victorious Arab armies or on the back of a UN decision or Great Power intervention.[82]

Morris shows that it was the Arabs, not the Jews, who had pressed the idea of expulsion and ethnic cleansing of enemy populations. According to Morris, the "gradual acceptance" of expulsion by the Zionists

> was in large part a response to the expulsionist ideology and violent praxis of al-Husseini and his followers during [the] previous two decades.
>   . . . Arab support for a Nazi victory and Haj Amin al-Husseini's employment by the Nazis in World War II Berlin also played a part in this thinking. Zionist expulsionist thinking was thus at least in part a response to expulsionist, or murderous, thinking [by Arab leaders].
>   Nonetheless, transfer or expulsion was never adopted by the Zionist movement or its main political groupings as official policy at any state of the movement's evolution—not even in the 1948 War.[83]

Recall that the Israeli decision not to allow the return of the Palestinian refugees was made against the background of post–World War II decisions by the allies, supported by the United Nations to remove millions of ethnic Germans from Czechoslovakia and other countries and resettle them in Germany. These Czech citizens had lived in the Sudetenland since the twelfth century and posed no realistic threat of violence.[84]

The Potsdam Agreement of 1945 stated that "the transfer to Germany of German populations, or elements thereof, remaining in Poland, Czechoslovakia, and Hungary, will have to be undertaken."[85] The Sudeten expellees first suffered brutal treatment and violence at the hands of the Czechs[86] and then food and housing shortages and unemployment in Germany, all after losing

25 to 30 billion marks' worth of capital left behind in their home country.[87] Tens of thousands may have died in the process of the transfer.[88] (The Palestinians suffered far less.)

Recall as well the expressed goal of the Arabs in the event they won the war of 1948:

> By contrast [to the policy of the Zionists to accept a significant Arab minority in its midst] expulsionist thinking and, where it became possible, behavior, characterized the mainstream of the Palestinian national movement since its inception. "We will push the Zionists into the sea—or they will send us back into the desert," the Jaffa Muslim-Christian Association told the King-Crane Commission as early as 1919.
>
> For the Palestinians, from the start, the clash with the Zionists was a zero-sum game. The Palestinian national movement's leader during the 1920s, 1930s, and 1940s, Haj Amin al-Husseini, consistently rejected territorial compromise and espoused a solution to the Palestine problem that posited all of Palestine as an Arab state and allowed for a Jewish minority composed only of those who had lived in the country before 1914 (or, in a variant, 1917). Thus he marked out all Jews who had arrived in the country after World War I and their progeny for, at the very least, noncitizenship or expulsion—or worse.[89]

This goal—the expulsion of more than 90 percent of Israel's Jewish population—became the central tenet of the Palestinian National Charter of 1964 and 1968.[90] Not only was the ethnic cleansing of the Jews the goal of the Arab war against Israel in 1948, it was implemented whenever possible:

> Such sentiments translated into action in 1948. During the "civil war," when the opportunity arose, Palestinian militiamen who fought alongside the Arab Legion consistently expelled Jewish inhabitants and razed conquered sites, as happened in the 'Etzion Bloc' and the Jewish Quarter of Jerusalem's Old City. Subsequently, the Arab armies behaved in similar fashion. All the Jewish settlements conquered by the invading Jordanian, Syrian, and Egyptian armies . . . were razed after their inhabitants had fled or been incarcerated or expelled.[91]

In fact, the Arab armies succeeded in expelling more than 70,000 Jews from their homes, largely in Jewish areas that had been allocated to Israel by the United Nations partition.[92] These forgotten refugees were absorbed into Israel, as were the hundreds of thousands of Jewish refugees who were forced to leave Arab countries in which their families had lived since well before the development of Islam and in some instances longer than the local Arab residents: "The immediate propellants to flight were the popular Arab hostility, including pogroms, triggered by the war in Palestine and specific governmental measures, amounting to institutionalized discrimination against the oppression of the Jewish minority communities."[93]

Israel's enemies sometimes compare the so-called Palestinian Nakba with the Holocaust. This is not only an obscenely false comparison, it is essentially a form of Holocaust denial or minimization. The Jews bear absolutely no responsibility for the catastrophe that resulted in the deliberate genocidal murder of six million innocent Jewish victims. In contrast, the Palestinians and their leaders and Arab supporters bear a large responsibility for the creation of the Palestinian refugee problem—a problem the Arabs have purposely refused to resolve for more than sixty years, treating the refugees as political pawns in their effort to deligitimate and destroy the Jewish state.

The 1947–1948 war, started by the Palestinians and the Arab nations, was a war of extermination conducted in part by Nazi war criminals intent on completing Hitler's final solution. It resulted in an exchange of populations—700,000 Palestinians left Israel under the pressures of the war, and approximately the same number of Jews were forced to leave Arab countries and areas of Israel that were captured by the Arabs. The Jewish state quickly settled the Jewish refugees, while the Arab states refused to settle the Palestinian refugees. This was a self-inflicted wound that bears no relationship to the Holocaust.

I welcome the commemorations of the Nakba on university campuses and in the media. Students and the world at large *should* learn more about "the Nakba," but they should learn the *truth*.

The myth of Palestinian noncomplicity in the Holocaust and nonresponsibility for the Nakba persists, despite the historical record. The hard left in particular is embarrassed by their uncritical support for a movement that has been allied so closely with Nazism. When I mention Husseini's role, as the leader of the Palestinian people, in Hitler's genocide (and in the attempted genocide against the Jews of Israel), the response is denial— another genre of Holocaust-related denial and part of a larger pattern of historical denial by many of Israel's enemies. It begins with denial that the Jews ever lived in what became Israel. In continues with a denial of Palestinian responsibility for refusing to accept statehood in 1938 and 1948 as proposed by the Peel Commission and the United Nations. It continues further with denial of Arab responsibility for the so-called Nakba or catastrophe suffered by the Palestinian people when Palestinian and Arab forces attacked Israel in 1947–1948, creating the refugee problem. It persists with the denial of Arafat's culpabilities for walking away from the Clinton-Barak proposal in 2000, which would have created a Palestinian state in all of Gaza and more than 95 percent of the West Bank. And it culminates in a denial of the future of Palestinian children by radical imams who teach them to prefer death over a compromise for peace. All of these denials are central to Ahmadinejad's program, which also includes the denial that Iran is developing nuclear weapons.

Following his encounter at Columbia, Ahmadinejad had a meeting with American Christian leaders, during which one cleric asked him, "Could there be an Iranian guarantee of no violence against Israel?" if there was a guarantee of no U.S. aggression against Iran? "Mr. Ahmadinejad responded by asking for a three-minute break 'for the interpreter.' After the break, he said that it was the United States and 'the Zionist regime' that had nuclear weapons, while Iran was seeking to enrich uranium only for 'fuel purposes.'"[94]

The nuclear standoff has continued, as have Ahmadinejad's inflammatory statements against Israel. In January 2008, as the UN Security Council considered new sanctions against Iran,

Ahmadinejad announced, "We have been promised that we will have nuclear power this time next year in our power grid." He then addressed Western nations: "I warn you to abandon the filthy Zionist entity, which has reached the end of the line. . . . It has lost its reason to be and will sooner or later fall. The ones who still support the criminal Zionists should know that the occupiers' days are numbered."[95]

Of late, Ahmadinejad seems to have been more candid in acknowledging his nuclear weapons program. When Iran was again implicated in supporting terror against Americans in Iraq, Ahmadinejad went on the offensive. "Iran is a nuclear country and if you continue your mischief, Iran will tomorrow conquer higher summits," he said in a televised address. "It will punch you [the West] in the mouth. . . . The Iranian nation will go on its war with power and will not stop until it conquers all the summits of honor. . . . If you think you can make the Iranian nation refrain from its resolute will through sanctions and heavy economic pressures, you're wrong."[96]

This came on the heels of the announcement that Iran was installing six thousand new centrifuges for uranium enrichment, in addition to its existing three thousand. Ahmadinejad, at a ceremony inaugurating their operation, claimed that the new centrifuges were five times more efficient than Iran's existing centrifuges; Western analysts said that was probably an exaggeration.[97]

Ahmadinejad also said that "The Iranian nation will bloody the enemy's [West's] nose if they want to violate an iota of our rights [to nuclear technology]. . . . We are standing firm and the West's misbehavior towards Iran will encourage the nation to capture higher summits. . . . It will not weaken our nation's will. . . . The era of oppression is finished."[98] The following day he continued, "The Iranian nation will not give up until the corrupt leadership in the world has been obliterated. . . . Our foes should know that threats, sanctions, and political and economic pressures cannot force our nation to back down. . . . We have two missions: to build Islamic Iran and to exert an effort to change the leadership in the world. We have to carry out both as well as we can. . . . The resolutions which are adopted against Iran are . . . scraps of papers."[99] In addition, he said, "[Israel is] weak, collapsing, and nothing will be able to save it. . . . The time of the weakening and collapse of the Zionist regime and its supporters has arrived."[100]

Some commentators have sought to explain Ahmadinejad's extremism as merely a cynical political strategy calculated to shore up his precarious position in Iran. His populist economic promises worried Iran's urban elite. The days following his election were bitter; according to the *New York Times*, he was "the subject of many jokes sent via text messages on cell phones across Iran . . . spoofed on television and radio . . . as a bumpkin and a bigot for declaring the Holocaust a myth and causing international outrage over Iran's nuclear program. One joke has the president combing his hair in a mirror and saying 'O.K., male lice to the left, female lice to the right,' ridiculing him as a religious fanatic who wants to separate the sexes in public places."

As Ahmadinejad's behavior and policies became more extreme—and as the domestic economic situation worsened—Iranians' amused distaste turned to anger.[101] At the height of the Israel-Lebanon war, reporters in Tehran found widespread discontent over Iran's support for Hezbollah. "Of course I am angry. . . . All our income is going to Palestine and Hezbollah," said one man who was interviewed.[102] Rising prices, unemployment (at 10 percent), inflation (more than 20 percent), food shortages, rising fuel costs, the jailing of dissidents, and a crackdown on speech and culture have led to public protests.[103] The *New York Times* reported that "when the president visited Amir Kabir University in Tehran . . . students burned his picture and chanted 'Death to the Dictator!' The protest . . . was featured on the evening news on state television . . . which is controlled by . . . Ayatollah Ali Khamenei. . . . Such publicity seemed to signal that someone fairly senior is less than enchanted with Ahmadinejad." "The perspective the U.S. has of Iran being a monolithic country under this demagogue is not correct,'" said Vali Nasr, a professor of Middle

Eastern politics at the Naval Postgraduate School, to the *New York Times*.[104]

The *Times* also reported that Ahmadinejad and friends, "increasingly nervous about losing . . . parliamentary elections [in March 2008] and next year's presidential vote . . . are pressing the vetting committees to keep a much higher than usual number of moderates and reform candidates off the ballot. Already large numbers of reformers have been told that they will not be allowed to run."[105]

Ultimately, 1,700 were rejected—"over a third of prospective candidates"—including 154 sitting members of Parliament.[106] Many of former president Khatami's supporters were barred from participating; Rafsanjani's supporters, according to the *Washington Post*, who had been "arrested in the past and charged with espionage," did not even bother trying.[107] Conservatives overall won 163 seats out of 260, a 70 percent majority—roughly "the same majority they held prior to the elections"—while reformists (all of whom were minor candidates) won 35, down from 40.[108] The reformists had expected to gain at least 10 seats, especially from districts in Tehran, where reformist support is strongest, but they won none. Conservatives won 19 of 30 seats in Tehran; the remainder were decided in runoff elections in late April 2008, where only one Tehran reformist prevailed.[109] Immediately, there were "questions . . . about the integrity of the vote."[110]

Official observers from reformist groups were reportedly made to leave some polling stations as counting began. Journalists were told to leave the Ministry of the Interior—which ran the election—on polling night.[111] According to one reformist candidate, "The reformists had received reliable reports as votes were being counted that 10 reformists were among the winners."[112] Somewhere between the count and the official results, those ten winners turned to zero.

The turnout also raised questions. Officials claimed 60 percent participation overall (although observers said that figure was inflated); in cities such as Tehran, where popular reformists were thrown off the ballot, turnout was less than 20 percent.[113] With a

25 percent threshold for election, the democratic legitimacy of the winners was deemed highly questionable.

Moreover, the conservative victory did not produce a bloc for Ahmadinejad—it was divided among the warring factions of the conservative wing and included several viable presidential hopefuls, even Ahmadinejad's archrival and former nuclear negotiator Ali Larijani, who won his seat with more than 70 percent of the vote in the "holy city" of Qom. According to one diplomat, the landslide for Larijani "sends the subliminal message that he has the backing of the religious mullahs."[114] More recently, in May 2008, Larijani was elected speaker of the parliament—a major victory that "may foreshadow Ahmadinejad's defeat in the presidential election scheduled for June 2009," according to some commentators.[115]

In sum, Ahmadinejad's grip on power at home—while tightening—is not absolute. His difficulties aren't only with the progressives, either. "On a political level," says a former Iranian vice president, "he does not have the support of the hard-liners."[116] Still, according to the *New York Times,* the extremist rhetoric "burnishes Mr. Ahmadinejad's populist image at home and adds to his aura on the Arab street," regardless of his actual effectiveness in Iran. Others have cast doubt on whether something was merely lost in translation. "Ahmadinejad did not say he was going to wipe Israel off the map because no such idiom exists in Persian," according to Professor Juan Cole, an anti-Israel extremist from the University of Michigan, who was quoted in the *New York Times.* He goes on to say, "He did say he hoped its regime, i.e., a Jewish-Zionist state occupying Jerusalem, would collapse," adding, "I smell the whiff of [U.S.] war propaganda." The same article cites ongoing debates as to whether "to wipe" or "must vanish" is a better translation from Persian (Ahmadinejad's own staff used "wiped away"); whether "the map" (Khomeini's formulation) or "the pages of history" (the literal translation) is more accurate; and thus whether Israel's destruction is imminent or in an unspecified future. It also questions whether "the occupying regime of Jerusalem" or "Israel" is more accurate, and thus whether Ahmadinejad was calling outright for war or merely a "regime change."[117] On June 2, 2008, the *New York Times* reported that Ahmadinejad once again threatened Israel with destruction. Addressing a group of foreign guests, he said, "You should know that the criminal and terrorist Zionist regime which has 60 years of plundering, aggression and crimes in its file has reached the end of its work and will soon disappear off the geographical scene."[118] What he meant by the "geographical scene," he left vague.

Hitler too often spoke in vague and euphemistic terms about ridding Europe of Jews. Israel certainly has no obligation to give Ahmadinejad the benefit of any doubts when it comes to interpreting threats of annihilation.

When I visited Israel in March 2008, I met with most of the Israeli political and many of the military leaders. Nearly all cautioned me that Ahmadinejad, despite his appearance of buffoonery, is a formidable and dangerous leader and that Iran is the "smartest" and "most technologically advanced" enemy Israel has ever faced. To a person, they believed that Iran was determined to obtain deliverable nuclear weapons that could be used against Israel, either directly or through surrogates like Hezbollah. To a person, they were shocked, disappointed, and appalled at the National Intelligence Estimate (NIE) released by the U.S. intelligence community in November 2007, which concluded that Iran had halted its nuclear weapons program in 2003, and that it therefore did not constitute a nuclear threat.[119]

I responded immediately to this report, arguing that this head-in-the-sand approach ignored something obvious and well known to all intelligence officials with an IQ above room temperature: that there are two tracks to building nuclear weapons. One is to conduct research and develop technology directly related to military use, as the United States did during the Manhattan Project. The second track is to develop nuclear technology for civilian (or dual) use and then transfer the civilian technology to military purposes.[120] What every intelligence agency knows is that the most difficult part of developing weapons corresponds precisely to what is essential for the second track: civilian use. In other words, it is relatively simple to move from track 1 to track 2 in a short period of time.

As Valerie Lincy and Gary Milhollin, both experts on nuclear arms control, put it in a *New York Times* op-ed on December 6, 2007:

> During the past year, a period when Iran's weapons program was supposedly halted, the government has been busy installing some 3,000 gas centrifuges at its plant at Natanz. These machines could, if operated continuously for about a year, create enough enriched uranium to provide fuel for a bomb. In addition, they have no plausible purpose in Iran's civilian nuclear effort. All of Iran's needs for enriched uranium for its energy programs are covered by a contract with Russia.
>
> Iran is also building a heavy water reactor at its research center at Arak. This reactor is ideal for producing plutonium for nuclear bombs, but is of little use in an energy program like Iran's, which does not use plutonium for reactor fuel. India, Israel and Pakistan have all built similar reactors—all with the purpose of fueling nuclear weapons. And why, by the way, does Iran even want a nuclear energy program, when it is sitting on an enormous pool of oil that is now skyrocketing in value? [Iran has the world's fourth-largest oil reserve.] And why is Iran developing long-range Shahab missiles, which make no military sense without nuclear warheads to put on them?
>
> The halting of its secret enrichment and weapon design efforts in 2003 proves only that Iran made a tactical move. It suspended work that, if discovered, would unambiguously reveal intent to build a weapon. It has continued other work, crucial to the ability to make a bomb, that it can pass off as having civilian applications.[121]

The NIE ignores all that. Instead, blinded by the "fog of peace," it concludes that Iran has been advancing its "civilian" nuclear program since 2003. Meanwhile, Iran is crowing about its hatred for Israel and is furiously and publicly claiming its right to civilian nuclear power. If Neville Chamberlain weren't long dead, I would wonder whether he had a hand in writing this "peace in our time" intelligence fiasco.

What, then, can explain so obvious an intelligence gaffe? One explanation could lie in the old saw that military intelligence is to intelligence as military music is to music. But I simply don't believe that our intelligence agencies are populated by the kind of nincompoops who would fall for this Iranian two-card monte. The more likely explanation is that there is an agenda hiding in the report. What might that agenda be?

To find a hidden agenda, one should always look for the beneficiaries. Who wins from this deeply flawed report? Well, certainly Iran does, but it is unlikely that Iranian interests could drive any U.S. agenda. Lincy and Milhollin surmise that "We should be suspicious of any document that suddenly gives the Bush administration a pass on a big national security problem it won't solve during its remaining year in office. Is the administration just washing its hands of the intractable Iranian nuclear issue by saying 'if we can't fix it, it ain't broke?'"[122]

My own view is that the authors of the report were fighting the last war. No, not the war in Iraq but rather what they believe was Vice President Dick Cheney's effort to go to war with Iran. This report surely takes the wind out of those sails. But that was last year's unfought war. Nobody in Washington has seriously considered attacking Iran since Condoleezza Rice and Robert Gates replaced Cheney as the foreign policy powers behind the throne.

Whatever the agenda and whatever the motive, this report may well go down in history as one of the most dangerous, misguided, and counterproductive intelligence assessments ever written. It may well encourage the Iranians to move even more quickly in developing nuclear weapons. If the report is correct in arguing that the only way of discouraging Iran from developing nuclear weapons is to maintain international pressure, then the authors of the report must surely know that they have single-handedly reduced any incentive by the international community to keep the pressure up.

I wish the intelligence assessment were correct. So do most of the media, which have accepted its naive conclusion with uncritical enthusiasm. The world would be a far safer place if Iran had indeed ended its efforts to develop deliverable nuclear weapons, as Libya did. But wishing for a desirable outcome does not make it so. Pretending that a desirable outcome is happening when the best information indicates that it's not only encourages the worst outcome.

One prominent public figure who seems entirely willing to pull the wool over his own eyes, and those of his readers, is former senator and once presidential hopeful Gary Hart. Hart defended the National Intelligence Estimate and castigated me for questioning its Pollyanna-ish conclusion. He compares those who are concerned about Iran with old-time cold warriors who are trying to fight "the Cold War all over again."[123] He went so far as to call my concern about Iran's nuclear ambitions "not only hysterical but almost catatonic."[124] (He must mean "paranoid" since catatonics manifest their illness by immobility and inaction.)

Now, however, my concerns about Iran have been echoed by the British Parliament's Foreign Affairs Committee and the chief UN nuclear inspector. Here is how the British committee's chairman put it, following a visit to Iran and based on the extensive evidence received by the group: "There is a strong possibility that Iran could establish a 'breakout' nuclear weapons capability by 2015." A "breakout capability" is "the ability to manufacture a nuclear device within a short period of time by virtue of its nonmilitary nuclear technical capabilities and assets."[125] This is precisely what I and other critics of the NIE have been saying! Mahmoud Ahmadinejad, the president of Iran, seems to agree. Following the release of the NIE, he boasted that Iran "will have the final victory in the nuclear arena."[126] This doesn't sound like he's talking about a peaceful nuclear alternative energy source in his oil-soaked nation. In a July 6, 2008, op-ed in the *Boston Globe*, Peter D. Zimmerman, a renowned nuclear physicist and former chief scientist for the Senate Foreign Relations Committee, marshaled the evidence that persuaded him and other scientists that "the real purpose of Iranian enrichment is to provide fuel for weapons." He also warned that Iran could produce low-cost nuclear weapons "on an assembly-line basis," which it could transfer to "groups such as Hezbollah and Hamas."

In February 2008, the chief UN nuclear inspector provided new evidence, including video from Iran's own military laboratories, that showed work "not consistent with any application other than the development of a nuclear weapon." The Iranian representative shouted out that the new evidence consisted of "baseless fabrications."[127] No one believed him.

No one except Gary Hart, who appears burdened by a conflict of interest when it comes to the Iranian nuclear program. For years now, Hart has been an advocate for the former Soviet Union, especially in the area of alternative energy. He is a founder of the United States–Russia Investment Fund. It is Russia that exports much of the material necessary for Iran's nuclear program. If Iran were forced to end its nuclear program, Russia would suffer and so would Hart. Despite this apparent conflict, which Hart failed to disclose, he has the temerity to accuse others (including me) of harboring hidden agendas and has urged "everyone to put their cards on the table."[128]

My cards are on the table. Yes, I worry that an Iran with nuclear weapons would become the first nation in the Middle East to use its nuclear arsenal, not only against Israel but against U.S. interests. I worry that if Iran gets the bomb, Saudi Arabia, Egypt, and other Middle Eastern nations will feel it necessary to go nuclear as well. I worry that Iran may hand off nuclear material to its surrogates, including Hezbollah. I worry than Iran will credibly threaten Israel with a nuclear strike in an effort to discourage tourism and encourage an exodus of frightened Israelis from their homeland. I worry that the deeply flawed and misleading National Intelligence Estimate—and the respected figures, such as Hart, who support its flawed conclusions—will make a preemptive attack against Iran more, not less, likely. The NIE will weaken the case for sanctions, as it already has, and will embolden Iran to move even more quickly toward developing nuclear weapons. I strongly prefer diplomacy and sanctions to a preemptive military strike. That, too, is why I am so critical of the highly politicized and misleading National Intelligence Estimate. I am certainly not a cold warrior—which is another reason I don't want to see a nuclear Iran. A cold war with a nuclear Iran would be even more dangerous than the one we had with the Soviet Union, because of Iran's suicidal and apocalyptic leadership.

Even before Ahmadinejad became president, I had been writing about the ominous development of Iran's nuclear program. At that time, I wrote that in light of the statements of then president Rafsanjani, Israel must have the right to protect its civilians from a nuclear holocaust, and that such a right must include the option to use preemptive military action of the sort taken by Israel against the Iraqi nuclear reactor at Osirak in 1981. (Israel's attack on the Iraqi reactor claimed only one life.) Despite the refrain that "Iran must not be allowed to develop a nuclear weapon," some people interpret international law—at least, as defined by the UN—as precluding a democracy that is threatened with nuclear annihilation from taking proportional, preventive military action to dissipate the threat to its civilians.[129]

Under this benighted view, the United States would not be able to take proactive steps against terrorist groups that threaten our civilians. We would have to wait until the terrorists attacked us first, even if they were suicide bombers with weapons of mass destruction. This unrealistic perversion of international law must be changed quickly to take into account situations in which deterrence simply cannot be counted on to work. Democracies must be authorized to take preemptive military actions against grave threats to their survival or to their civilian population. (In an important sense, an Israeli attack on Iran would be neither preventive nor preemptive. It would be retaliatory, since Iran attacked the Israeli embassy in Buenos Aires and Iran assisted Hezbollah in its attack against Israel in 2006. Iran is already in a state of war with Israel, having engaged in more than one casus belli, but the international community would likely reject this analysis and insist that an Israeli attack on Iran's nuclear weapons program be deemed preventive and unlawful under the circumstances.)

Current international law is woefully inadequate for the task of preventing the deployment of weapons of mass destruction. It requires that the threat be immediate, as it was when Israel preempted an imminent coordinated attack by Egypt and Syria in 1967.

But the threat posed by the future development of nuclear weapons does not fit this anachronistic criterion. It is the nature of the threat—the potential for mass casualties and an irreversible shift in the balance of power—that justifies the use of preventive self-defense with regard to the Iranian threat. International law must be amended to reflect this reality, but it is unlikely that any such changes will take place if it is seen as benefiting Israel. (As the late Abba Eban, the early Israeli ambassador to the UN, once put it: "If Algeria proposed a resolution that the Earth was flat and that Israel flattened it, it would pass by a vote of 120 to 3, with 27 abstentions.")[130]

Although military preemption and prevention have gotten a bad name among some people following the U.S. attack on Iraq, they must remain an option in situations where deterrence is unrealistic and the threat is sufficiently serious.

If the Iranian nuclear facilities were located in one place, away from any civilian population center, it would be moral—and, under any reasonable regime of international law, legal—for Israel to destroy them. (Whether it would be tactically wise is another question.) But the ruthless Iranian militants have learned from the Iraqi experience and, according to intelligence reports, deliberately have spread Iran's nuclear facilities around the country, including in heavily populated areas.[131] This would force Israel into a terrible choice: either allow Iran to complete its production of nuclear bombs aimed at the Jewish state's civilian population centers or destroy the facilities despite the inevitability of Iranian civilian casualties.

The laws of war, as described in the previous chapter, prohibit the bombing of civilian population centers for the purpose of killing noncombatants, but they permit the bombing of military targets, and this certainly includes nuclear facilities that are capable of producing weapons of mass destruction. By deliberately placing nuclear facilities in the midst of civilian population centers, the Iranian government has made the decision to expose its civilians to attacks, and it must assume all responsibility for any casualties caused by such attacks. Israel, the United States, and other democracies always locate their nuclear facilities away from population centers, precisely in order to minimize danger to their civilians. Iran does precisely the opposite because its leaders realize that decent democracies—unlike indecent tyrannies—would hesitate to bomb a nuclear facility located in an urban center.

Israel, with the help of the United States, should first try everything short of military action: diplomacy, threats, bribery, sabotage, targeted killings of individuals who are essential to the Iranian nuclear program, and other covert actions. But if all else fails, Israel or the United States must be allowed under international law to take out the Iranian nuclear threat before it is capable of the genocide for which it is being built.

The Iranians would probably give up their nuclear weapons program if their leaders truly believed that refusal to do so would produce an Iraq-like attack—an all-out invasion, a regime change, and occupation. But the continuing war in Iraq has made it nearly impossible for the United States to mount a credible threat because American public opinion—and now U.S. intelligence services—will not accept a second war (or so the Iranians believe). Moreover, America's allies in the war against Iraq—most particularly, Great Britain—would not support an attack on Iran.

That is precisely why the Bush administration was barking so loudly, at least until the release of the NIE. It wanted to convince Iranian leaders that it is preparing to bite—to attack, invade, and destroy their regime, perhaps even with the use of tactical nuclear weapons. But the threat wasn't working. It only caused the Iranian leaders themselves to bark louder, to exaggerate their progress toward completing a nuclear weapon and to threaten terrorist retaliation by their suicide volunteers if Iran were to be attacked.

The war in Iraq is a two-edged sword when it comes to Iran. One edge demonstrates that the United States is willing and able to topple dictatorial regimes that it regards as dangerous. That is the edge the Bush administration was trying to showcase. The other edge represents the failure of Iraq—widespread public distrust of intelligence claims, fear of becoming bogged down in another endless war, and strident opposition at home and abroad. That is the edge being seen by the Iranian leaders. The U.S. threat is seen as hollow—especially now, in the aftermath of the NIE report.

The authors of that perverse report, which influenced policy so immediately and negatively, will have much to answer for if their assessment results in a reduction of pressure on Iran to stop its obvious march toward becoming the world's most dangerous nuclear military power. Iran is the only nation that has actually threatened to use nuclear weapons to attack its enemies.

In May 2008, the International Atomic Energy Agency—which was long perceived as far more cautious than the United States—issued a dire warning about the status of Iran's nuclear weapons ambitions. The *New York Times* reported:

> On the basis of that combination of new and old evidence, over the last few months, the inspectors of the International Atomic Energy Agency have come to worry that Iran—before suspending its work nearly five years ago—may have made real progress toward designing a deadly weapon. . . . [T]he issue crystallized publicly when the inspectors issued an uncharacteristically blunt demand for more information from Tehran and, even more uncharacteristically, disclosed the existence of 18 secretly-obtained documents that suggest Tehran had high interest in designing a nuclear weapon before the program was suspended.
>
> In their report, . . . the Vienna-based investigators called the evidence of the early warhead work "a matter of serious concern," and said that uncovering the real story "is critical to an assessment of the nature of Iran's past and present nuclear program."

The Iranians, as usual, denied any interest in developing nuclear weapons, but a "senior official close to the agency" responded that "the Iranians 'lied, obfuscated and didn't tell us for 20 years what they were doing.'"

The International Atomic Energy Agency was apparently concerned that the widely discredited National Intelligence Estimate, issued in December 2007, "did not mention the possibility that now seems to concern the international inspectors—that Iran had perhaps made enough progress that it could afford to slow down or stop."

Now some senior officials who worked on the National Intelligence Estimate "say Iran's weapon-design work, with the right fuel, might have progressed enough by 2003 to make a bomb comparable to the five-ton blunderbuss dropped on Hiroshima." They worry that if Iran develops a nuclear bomb that can be placed on a missile, such a weapon "can change a region's balance of power without even being fired."[132]

U.S. Intelligence agencies estimate that Iran could have a nuclear bomb ready by 2009, "but 2010 to 2015 is a more likely time frame."[133] This "could put the potential for a crisis squarely on the agenda of the next American president"—unless Israel were to act even sooner.

The U.S. failure to stand up to Ahmadinejad and Iran may compel Israel to defend itself. Israel's military threat to Iran is real but limited. Who could blame Israel for seeking to destroy the emerging nuclear capacity of an enemy nation whose leader, in April 2006, threatened to eliminate "the Zionist regime" by "one storm"—a clearly intended reference to a nuclear attack?[134] As was previously mentioned, Ahmadinejad's predecessor, the more moderate Hashemi Rafsanjani, "speculated [in 2001] that in a nuclear exchange with Israel his country might lose 15 million people, which would amount to a small 'sacrifice' from among the one billion Muslims worldwide in exchange for the lives of five million Israeli Jews." According to the journalist, "he seemed pleased with his formulation."[135] Iran has already developed and displayed its long-range missiles, which are capable of striking Israeli cities with nuclear warheads.

These threats of a nuclear attack are being taken seriously by Israeli leaders, even if they are neither imminent nor certain. Israelis remember apocalyptic threats from an earlier dictator that were not taken seriously. This time, those who are threatened have the military capacity to confront the danger and are likely to do so if it becomes more likely. Even if Israelis believe there is only a 5 percent chance that Iran would attack Israel with nuclear weapons, the risk of national annihilation would be too great for any nation to ignore—most especially one built on the ashes of the Holocaust.

The Iranian leaders understand this. They take seriously the statements made by Israeli leaders that they will never accept a nuclear Iran under its present leadership.

Iranian leaders fully expect an attack from Israel when they come close to producing a nuclear weapon. They have already threatened to respond with nuclear weapons. On June 28, 2008, the Associated Press reported:

> Iran's Parliament speaker yesterday warned that the West could face a "done deal" if it provokes Iran, in a rare hint by an Iranian official that Tehran could build nuclear weapons if attacked. . . .
>
> He cited comments by Mohamed ElBaradei, the UN nuclear watchdog chief, who said in an interview last week that a military strike on Iran could turn the Mideast into a "ball of fire" and "prompt Iran, even if it didn't produce a nuclear weapon today, to resort to an emergency plan to produce a nuclear weapon."
>
> "Take Mr. ElBaradei's warnings seriously," Larijani said, addressing the West.

This statement would seem to confirm the widespread belief among intelligence agencies that Iran could quickly convert its dual-track nuclear developments into deliverable weapons.

Why, then, are the Iranians not deterred by the realistic prospect of an Israeli preemptive (or preventive) strike? First, an Israeli attack would be a limited, surgical strike (or series of strikes). It would not be accompanied by a full-scale invasion, occupation, and regime change. Second, it would only delay production of a nuclear bomb because it would be incomplete. Some nuclear facilities would be missed or only damaged because they are "hardened" and/or are located in populated areas.[136]

The third and most important reason is that an attack by Israel would solidify the Iranian regime. It would make Iran the victim of "Zionist aggression" and would unify Muslims, both inside and outside Iran, against their common enemies. I say "enemies" because regardless of what role the United States played or did not play in an Israeli attack, the United States would share the blame in the radical Islamic world.

I am not going so far as to argue that the Iranian leadership would welcome an Israeli attack, but it would quickly turn such an attack to its advantage. If matters get worse domestically for the

Iranian regime—if the nascent anti-Ahmadinejad "democratic" or "secular" movements were to strengthen—Ahmadinejad might actually get to the point of welcoming, even provoking or faking, an attack from Israel. This is why the threat from Israel will probably not be a sufficient deterrent.

So we have two threats: one from a superpower—the United States—that can but won't bring about regime change. The other from a regional power—Israel—that may well attack but, if it does, will not only fail to produce regime change but may actually strengthen Ahmadinejad's existing regime.

The Iranians will persist, therefore, in their efforts to secure nuclear weapons. Unless they are stopped or significantly delayed by military actions, they will become a nuclear power within a few years—precisely how many is unknown and probably unknowable.

Armed with nuclear weapons and ruled by religious fanatics, Iran will become—if it is not already—the most dangerous nation in the world. There is a small but still real possibility that it could initiate a suicidal nuclear exchange with Israel. There is a greater likelihood that it could hand over nuclear material to one of its terrorist surrogates or that some rogue elements could steal nuclear material. This would pose a direct threat to the United States and all of its allies.

The world should not accept these risks if there are reasonable steps available to prevent or reduce them. The question remains: are any such steps feasible? Probably not, as long as the United States remains bogged down in Iraq. History may well conclude that the United States and Britain fought the wrong preventive war against a country that posed no real threat, and that fighting that wrong war stopped them from fighting the right preventive war against a country that did pose a danger to world peace.

Although the doctrine of preventive war is easily abused—as it was in Iraq—sometimes it is a necessary evil. The failure of Britain and France to wage a preventive war against Nazi Germany in the mid-1930s cost the world tens of millions of lives. Will the same be said someday about the failure to prevent Mahmoud Ahmadinejad's Iran from developing nuclear weapons?

Conclusion

The Case against Simple-Minded, One-Sided Solutions to Complex, Multifaceted Problems

The question of how to resolve the Arab-Israeli, Palestinian-Israeli, Muslim-Israeli conflict (or conflicts) is extraordinarily complex. There used to be a relatively simple answer: two states, one Jewish and the other Arab, on roughly the land areas that each side controlled before the Six-Day War (with a few small mutual adjustments that reflect practical realities on the ground). This is the resolution that was proposed by President Bill Clinton and Prime Minister Ehud Barak in 2000–2001 but was rejected by Yasser Arafat. Since that time, much has changed. Arafat died, Israel ended its occupation of Gaza, and Hamas defeated the Palestinian Authority in an election and took over Gaza by force. Hamas then used Gaza as a launching pad for rockets, suicide bombings, and kidnapping (as Hezbollah did when Israel left southern Lebanon).

The Israeli government can no longer make peace with the Palestinian Authority alone. Hamas, too, must be willing to

224

abide by any agreement, but its charter doesn't recognize Israel's right to exist and calls for the military destruction of the Jewish state. Nor can Israel make peace by unilateral actions, as former Prime Minister Ariel Sharon tried to do by ending Israel's occupation of Gaza and moving toward ending its occupation of the West Bank. As one of the most influential imams in Gaza told a reporter for the *Atlantic*, "It does not matter what the Jews do. We will not let them have peace. . . . They can be nice to us or they can kill us, it doesn't matter. . . . If we have a cease-fire with the Jews, it is only so that we can prepare ourselves for the final battle."[1]

The imam said that in a crowded mosque, during a conversation in which he described Jews as "the sons of apes and pigs." In light of these new realities, it will be much more difficult to implement a two-state solution, especially since Hamas refuses to recognize Israel and to end its terrorism.

On April 27, 2008, the *New York Times* reported that Khaled Meshal, the leader of Hamas, also said that any "truce" or "cease-fire" with Israel would merely be a "tactic," allowing his terrorists to rearm and prepare themselves to destroy Israel militarily.[2]

The issues, therefore, have become far more complicated and nuanced, but you wouldn't know that from listening to Israel's enemies, nearly all of whom offer simple-minded, one-sided, and unrealistic solutions. Jimmy Carter says that if only Israel ended the occupation, there would be peace. Israel did end its occupation of Gaza and Lebanon, but instead there were rocket attacks, kidnappings, and terrorism. If Israel were now to end its occupation of the West Bank, it is likely that Hamas would seize control over that area as well. Rockets from the West Bank could hit Jerusalem, Tel Aviv, and Ben-Gurion Airport and would place nearly all of Israel's civilians in harm's way. This does not mean that Israel should expand, or even maintain, civilian settlements in the heart of the West Bank. In my view, it should not. But some military presence may still be required to prevent terrorism and rocket attacks, at least until the Palestinian Authority demonstrates the capacity and will to do so, or Israel develops a technological defense against rockets and missiles. It's a bit more complicated than you suggest, Mr. Carter!

Stephen Walt and John Mearsheimer argue that if only the Israel Lobby were to stop coercing the United States into supporting Israel, the threat of international terrorism would abate, America's position in the world would be restored, and peace would break out. Yet international terrorism since 9/11 (which had little to do with the Israeli-Palestinian conflict and much to do with the U.S. relationship with Saudi Arabia) has been directed against Spain, England, Australia, and other nations far less supportive of Israel than is the United States. Moreover, it now turns out that Israel, speaking through its prime minister, opposed the U.S. invasion and occupation of Iraq. Its not as simple as that, Professors Walt and Mearsheimer!

Those who believe that academic boycotts or divestment campaigns directed only at Israel will either bring peace to the region or improve the human rights situation around the world are kidding themselves—or, more likely, are trying to mislead others. These campaigns only encourage terrorists to persist in their efforts to take lethal actions against Israeli civilians, which then forces Israel to respond in ways that escalate the demand for sanctions. Indeed, the intensity of these immoral boycott and divestment campaigns tends to vary inversely with Israeli actions, often increasing when Israel makes concessions. (The latest proposal for a boycott, voted in late May 2008, coincided with Israeli proposals to reach peaceful resolutions with Syria and the Palestinian Authority.) It is almost as if the anti-Israel zealots who are pushing boycotts and divestment want Israel to become more repressive. It's more complicated than the self-righteous advocates of immoral boycotts and divestments try to convey to their often naive religious and ideological followers!

On college and university campuses, the rhetoric is becoming increasingly simple-minded and slogan-driven. Shouts of "Nazi," "Apartheid," and "Racist" have replaced reasoned discourse, not only at political forums, but increasingly in the classrooms of such institutions of learning as Columbia University, the University of California, the University of Michigan, and Oxford University. Books are being published by university presses that contain crass anti-Israel propaganda instead of balanced scholarship. The intellectual and political challenges forcing those who would try to make peace in the Middle East have been dumbed down by academic ideologues, who see their mission as proselytizing instead of educating. It's more nuanced than these slogans and propaganda screeds suggest!

Israel's military enemies have learned from their academic and media supporters. They understand that by using clichés to portray themselves as David fighting Goliath or freedom fighters struggling against repression or a national liberation movement resisting colonialism, they can justify any immoral tactic, ranging from suicide terrorism to firing rockets from behind human shields to threatening nuclear genocide. With the support of a UN rapporteur like Richard Falk, Islamic terrorists can see themselves as the Jews of the Warsaw Ghetto resisting the "Nazi Holocaust" or as African victims of the Rwandan and Darfur "genocides" or of the South African "apartheid." Even Mahmoud Ahmadinejad can view himself as a nuclear liberator of the victims of "crimes against humanity." But the situation is not subject to those sorts of inapt and immoral analogies!

Israel is the only country in the world that is accused by its enemies of practicing apartheid without racism; of perpetrating a Holocaust without gas chambers; of engaging in genocide without mass murder; of committing war crimes without targeting civilians; and of being the worst human rights violator in the world, while having one of the most responsive legal systems in the world. This is accusation by metaphor, prosecution by propaganda, trial by bigotry, guilt by hyperbole, and sentence by sloganeering. In demeaning these historically contingent and emotionally powerful terms, those enemies of Israel deflect attention away from genuine apartheid regimes, actual practitioners of genocide, real war criminals, and grievous human rights violators. They have succeeded in hijacking the human rights agenda of the United Nations, of many nongovernmental organizations, and of several religious groups. The real victims of this double standard have been the millions of innocent Africans, Asians, and others who have been murdered, raped, and maimed—while the international community has stood silently by, smugly focusing nearly all of its condemnatory resources on one imperfect democracy that contributes so much to the world while closing its eyes to so many perfect tyrannies that inflict so much harm on the world.

If peace is to come to the Middle East, this brand of simple-minded sophistry must stop. The time has come for people of goodwill and common sense to insist that rationality be restored to discussions of the Mideast conflict. The blame-everything-on-Israel approach that is characteristic of so many of Israel's enemies is incompatible not only with reasoned discourse but also with a compromise peace. We must recognize the complexity of the situation and the calibrated measures required to address it.

I call on all people of goodwill, everyone who truly wants a peaceful resolution to the Middle East conflict, to stop demonizing Israel, to end the double standard that has been imposed on Israel, to cease the name-calling, to terminate the bigoted calls for boycotts and divestment against the Jewish state, and to stop encouraging terrorism, and instead to propose constructive, realistic steps that can be taken toward a compromise peace that produces a secure Israel and an economically viable, peaceful, and democratic Palestinian state—and that finally allows the beleaguered people of this war-torn part of the world to enjoy the blessings and benefits of peace, *salaam,* and *shalom.*

Why Jimmy Carter Is Wrong: The Facts

FALSEHOODS AND MORE FALSEHOODS

Chief among the myriad defects of Jimmy Carter's book is the fundamental problem of its many factual errors concerning the Arab-Israeli conflict—errors related to historical events, international agreements, national policies and recent occurrences. Identifying these many inaccurate statements and refuting them serves to highlight the fallacious underpinnings of Carter's overall analysis, in particular his gross mischaracterizations of the actions of Israel and that nation's adversaries, and the false premises of his prescriptions for achieving peace.

Despite widespread criticism of the factual shoddiness of *Palestine: Peace Not Apartheid*, Carter has regularly boasted in press appearances and lectures of the allegedly pristine accuracy of his book. In an appearance on "Larry King Live" on Nov. 27, 2006, for instance, he insisted: "Everything in the book, I might say, is completely accurate." . . .

Adapted with permission from *Bearing False Witness: Jimmy Carter's Palestine, Peace Not Apartheid* by Gilead Ini, Alex Safian, PhD, Andrea Levin, Tamar Sternthal. Copyright Committee for Accuracy in Middle East Reporting in America (CAMERA) 2007, published by CAMERA. Notes to this appendix begin on page 248.

He told CNN's Soledad O'Brien on December 13, 2006: "I know what I'm talking about and the book is completely accurate."

In the *Washington Post* (January 18, 2007), he declared that "most critics have not seriously disputed or even mentioned the facts."

In reality, of course, much of the criticism of the book has focused on its pervasive and serious misrepresentations of fact. Moreover, Carter has frequently reiterated the same falsehoods and distortions proffered in the book in television, radio, and print appearances, as well as for numerous audiences at bookstores, college campuses, symposia and other venues.

Following is a review of many of the factual errors in *Palestine: Peace Not Apartheid* along with some of Carter's false statements made in the media and elsewhere, mainly while promoting the book. The list is not comprehensive; it would be virtually impossible to cite every inaccurate or distorted statement made in the book and in the author's public appearances. The errors cited are organized by category.

INTERNATIONAL AGREEMENTS AND BORDERS

Carter continually misrepresents the contents of peace agreements, peace proposals and U.N. Security Council Resolution 242, then falsely casts Israel as violating the letter and spirit of international law and betraying American administrations and the world community in general. Thus, for instance, Carter writes on page 208, in a concluding chapter, that: "The overriding problem is that, for more than a quarter century, the actions of some Israeli leaders have been in direct conflict with the official policies of the United States, the international community, and their own negotiated agreements."

Errors Concerning UN Resolution 242

CARTER:
Palestine: Peace Not Apartheid, page 38: ". . . U.N. Resolution 242, which confirmed Israel's existence within its 1949 borders."

Palestine: Peace Not Apartheid, page 215: "[An option for Israel is] withdrawal to the 1967 border specified in U.N. Resolution 242 and as promised in the Camp David Accords and the Oslo Agreement . . . "

PBS NewsHour, November 28, 2006: "The demand is for them [the Israelis] to give back all the land. The United Nations resolutions that apply, the agreements that have been made at Camp David under me and later at Oslo for which the Israeli leaders received the Nobel Peace Prizes, was based [sic] on Israel's withdrawal from occupied territories."

Canadian Broadcasting Corporation, December 8, 2006: "It's a minority of Israeli leaders who prefer to occupy Palestinian land that is the obstacle to peace. It's a violation of United Nations resolutions. It's a violation of the agreements that were worked out at Camp David. It's a violation of the agreement that Israeli leaders and Parliament accepted in Oslo because of the Norwegians. It's a violation of the international Quartet's Road Map, all of which call for Israel to withdraw from occupied territories."

FACT:
All the agreements Carter cites are predicated on U.N. Security Council Resolution 242 and none—the Camp David Accords, the Oslo Accords, the Road Map—requires Israel to "give back all the land" and return to the vulnerable pre-1967 armistice lines. Nor in its continuing presence in the West Bank is Israel in "violation" of the agreements cited.

Resolution 242 calls on Israel to withdraw from territory in the context of negotiations that assure the "right to live in peace within secure and recognized boundaries free from threats or acts of force."[1] Despite many efforts, peace summits and signed accords there has yet to be a conclusive agreement defining "secure and recognized boundaries."

And, contrary to the ex-President, UNSCR 242 does not specify the extent of Israel's withdrawal from the West Bank. The drafters of 242 repeatedly, explicitly and emphatically spelled out their reasoning. For example, Lord Caradon, the chief architect of the resolution, observed:

> We could have said: well, you go back to the 1967 line. But I know the 1967 line, and it's a rotten line. You couldn't have a worse line for a permanent international boundary. It's where the troops happened to be on a certain night in 1948. It's got no relation to the needs of the situation. Had we said that you must go back to the 1967 line, which would have resulted if we had specified a retreat from all the occupied territories, we would have been wrong.
>
> In New York, what did we know about Tayyibe and Qalqilya? If we had attempted in New York to draw a new line, we would have been rather vague. So what we stated was the principle that you couldn't hold territory because you conquered it, therefore there must be a withdrawal to—let's read the words carefully—"secure and recognized boundaries." They can only be secure if they are recognized. The boundaries have to be agreed; it's only when you get agreement that you get security. I think that now people begin to realize what we had in mind—that security doesn't come from arms, it doesn't come from territory, it doesn't come from geography, it doesn't come from one side dominating the other, it can only come from agreement and mutual respect and understanding.[2]

Lord Caradon reiterated the argument on a 1978 PBS segment:

> We didn't say there should be a withdrawal to the '67 line; we did not put "the" in, we did not say all the territories deliberately. We all knew that the boundaries of '67 were not drawn as permanent frontiers, they were a cease-fire line of a couple of decades earlier. . . . We did not say that the '67 boundaries must be forever.[3]

Errors Concerning "Borders"

In conjunction with many of the distortions about 242, Carter continually injects inaccurate references to Israel's supposedly established and internationally recognized eastern "borders" along the West Bank. However, no such borders have ever been finalized. The Camp David Accords, signed by Carter himself, state: "The negotiations [concerning the West Bank and Gaza] will resolve, among other matters, the location of the boundaries. . . ." The Oslo Agreements deferred "borders" as one of the "issues that will be negotiated in the permanent status negotiations" (Article XVII, 1, a). Similarly, the Road Map of 2003 invokes 242 and states that a "process" would begin in 2004 "leading to a final, permanent status resolution in 2005, including on borders, Jerusalem, refugees, settlements."

No permanent status resolution on these issues has yet occurred.

CARTER:
Palestine: Peace Not Apartheid, Page 57: "The 1949 armistice demarcation lines became the borders of the new nation of Israel and were accepted by Israel and the United States, and recognized officially by the United Nations."

Palestine: Peace Not Apartheid, Page 190: "[Israel's security barrier] is projected to be at least three and a half times as long as Israel's internationally recognized border . . ."

Palestine: Peace Not Apartheid, Page 207: "The unwavering official policy of the United States since Israel became a state has been that its borders must coincide with those prevailing from 1949 until 1967 (unless modified by mutually agreeable land swaps). . . . Also as a member of the International Quartet that includes Russia, the United Nations, and the European Union, America supports the Roadmap for Peace, which espouses exactly the same requirements."

Palestine: Peace Not Apartheid, Page 216: "The bottom line is this: Peace will come to Israel and the Middle East only when the Israeli government is willing to comply with international law, with the Roadmap for Peace, with official American policy, with the wishes of a majority of its own citizens—and honor its own previous commitments—by accepting its legal borders."

Tavis Smiley Show, PBS, December 11, 2006: ". . . twenty-three Arab countries agreed to recognize Israel's right to exist in peace inside their legal borders. . . . But that's not something that Israel is willing to accept, to live inside their own borders. The international borders."

Lecture at George Washington University, March 7, 2007: "Condoleezza Rice has called for early U.S.-Israeli-Palestinian peace talks. She recommended, by the way, as a basis for peace, the 2002 offer of all 23 Arab nations—that is, full recognition of Israel, based on a return to its internationally recognized borders. And this recommendation is compatible with all U.S. official policy of our government since before I became president and since, also is compatible with United Nations resolutions and also with previous agreements which the Israeli government has approved overwhelmingly in 1978, as I've already mentioned, and later, in 1993, with the Oslo agreement."

FACT:
The 1949 armistice lines separating the West Bank from Israel never became permanent borders recognized by Israel, the United States or the U.N. Security Council. Israel's only internationally recognized borders are those between Israel and Egypt and Israel and Lebanon. Indeed, the Jordanian-Israeli General Armistice Agreement of April 3, 1949 specifically notes that the lines are not borders: "The Armistice

Demarcation Lines defined in articles V and VI of this Agreement are agreed upon by the Parties without prejudice to future territorial settlements or boundary lines or to claims of either Party relating thereto." Nor, obviously, was there any "unwavering official policy," as Carter alleges, defining Israel's eastern "borders."

President Johnson said on June 19, 1967: "The nations of the region have had only fragile and violated truce lines for 20 years. What they now need are recognized boundaries and other arrangements that will give them security against terror, destruction, and war."

Arthur Goldberg, the U.S. ambassador to the United Nations from 1965–1968, explained in a March 12, 1980 letter to the *New York Times:* "In a number of speeches at the U.N. in 1967, I repeatedly stated that the armistice lines fixed after 1948 were intended to be temporary."

Errors Concerning Camp David

CARTER:
Palestine: Peace Not Apartheid, Pages 51–52: . . . [I]mportant provisions of our [1978/79] agreement have not been honored since I left office. The Israelis have never granted any appreciable autonomy to the Palestinians . . .

FACT:
Obviously, after 1993 the Palestinians gained "appreciable autonomy." The Oslo process created the Palestinian Authority, giving Palestinians control of political, civic, security, medical, educational and media institutions. Under the Accords, Israel ceded 40 percent of the West Bank, and unilaterally pulled out from Gaza entirely. About 98 percent of the Palestinian population lived in the areas of Palestinian self-rule. Any subsequent Israeli military incursions into these areas have been in response to their use by Palestinians as bases for terrorism.

With regard to Palestinian autonomy and the original Camp David agreements, Carter grossly distorts the facts. Efforts to negotiate details of an autonomy agreement failed then not because of Israel, but because Yasir Arafat and his lieutenants publicly denounced such efforts and any Palestinians who supported them were killed.

For example, the *New York Times* reported on a Christian Palestinian from Ramallah who had publicly rejected the PLO in favor of seeking peace via the path of Begin and Sadat. "Defying the PLO," by *Times*' senior editor John Oakes (December 21, 1977) told of Abdel-nur Khalil Janho, who was said to be:

> . . . typical of those Palestinian Arabs of the West Bank who have no use for the PLO's extreme position and terrorist tactics, who fear its radicalism and who do not accept the dogma that it is in fact the sole legitimate representative of the Palestinian people. . . . this position, rarely expressed openly by Arabs in the occupied territories prior to the Sadat peace initiative, has suddenly come alive not only with Mr. Sadat's downgrading of the PLO, but especially since President Carter stated that moderate Palestinians now must be included in the discussions at the Cairo conference, which the PLO has rejected.

According to Mr. Janho,

> the Sadat-Begin approach now gives a unique opportunity for the 750,000 West Bank Arabs to be liberated from the occupation and at the same time help along in

the process of reconciliation by holding out a friendly hand to the Israelis. And if this opportunity isn't made the most of by the Arabs who live inside the West Bank, the PLO outside will again seize the initiative, the whole peace effort will collapse and the radicals will take over.

Questioned by Oakes about the many West Bank mayors who supported the PLO, Janho replied,

> they were elected at a time when West Bank Arabs could see no possibilities of a peaceful settlement with the Israelis . . . but all that's changed now, as a result of Sadat. There is an alternative to [the] PLO; we have a chance to regain our identity and our dignity without war. Petitions in support of Mr. Sadat's moves, signed by 9,000 Arab citizens of Nablus, the West Bank's largest city and center of PLO sentiment, would seem to bear him out.

Regrettably, however, only a few weeks later a PLO hit-squad gunned down Mr. Janho.

Shortly after the *Times* story, the PLO press agency WAFA announced on December 26, 1977 that orders had been given to "liquidate a number of agents," and on that very day the PLO announced in Beirut its responsibility for the murder of Hamdi Kadi, a Palestinian resident of Ramallah who was willing to work with the Israelis. According to the *Washington Post,* "The announcement of Kadi's assassination followed a PLO statement rejecting Israel's latest proposals for limited Arab self-rule on the West Bank." (December 27, 1977)

Ironically, Carter was to become an advisor, friend and advocate of Yasir Arafat, even though it was the PLO leader who undermined Camp David's autonomy components and whose minions liquidated courageous moderates who embraced the president's proposals. In his reflexive blaming of Israel and whitewashing of the PLO's role regardless of the facts, as illustrated in this episode, Carter reveals his sharp bias against the Jewish state.

CARTER:
Palestine: Peace Not Apartheid, Page 50: "Perhaps the most serious omission of the Camp David talks was the failure to clarify in writing Begin's verbal promise concerning the settlement freeze during subsequent peace talks."

Washington Post Op-Ed, Nov. 26, 2000: "Prime Minister Begin pledged that there would be no establishment of new settlements until after the final peace negotiations were completed. But later, under Likud pressure, he declined to honor this commitment. . . ."

FACT:
Menahem Begin promised in the Camp David discussions to maintain a three month settlement freeze and he adhered to his commitment. This was dramatically underscored in a public forum about the Camp David agreements on September 17, 2003 at the Woodrow Wilson Center. A member of the panel, Israeli jurist Aharon Barak, explained he had attended the relevant meeting at which the settlement freeze discussion transpired, had been the only one present taking notes, and that his notes showed Begin had agreed only to a three month freeze.

In the background, Carter is heard to state, "I don't dispute that." William Quandt then added that while he had not been in the meeting, Secretary of State Cyrus Vance had, and told him immediately afterwards that Begin had agreed to a three month freeze, but they hoped to get it lengthened the next day. Neither Carter, nor Barak, nor Quandt indicated that Begin had ever agreed to extend the freeze.

Errors Concerning the Road Map

In a pattern apparent throughout Carter's formulations, the Palestinians are, regardless of the facts, cast as near perfect in fealty both to agreements and to the cause of peace, while Israel is condemned for violating both.

CARTER:
Palestine: Peace Not Apartheid, Page 173: "[Abbas and his key advisers] pointed out that Palestinian leaders had accepted all provisions of the Quartet's Roadmap for Peace, but that Sharon had publicly rejected most of its key provisions. There was no doubt that Abbas had the support and respect of his people and was dedicated to the immediate pursuit of a peace agreement in accordance with the Roadmap."

Palestine: Peace Not Apartheid, Page 187: "He [Abbas] has publicly endorsed the international community's Roadmap for Peace without equivocation and has been eager to negotiate with Israel since first becoming prime minister three years before being elected president."

Palestine: Peace Not Apartheid, Page 207: "Palestinian leaders unequivocally accepted this proposal, but Israel has officially rejected its key provisions with unacceptable caveats and prerequisites."

CNBC, The Tim Russert Show, Dec. 2, 2006: "[The Road Map peace plan] was immediately adopted in its totality by the Palestinians, who still have no caveats and no objections to the Road Map terms."

FACT:
Mahmoud Abbas did, indeed, verbally express his support for the June 2003 document. But there is no evidence that the Palestinian Authority cabinet or parliament ever approved the Road Map, as would be required for such an international agreement. Indeed, there's no evidence it was ever even discussed by these bodies. Nor was Abbas clearly "dedicated" to achieving an "agreement in accordance with the Road Map."

He attached caveats to PA implementation of the Road Map. He insisted, for example, that Palestinian prisoners be released before he would take any required steps, even though prisoners were not mentioned in the agreement. He also flatly ruled out taking forcible action to disarm and dismantle the infrastructure of terror, saying he would rely on persuasion alone; Abbas thus flouted the most essential Palestinian commitment to the agreement and to achieving a stable peace. Violence against Israelis actually increased almost immediately after the signing of the Road Map. On June 11, 2003, Hamas blew up a bus in Jerusalem, killing 17 and wounding 100.

Regarding Ariel Sharon's response to the U.S. initiative, American officials made clear at the outset they expected feedback from the parties. A statement by Secretary of State Colin Powell and National Security Advisor Condoleezza Rice on May 23, 2003 underscored this:

> The roadmap was presented to the Government of Israel with a request from the President that it respond with contributions to this document to advance true peace. The United States Government received a response from the Government of Israel, explaining its significant concerns about the roadmap.
>
> The United States shares the view of the Government of Israel that these are real concerns, and will address them fully and seriously in the implementation of the roadmap to fulfill the President's vision of June 24, 2002.

Despite concerns, the Israeli Cabinet promptly endorsed the plan. As *Ha'aretz* reported on May 25, 2003:

> . . . the Israeli cabinet formally approved the U.S.-backed road map for an Israeli-Palestinian settlement yesterday. The cabinet approved the map—a three-phase plan that calls for a settlement freeze and an end to terror attacks in the first stage, a Palestinian state with temporary borders in the second and a final-status agreement by 2005—by a vote of 12–7, with four abstentions, at the end of a stormy six-hour debate . . .

Errors Concerning U.N. Resolution 425 and Lebanon

Carter misrepresents the facts regarding Israel's complete withdrawal from Lebanon in the spring of 2000, a withdrawal certified by the United Nations. Echoing allegations of some Arab groups, including Hezbollah, Carter claims Israel has not completely withdrawn from Lebanon.

CARTER:
Palestine: Peace Not Apartheid, Page 71: Israel has relinquished its control over . . . almost all of Lebanon . . .

Palestine: Peace Not Apartheid, Page 98: [A number of events influenced] Israel's decision in May 2000 to withdraw almost completely from Lebanon after eighteen years of occupation, retaining its presence only in Shebaa Farms.

FACT:
Israel did not "withdraw almost completely" from Lebanon. On June 16, 2000, United Nations Secretary General Kofi Annan reported to the Security Council that "Israeli forces have withdrawn from Lebanon in compliance with resolution 425" and "in compliance with the line of withdrawal identified by the United Nations."

(Security Council Resolution 425 called on Israel to "withdraw forthwith its forces from all Lebanese territory." The line identified by the United Nations "conform[ed] to the internationally recognized boundaries of Lebanon based on the best available cartographic and other documentary material.")

Two days later, the Security Council endorsed the Secretary General's conclusion that Israel had withdrawn from all Lebanese territory.

Errors Concerning U.N. Resolution 1701 and Hezbollah

CARTER:
Palestine: Peace Not Apartheid, Page 200: "Finally, on August 11, the United Nations Security Council passed resolution 1701, which provided that combat would cease and that 15,000 Lebanese troops and an equal number from the international community would be deployed in Southern Lebanon as both Israeli and Hezbollah military forces withdrew. *The key issues of prisoner exchange . . . and the disarming of Hezbollah were postponed . . .*" (emphasis added)

FACT:
In fact, an operative paragraph of UNSC Resolution 1701 calls for "full implementation of the relevant provisions of the Taif Accords, and of resolutions 1559 (2004) and 1680 (2006), that require the disarmament of all armed groups in Lebanon, so that, pursuant to the Lebanese cabinet decision of 27 July 2006, there will be no weapons or authority in Lebanon other than that of the Lebanese State."

And the third paragraph of the resolution emphasizes the need for an "unconditional release of the abducted Israeli soldiers," while the fourth paragraph also encourages "the efforts aimed at urgently settling the issue of the Lebanese prisoners detained in Israel."

MISREPRESENTING PEACE PROPOSALS, NEGOTIATIONS, AND OTHER INITIATIVES

. . .

Camp David/Taba Negotiations

CARTER:
Palestine: Peace Not Apartheid, Pages 150–51: "Later, during his last months in Washington, President Clinton made what he called his final proposal. Eighty percent of Israeli settlers would remain in the West Bank, and Israel could maintain its control of the Jordan River valley. . . .

"There was no clear response from Prime Minister Barak, but he later stated that Israel had twenty pages of reservations. President Arafat rejected the proposal. . . .

"The best offer to the Palestinians—by Clinton, not Barak—had been to withdraw 20 percent of the settlers, leaving more than 180,000 in 209 settlements, covering about 10 percent of the occupied land, including land to be 'leased' and portions of the Jordan River valley and East Jerusalem."

CNN, The Situation Room, Nov. 28, 2006: "You could check with all the records. Barak never did accept [the Clinton parameters]."

CNBC, The Tim Russert Show, Dec. 2, 2006: "The fact is that the proposals [Clinton] made were never accepted by either Barak on behalf of the Israelis or by the Palestinians' Arafat."

FACT:

Carter gets both the terms of the proposals and the responses of the Israelis and Palestinians wrong. For instance, according to Clinton's parameters, Israel would not "maintain its control of the Jordan Valley" as it had in the past. The proposal entailed "a small Israeli presence" under the authority of an international force that could remain in "fixed locations" but that would withdraw after a maximum of 36 months. Israel would withdraw from "between 94 and 96 percent of West Bank territory" and there would be a land swap of 1 to 3 percent.

Israeli Prime Minister Ehud Barak's response was clear—he accepted the parameters, as Dennis Ross, the chief U.S. negotiator, described in *The Missing Peace*, his definitive account of those discussions. Ross has also reiterated the facts in interviews since Carter's book appeared. In a December 8, 2006 segment on CNN's "Situation Room with Wolf Blitzer," there was the following exchange:

> **Blitzer:** Who is right, Jimmy Carter or Bill Clinton on this question which is so relevant as to whether or not the Israelis at Camp David at the end of the Bill Clinton administration accepted the proposals the U.S. put forward?
>
> **Ross:** The answer is President Clinton. The Israelis said yes to this twice. First at Camp David there were a set of proposals that were put on the table that they accepted. And then were the Clinton parameters, the Clinton ideas which were presented in December. Their government, meaning the cabinet, actually voted it. You can go back and check it, December 27th the year 2000, the cabinet voted to approve the Clinton proposal, the Clinton ideas. So this is—this is a matter of record. This is not a matter of interpretation.
>
> **Blitzer:** So you're saying Jimmy Carter is flat wrong.
>
> **Ross:** On this issue, he's wrong.

CARTER:

Palestine: Peace Not Apartheid, Page 148: Maps on this page are labeled: "Palestinian Interpretation of Clinton's Proposal 2000" and "Israeli Interpretation of Clinton's Proposal 2000."

FACT:

The maps are mislabeled. Dennis Ross, the U.S. peace negotiator who drew up the original version of Carter's maps, explained:

> The problem is that the "Palestinian interpretation" is actually taken from an Israeli map presented during the Camp David summit meeting in July 2000, while the "Israeli interpretation" is an approximation of what President Clinton subsequently proposed in December of that year. Without knowing this, the reader is left to conclude that the Clinton proposals must have been so ambiguous and unfair that Yasir Arafat, the Palestinian leader, was justified in rejecting them. But that is simply untrue.[4]

Prisoners' Proposal

CARTER:
Palestine: Peace Not Apartheid, Page 214: "The prisoners' proposal called for a unity government with Hamas joining the PLO, the release of all political prisoners, acceptance of Israel as a neighbor within its legal borders . . ."

FACT:
While calling for a Palestinian state in the West Bank and Gaza Strip, the so-called prisoners' proposal, formulated by Palestinians without any involvement of Israel, says nothing about "acceptance of Israel as a neighbor." Many Palestinian leaders have emphasized that the document entails no recognition of Israel whatsoever.

Abdul Rahman Zidan, a Palestinian government minster from Hamas's "Change and Reform" list, told the BBC: "You will not find one word in the document clearly stating the recognition of Israel as a state."[5]

Hamas leader Khalil Abu Leila said that "Fatah wants from us more than what is in this document. They want Hamas to recognize Israel and be a copy of Fatah, something that will not happen. . . . We will never recognize Israel."[6]

Salah Bardaweel, the leader of the Hamas faction in parliament, said: "We accept a state in [territory occupied] in 1967, but we did not say we accept two states."[7]

Syria's Assad and Negotiations

CARTER:
Palestine: Peace Not Apartheid, Page 130: ". . . when I visited Damascus in 1990, President Assad informed me that he was willing to negotiate with Israel on the status of the Golan Heights. His proposal was that both sides withdraw from the international border . . . [and] Syria might move its troops farther from the border because of the terrain."

FACT:
Former executive director of the Carter Center Kenneth Stein, who participated in the meeting with Carter and Assad, explained in a *Los Angeles Times* article that:

> his own notes of the Damascus meeting show that Assad, in response to a question from Carter, replied that Syria could not accept a demilitarized Golan without "sacrificing our sovereignty." Stein also disputed Carter's statement in the book that Assad expressed willingness to move Syria's troops farther from the border than Israel should be required to do.[8]

Errors Concerning Israel's Security Barrier

Much of Carter's commentary about the security barrier Israel erected as a defense against unprecedented terrorism originating from the West Bank echoes extreme anti-Israel propaganda. He terms the barrier an "imprisonment wall,"[9] a "segregation wall"[10] and a "segregation barrier;"[11] claims its purpose is "the acquisition of land"[12] and grossly misrepresents its location. He includes only passing and oblique mention of the actual purpose of the barrier in reducing death and destruction in Israel by Palestinian infiltrators. In the briefest of sanitized terms, he notes, for instance, that Israel drew lessons about the utility of constructing a barrier from the fence already built around Gaza, which had led to "a substantial decrease in *cross-border raids*."[13] Obviously, "cross-border raids" conveys little about the reality of terrorists murdering civilians. (And, of course, there's the misnomer in citing a "border.")

Likewise, he refers to "Israeli *arguments* that the wall is to keep Palestinian suicide bombers from Israel,"[14] as though Israel had contrived the excuse of terrorist infiltrators to launch its callous building project and as though the lives saved and attacks prevented were undocumented and debatable. Nearly a thousand Israelis had been murdered in terrorist attacks and thousands more injured in a span of three years beginning in September 2000, an onslaught that led to erecting the barrier. Within the first year, when significant portions were completed, the incidence of attacks had declined by nearly 90%. The book contains no data about the sharp reduction in deaths and injuries to Israelis. Nor is there any reference whatever to the bomb factories and terror-training in West Bank towns that spawned attackers who crossed sometimes within minutes into Israel to blow up Israeli civilians in buses, cafes and at religious events. The barrier is portrayed as one more gratuitous and cruel policy of a monstrously selfish Israel.

CARTER:

Palestine: Peace Not Apartheid, Page 189: "Their presumption is that an encircling barrier will finally resolve the Palestinian problem. Utilizing their political and military dominance, they are imposing a system of partial withdrawal, encapsulation, and apartheid on the Muslim and Christian citizens of the occupied territories. The driving purpose for the forced separation of the two peoples is unlike that in South Africa—not racism but the acquisition of land."

Palestine: Peace Not Apartheid, Page 190: "The governments of Ariel Sharon and Ehud Olmert have built the fence and wall entirely within Palestinian territory, intruding deeply into the West Bank to encompass Israeli settlement blocs and large areas of other Palestinian land."

CNBC, The Tim Russert Show, Dec. 2, 2006: "And this wall, unlike the Berlin Wall, which was built on East German territory, none of this wall is built on Israeli territory. It's all built inside the West Bank. . . . And in no place along that wall does it separate Palestinians from Israelis to protect Israelis. Everywhere the wall separates Palestinians from other Palestinians."

CSPAN2, Book TV, Dec. 3, 2006: ". . . this wall is not built between Palestinian land and Israeli land. No place does the wall touch Israel. The wall is entirely inside Palestine. And the wall is designed as it's presently planned and being built completely inside Palestine not to protect Israelis but to take Palestinian land, and all you have to do is look at a map . . . it shows the route of the wall."

Tavis Smiley Show, PBS, December 11, 2006: "In every inch of it, it separates Palestinian land from from other Palestinian land. And it's not designed to protect

Israelis from Palestinian attacks . . . What it's designed to do is to take away Palestinian land and that's what I'm trying to reveal in this book."

University of California, Berkeley, May 2, 2007: "In some cases [the wall] completely surrounds a city. For Qalia (sic) which is up in the northern part of the West Bank is wholly surrounded by a fence. It's well inside Palestinian territory . . . Bethlehem is completely surrounded by wall deep inside the West Bank."

FACT:
Carter's many assertions about the path and purpose of the barrier are totally spurious and divorced from reality. United Nations maps and numbers confirm that the barrier adheres to the "green line"—the armistice line marking the boundaries of the West Bank—along about 140 km (45 percent) of the green line's path. Contrary to Carter's obsessively-repeated and absurd contention that "in no place along that wall does it separate Palestinians from Israelis" but rather separates Palestinians from Palestinians—the barrier is situated between Israelis and Palestinians along most of its path.

Moreover, in some places the barrier also veers into Israeli territory. (For example, near Tulkarm and Al Mughayyir Al Mutilla.)

Carter's statements at Berkeley about Qalquilya are totally deceptive and distorted. Indeed, the town is essentially surrounded by the barrier because geographically it juts into Israel; it is not "well inside Palestinian territory" but the opposite. It directly abuts the Green Line on its western side and is adjacent to the Israeli city of Kfar Sava. Because of shooting by Palestinian gunmen from the Arab town into Israel, the wall is concrete in this stretch. Carter is equally inaccurate in describing Bethlehem. There the barrier curves along the northern half of the city, from which multiple suicide bombers have come. Bethlehem is not "completely surrounded."

CARTER:
Palestine: Peace Not Apartheid, Page 190: [The barrier] is projected to be at least three and a half times as long as Israel's internationally recognized border . . .

FACT:
The United Nations Office for the Coordination of Humanitarian Affairs notes that "Because of its meandering path into the West Bank, the [total 703 km length of the route] is more than twice the length of the "Green Line"—315 km."

MINIMIZING AND OMITTING ANTI-ISRAEL VIOLENCE AND ARAB REJECTIONISM

One of the most striking features of Carter's book is the near total omission of reference to the hatred and aggression directed against Israelis and Jews by Arab states and groups. A chronology of historical events omits Arab aggression in the 1930's as well as during the decades of international terrorism against Israelis and others that made aircraft hijacking and suicide bombing synonymous with the Palestinian cause. Israel's extreme adversaries, including those advocating the nation's destruction, are cast as benign and reasonable. Demonization of Jews in the media, mosques and political discourse of the Arab world is omitted completely. The net effect is to frame Israeli actions taken in self-defense against aggression as irrationally violent and those of Arafat, Hafez al Assad, Hamas, Hezbollah and other Arab actors as harmless and reasonable.

Whitewashing Arafat and Hamas

CARTER:
Palestine: Peace Not Apartheid, Page 62: When I met with Yasir Arafat in 1990, he stated, "The PLO has never advocated the annihilation of Israel. The Zionists started the 'drive the Jews into the sea' slogan and attributed it to the PLO."

FACT:
Were Carter to present Arafat's bizarre statement as a point of departure for exploring the man's view of events with a corrective reference to the full truth, the observation about the PLO and its leader never advocating annihilation of Israel—and claiming Zionists started slogans about their own destruction—would be of interest. But Carter presents such statements (including a litany of accusation against Israel by Syria's Hafez al Assad) as having merit.

The Palestinian cause as expressed by Arafat and the PLO is rooted in the goal of destroying Israel. The founding PLO charter speaks almost exclusively of "the liberation of Palestine" and calls on Palestinians to "move forward on the path of jihad until complete and final victory has been attained." (This was written in 1964, before Israel controlled the West Bank and Gaza Strip. Liberating "Palestine" referred not only to these areas but to all the territory between the Jordan River and the Mediterranean Sea—including Israel.) It adds: "The partitioning of Palestine, which took place in 1947, and the establishment of Israel are illegal and null and void . . ."

Likewise, the 1968 version of the charter describes "Palestine" as the area encompassing the West Bank, Gaza Strip and Israel, then states: "Armed struggle is the only way to liberate Palestine. This is the overall strategy, not merely a tactical phase."

Arafat himself frequently called for destroying Israel. An extensive interview in the March 29, 1970 *Washington Post* with famed journalist Oriana Fallaci contains multiple such statements, including:

> We shall never stop until we can go back home and Israel is destroyed.
>
> The goal of our struggle is the end of Israel, and there can be no compromises or mediations. Whether our friends like it or not, the dimensions of our struggle will always remain those outlined by the principles of Al Fateh: First, revolutionary violence is the only means for the liberation of the land of our forefathers; second, the goal of this violence is the elimination of Zionism from Palestine in all its political, economic and military aspects . . .

We don't want peace; we want victory. Peace for us means Israel's destruction and nothing else.

Similar statements appear through the decades as in "[p]eace for us means the destruction of Israel. We are preparing for an all-out war, a war which will last for generations" (*El Mundo* [Venezuela], Feb. 11, 1980). Arafat also regularly called for Jihad against Israel[15] and promoted the so-called phased plan to destroy Israel.[16]

And, contrary to Carter/Arafat, Arabs had long invoked the image of throwing the Jews into the sea. A *New York Times* column by Flora Lewis on April 10, 1988 recounted that Ahmed Shukairy, a founder of the PLO, had, "preached holy war at the Great Mosque in East Jerusalem the Friday before the Six-Day war began, promising to 'throw the Jews into the sea.' "

More recently, Lieutenant-Colonel Munir Maqdah, who had commanded Arafat's Fatah army in Lebanon before being suspended, said his forces would continue fighting "the Jews and their agents" despite any peace talks, promising that "[s]ooner or later we will throw the Zionists into the sea." (Reuters, Oct. 8, 1993)

CARTER:
Palestine: Peace Not Apartheid, Page 179: "Hamas was now [January 2006] holding many local posts, and their incumbent officials had been free of any allegations of corruption and, for sixteen months, had meticulously observed a cease-fire commitment, which they called hudna."

Palestine: Peace Not Apartheid, Page 184. "When I questioned him about the necessity for Hamas to renounce violence and recognize Israel, [Hamas member Dr. Mahmoud Ramahi] responded that they had not committed an act of violence since a cease-fire was declared in August 2004 . . ."

CNN, Larry King Live, Nov. 27, 2006: ". . . since August of 2004 . . . Hamas has not been guilty of an act of terrorism that cost an Israeli life."

PBS, NewsHour, November 28, 2006: Carter: ". . . since August of 2004, Hamas has not committed a single act of terrorism that cost an Israeli life, not a single one."

Canadian Broadcasting Corporation, December 8, 2006: "You have to look at the facts. That is, take Hamas, for instance, the number one organization that is accused. There hasn't been an Israeli life lost from Palestinian terrorism—that is Hamas—since August of 2004. They imposed unilaterally a cease-fire, which they call a hudna."

Tavis Smiley Show, PBS, December 11, 2006: ". . . almost a year and a half ago, Hamas declared a unilateral cease-fire. They call it a 'hudna.' And there hasn't been a single Israeli killed with a Hamas terrorist attack since August of 2004."

FACT:
At least a dozen Israeli civilians were murdered by Hamas members during the period in which, according to Carter's repeated statements, the group had "meticulously"

observed a cease-fire and had not "committed a single act of terrorism that cost an Israeli life, not a single one."

On Sept. 29, 2004, two preschool children, Yuval Abebeh, 4, and Dorit Benisian, 2, were killed by a Qassam rocket fired from Gaza into the Israeli town of Sderot. Hamas claimed responsibility.

On October 6, 2004, a 24 year-old greenhouse worker, Pratheep Nanongkham, was killed by a Hamas terrorist.

On January 2, 2005, 25 year-old Nissim Arbiv was killed in a Hamas attack while working at the Erez Industrial Park.

On Jan 13, 2005, Palestinian terrorists attacked the Karni crossing between the Gaza Strip and Israel, killing 6 civilians. The victims were Dror Gizri, 30, of Sderot; Ibrahim Kahili, 46, of Umm al-Ghanem; Munam Abu Sabia, 33, of Daburiyeh; Ivan Shmilov, 53, of Sderot; Herzl Shlomo, 51, of Sderot; and Ofer Tiri, 23, of Ashkelon. Hamas claimed joint responsibility.

On July 14, 2005, Dana Galkowicz, 22, was killed by a Qassam rocket fired from Gaza into Israel. Hamas claimed responsibility.

On September 21, 2005, Sasson Nuriel, 55, was kidnapped and murdered. Hamas claimed responsibility. . . .

CARTER:
In a dramatic instance of Carter's extreme efforts to deny reality, he argued with a radio interviewer who confronted him with a current example of Hamas Prime Minister Ismail Haniyeh reiterating the group's rejection of Israel's legitimacy and existence. The exchange went as follows:

KHOW-AM, The Caplis & Silverman Show (Denver), Dec. 12, 2006:

Silverman: Didn't the head of Hamas, the elected leader of the Palestinians, go to Tehran last week and say, "We will never recognize the usurper Zionist government. . . ."

Carter: No, he didn't.

Silverman: . . . and we will continue our jihad-like movement . . .

Carter: No, he didn't do that.

Silverman: until the liberation of Jerusalem?

Carter: No, he didn't do that. I saw no report about that.

FACT:
Many media outlets reported the statements of Haniyeh. The *International Herald Tribune*, for instance, carried an Associated Press account on December 8, 2006 whose essentials were similarly cited as well by many other newspapers and electronic media:

"Haniya soundly rejected such steps as he addressed thousands of worshipers at Tehran University. The United States and Israel, he said, 'want us to recognize the usurpation of the Palestinian lands and stop jihad and resistance and accept the agreements reached with the Zionist enemies in the past."

He added: "We will never recognize the usurper Zionist government and will continue our jihad-like movement until the liberation of Jerusalem."

Haniya said the policy of not recognizing Israel was "irreversible."

CARTER:
Palestine: Peace Not Apartheid, Page 8: "1996: Palestinians elect Yasir Arafat as president and elect the members of a legislative council. Israelis return the Likud Party to power, which stalls the Oslo process."

FACT:
In a chronology of events, Carter distorts cause and effect, omitting entirely the milestone terror attacks by Palestinians in February and March 1996 that killed 60 Israelis and derailed the Oslo process. As Reuters reported on March 3, 1996, "After last Sunday's Hamas bombings killed 26 people, [Labor leader Shimon] Peres lost a commanding lead in opinion polls."

CARTER:
Palestine: Peace Not Apartheid, Page 145: "Of 1,696 voting places outside Jerusalem [during the 1996 Palestinian elections], there were problems in only two. Three Palestinians were shot and killed by Israeli police at a checkpoint at Jenin . . ."

FACT:
Here Carter makes a gross error of omission. The Associated Press, *New York Times,* Agence France Press and others reported at the time that the Palestinians at the checkpoint were killed after opening fire on Israeli security forces. According to the *Boston Globe* on January 21, 1996, an Israeli soldier was wounded when the three—all Hamas members—"tried to shoot their way past an Israeli roadblock."

ISRAELI POLICIES AND MILITARY ACTIONS

In many passages, Carter makes false and derogatory references to Israel, whether in his recalled conversation with Hafez al Assad, who is said to have lamented Israeli racism and injustice, or in various baseless charges related to Israel's treatment of Palestinians, its participation in hostage negotiations and its actions in the Hezbollah war of 2006.

Land and Water Issues

CARTER:
Palestine: Peace Not Apartheid, Page 168: "Living among 1.3 million Palestinians, the 8,000 Israeli settlers [in the Gaza Strip] were controlling 40 percent of the arable land and more than one-half the water resources . . ."

FACT:
Settlers lived on roughly 15–20 percent of Gaza land, and controlled little of its water. In fact, Israel supplied, and continues to supply, large amounts of water to Palestinians in the Gaza Strip.

The *American Journalism Review* in August/September 2004 published the following correction after similarly mis-stating Gaza statistics: "In 'Caught in the Crossfire' (June/July 2004), Barbara Matusow wrote that Israeli settlers occupy

25 percent of the land in the Gaza Strip and control most of the water resources. According to the Institute of Applied Research in Jerusalem, the Palestinians control 95 percent of the water resources in Gaza. Estimates vary widely when it comes to control of the land, however. A June 2004 report on Gaza by the World Bank states that 15 to 20 percent of the land is occupied by settlements."

CARTER:
Palestine: Peace Not Apartheid, Page 121: "Each Israeli settler uses five times as much water as a Palestinian neighbor, who must pay four times as much per gallon."

FACT:
According to Sharif Elmusa, who was a water negotiator for the Palestinian side in talks with Israel, Palestinians in the West Bank pay approximately $1 per cubic meter for domestic water, "virtually identical with the price in Israel . . ."[17] While both Arab and Jewish Israelis use more water per capita than Palestinians, the ratio is just half of what Carter claims.[18]

Similarly, with regard to agricultural water, Elmusa writes: ". . . in absolute terms, the price of irrigation water in Israel, the West Bank, and Jordan converged, and water prices could not have affected competitiveness in any significant way."[19]

In fact, some Palestinians—those in Jericho, Tulkarm and Gaza—have paid substantially less for water than the typical Israeli household.

CARTER:
Palestine: Peace Not Apartheid, Page 151: "There is a zone with a radius of about four hundred meters around each settlement within which Palestinians cannot enter."

FACT:
Not only do Palestinians routinely enter within four hundred meters of Israeli settlements, they frequently enter into the settlements. For example, Palestinians from villages near the Israeli settlement of Ariel work alongside Israelis at a textile factory in the settlement.

Interrogation Legalities

CARTER:
Palestine: Peace Not Apartheid, Page 197: "Confessions extracted through torture are admissible in Israeli courts."

FACT:
Under Israeli criminal procedures, when a person claims that his confession was extracted via torture, a "trial-within-a-trial" is immediately held (in Hebrew mishpat zuta) in which the prosecution must prove that torture or other illegitimate means were not used. If the prosecution is unable to disprove claims of torture the confession is thrown out. In addition, if it appears that other illegal means short of torture were used, the confession can be admitted, but only if the court finds that the interrogation did not prejudice the defendant's free will.[20]

GILAD SHALIT KIDNAPPING

Typical of factual errors that minimize Israeli vulnerability and denigrate the nation's efforts to cope with violence is Carter's account of the June 2006 kidnapping of Gilad Shalit and killing of two Israeli soldiers in Israel by Palestinians from Gaza. He neglects to mention the killings, then misrepresents the Palestinians' terms for a prisoner swap and wrongly claims Israel "rejected any negotiations."

CARTER:

Palestine: Peace Not Apartheid, Page 197: "The cycle of violence erupted once more in June 2006, when Palestinians dug a tunnel under the barrier that surrounds Gaza and attacked some Israeli soldiers, capturing one of them. They offered to exchange the soldier for the release of 95 women and 313 children who are among some 8,500 Palestinians in Israeli prisons. Israel rejected any negotiations . . ."

CSPAN2, Book TV, December 3, 2006: ". . . And what the Palestinians asked for is, 'We'll swap you this one soldier [Gilad Shalit] if you'll just release some of the hundred women you're holding—about a hundred—or some of the little children you're holding . . . ,' and the Israeli government refused to swap. . . . "

FACT:

On June 26, 2006, CNN reported: "Palestinian militants distributed a statement Monday saying they will provide *information* about a kidnapped Israeli soldier if Israel agrees to release all female prisoners and all children under 18 being held in Israeli jails." (Emphasis added.)

Israel's *Ha'aretz* newspaper on July 12, 2006 subsequently reported: "For its part, Hamas is demanding that 400 prisoners be freed in the first part of the deal, and 500 each in the two subsequent parts of the exchange. Israel would like to limit that figure. However, a senior Israeli source said this week that it is possible that Israel will agree to the release of as many as 1,000 Palestinians." According to the same *Ha'aretz,* story, one of the prisoners Hamas demanded Israel release is "Abbas Sayed, the mastermind of the massacre at the Park Hotel in Netanya over Passover in 2002, in which 29 civilians were killed."

A January 3, 2007 *Jerusalem Post* story reported: "A senior Hamas official said Thursday his group was ready to give Israel a videotape of the soldier if it agreed to release Palestinian women prisoners and other detainees." The article suggests the videotape-prisoner swap would be prelude to a further exchange. Ahmed Youssef, political advisor to Palestinian Authority Prime Minister Ismail Haniyeh, "claimed that Israel had agreed to release 200 prisoners who had been sentenced to long prison terms, including senior officials from Hamas and other Palestinian factions."

Finally, regarding Carter's charge that Israel holds over 300 Palestinian "children" or "little children", it's not clear exactly what age he is referring to, but in 1967, under Jordan and Egypt, the "age of criminal responsibility" in the West Bank and Gaza was nine. Israel raised it to 12, and rarely if ever prosecutes any children under the age of 14.[21] Thus, even according to Palestinian statistics, as of July 2005 there was just one detainee between the ages of 12 and 13, and three between the ages of 13 and 14; the largest number by far, 130, were at least 17 years old.[22] In 2006, also according to Palestinian statistics, no children 14 years or younger were sentenced by Israel. To put these ages in context, it should be noted that in the PA under Article 67 of the Palestinian Child Law, the age of criminal responsibility is just nine, while in Mr. Carter's home state of Georgia, where he served as governor, the age is as low as 13 for serious crimes.

Hezbollah War

CARTER:
Palestine: Peace Not Apartheid, Page 201: "What were the causes and results of the Israeli-Lebanese war? The conflict began when Hezbollah militants attacked two Israeli vehicles, killing three soldiers and capturing two others. . . . Israel . . . surprisingly declared that it had been assaulted by the entire nation of Lebanon, and launched an aeriel bombardment . . ."

FACT:
Carter omits mention that the attack was in Israel, and Hezbollah fired rockets across northern Israel as part of the assault, one of them scoring a direct hit on a home and wounding four. As far as his surprise that Israel held Lebanon responsible, Hezbollah was a key member of the Lebanese government, and that government's Policy Guidelines stated support for Hezbollah's attacks against Israel: "Protection of [Hezbollah] and recognition that it is a genuine Lebanese manifestation of our right to liberate our lands from any occupation." Notwithstanding Hezbollah's political role in Lebanon, Israel confined its retaliation to Hezbollah strongholds and left unscathed most of the nation.

---

1. United Nations Security Council Resolution 242, November 22, 1967
   The Security Council,
   Expressing its continuing concern with the grave situation in the Middle East,
   Emphasizing the inadmissibility of the acquisition of territory by war and the need
       to work for a just and lasting peace in which every State in the area can live in
       security,
   Emphasizing further that all Member States in their acceptance of the Charter of the
       United Nations have undertaken a commitment to act in accordance with Article
       two of the Charter,

   > *Affirms* that the fulfillment of Charter principles requires the establishment of
   > a just and lasting peace in the Middle East which should include the application of both the following principles:

   >> Withdrawal of Israeli armed forces from territories occupied in the recent
   >> conflict;
   >> Termination of all claims or states of belligerency and respect for and
   >> acknowledgement of the sovereignty, territorial integrity and political independence of every State in the area and their right to live in peace within
   >> secure and recognized boundaries free from threats or acts of force;

   > *Affirms further* the necessity

   >> For guaranteeing freedom of navigation through international waterways
   >> in the area;

For achieving a just settlement of the refugee problem;

For guaranteeing the territorial inviolability and political independence of every State in the area, through measures including the establishment of demilitarized zones;

Requests the Secretary General to designate a Special Representative to proceed to the Middle East to establish and maintain contacts with the States concerned in order to promote agreement and assist efforts to achieve a peaceful and accepted settlement in accordance with the provisions and principles in this resolution;

Requests the Secretary-General to report to the Security Council on the progress of the efforts of the Special Representative as soon as possible.

2. *Journal of Palestine Studies,* "An Interview with Lord Caradon," Spring–Summer 1976, pp. 144–145.
3. The MacNeil-Lehrer Report, March 30, 1978.
4. *New York Times,* January 9, 2007.
5. *Philadelphia Inquirer,* June 28, 2006.
6. *Boston Globe,* June 29, 2006.
7. *Chicago Tribune,* June 29, 2006.
8. *Los Angeles Times,* January, 17, 2006.
9. *Palestine: Peace Not Apartheid,* page 174.
10. Ibid, page 191.
11. Ibid, page 192.
12. Ibid, page 190.
13. Ibid, page 190.
14. Ibid, page 194.
15. *Yediot Ahronot,* October 23, 1996: "We know only one word—jihad. jihad, jihad, jihad. Whoever does not like it can drink from the Dead Sea or from the Sea of Gaza."
16. Radio Monte Carlo, September 1, 1993: "[The Oslo agreement] will be a basis for an independent Palestinian state in accordance with the Palestinian National Council resolution issued in 1974 . . . The PNC resolution issued in 1974 calls for the establishment of a national authority on any part of Palestinian soil from which Israel withdraws or which is liberated."
17. Sharif S. Elmusa, *Water Conflict: Economics, Politics, Law and Palestinian-Israeli Water Resources,* page 144.
18. Statistical Abstract of Israel, 1996.
19. Elmusa, page 173.
20. See for example, *The Right to a Fair Trial,* D. Weissbrodt and R. Wolfrum, eds., Springer, 1997.
21. Human Rights in the Administered Areas, Justus Reid Weiner, Wisconsin International Law Journal, Vol. 10, No. 2, Spring 1992, pp 221–222.
22. Palestinian Political Child Prisoners in Israeli Prison—Monthly Update Until 5 of July 2005, Child and Youth Department, Ministry of Detainees and Ex-Detainees Affairs; http://www.edrp.gov.ps/CYD/CYD%20Report%20705.pdf.

NOTES

INTRODUCTION

1. William J. Brennan, "The Quest to Develop a Jurisprudence of Civil Liberties in Times of Security Crisis," paper delivered in Jerusalem, December 22, 1987. Thanks to Einer Elhaugue for bringing this to my attention.
2. Jeffrey Goldberg, "Is Israel Finished?" *Atlantic*, May 2008, p. 40.
3. Susannah Heschel, "Ad Condemning Anti-Semitism on Campuses Misses the Point," JTA, October 14, 2002, www.jta.org/cgi-bin/iowa/news/article/20021015AdcondemningantiS.html.
4. J. Lorand Matory, "Israel and Censorship at Harvard," *Harvard Crimson*, September 14, 2007.
5. Thomas L. Friedman, "Campus Hypocrisy," *New York Times*, October 16, 2002.
6. Phyllis Chesler and Nancy Kobrin, "Psychological Roots of Islamic Rage," *Jewish Press*, August 9, 2006.
7. Protests before a Berkeley, California, speech by Benjamin Netanyahu in 2000 were so out of control that the talk was canceled for security reasons, as were two others scheduled in the area. See Charles Burress, "Security Fears Cancel Speeches by Netanyahu," *San Francisco Chronicle*, November 30, 2000; also Charles Burress, "Infringing on Free Speech," *San Francisco Chronicle*, December 10, 2000. His speech, as well as one by Ehud Barak, were canceled by Concordia University.
8. This anti-Israel atmosphere was well captured by an editorial cartoon in the October 6, 2007, *Boston Herald* that showed former Harvard president Lawrence Summers, whose scheduled speech had been canceled by the University of California Board of Regents, imploring the university to change its mind by saying: "I didn't mean that men are more interested in science than women. What I really meant was that Israel should be wiped off the map. Now can I speak at your university?"
9. Daniel Schwammenthal, "The Israel-Bashing Club," *Wall Street Journal*, September 3, 2007.
10. Barbara Amiel, "Islamists Overplay Their Hand but London Salons Don't See It," *Daily Telegraph* (UK), December 17, 2001.

11. "'Anti-Semitic' French envoy under fire," *BBC News,* December 20, 2001.
12. I have repeatedly been asked to compile a book of the hate mail I have received over the years, mostly regarding Israel. It would be a fascinating and informative collection, but I have hesitated out of concern for giving the haters a platform.
13. Alan M. Dershowitz, *Preemption: A Knife That Cuts Both Ways* (New York: W. W. Norton, 2006), p. 175.
14. Charles Krauthammer, "In Iran, Arming for Armageddon," *Jewish World Review,* December 16, 2005 (www.jewishworldreview.com/1205/krauthammer121605. php3?printer_friendly).

1. THE CASE AGAINST PRESIDENT JIMMY CARTER

1. Susan Fraker, "The Carter Brain Trust," *Newsweek,* June 21, 1976.
2. Jewish Agency for Israel, "1978," www.jewishagency.org/JewishAgency/English/ Jewish+Education/Compelling+Content/Jewish+History/Zionist+Institutions/ JAFI+Timeline/1978.htm.
3. Daniel Freedman, "President Carter Interceded on Behalf of Former Nazi Guard," *New York Sun,* January 19, 2007, www.nysun.com/article/46972?page_no=1.
4. Associated Press, "Carter Says It Is Necessary to Talk with Hamas," *International Herald Tribune,* April 13, 2008.
5. Jimmy Carter, on the *Tavis Smiley Show,* Public Broadcasting Service, December 11, 2006, www.pbs.org/kcet/tavissmiley/archive/200612/20061211_carter.html.
6. Farah Stockman and Marcella Bombardieri, "Carter Book Won't Stir Brandeis Debate," *Boston Globe,* December 15, 2006, www.boston.com/news/education/ higher/articles/2006/12/15/carter_book_wont_stir_brandeis_debate/?page=2.
7. Alan Dershowitz, "The World According to Jimmy Carter," *Huffington Post,* November 22, 2006, www.huffingtonpost.com/alan-dershowitz/the-world-according-to-ji_b_ 34702.html.
8. Jimmy Carter, in Stockman and Bombardieri, "Carter Book Won't Stir Brandeis Debate," n. 5.
9. Alan Dershowitz, "Why Won't Carter Debate His Book?" *Boston Globe,* December 21, 2006, p. A15.
10. Alan Dershowitz, remarks at Brandeis University, January 23, 2007, www.brandeis. edu/offices/communications/events/200701carter.html.
11. Jennifer Hoar, "Carter: 'Apartheid' Is Apt for West Bank," *CBS News,* March 8, 2007, www.cbsnews.com/stories/2007/03/08/politics/main2550072.shtml?source= RSSattr=World_2550072. Carter stated the following at Brandeis:

> But let the debate take place, and I've never responded to any of the people that have made their attacks on me. I understand there is a Harvard professor that has done so. I turned down a meeting with him; I felt, I didn't think that Brandeis needed a Harvard professor to come here and tell you how to ask questions. But to summarize my answer I think it is going to be much easier in the future not only in this campus but around the nation to debate these issues.

For a full transcript of Carter's remarks at Brandeis, see http://my.brandeis.edu/ news/item?news_item_id=7816. For a video of both his speech and my own, see www. brandeis.edu/offices/communications/events/200701carter.html.
12. David Abel, "Carter Agrees to Speak at Brandeis," *Boston Globe,* January 11, 2007, www.boston.com/news/local/articles/2007/01/11/carter_agrees_to_speak_at_ brandeis/. Another article stated, "A member of Carter's staff later asked whether

Reinharz could extend an invitation, instead, so [Eisenstadt] said he approached Reinharz with an idea: invite Carter to debate Dershowitz, who had recently reviewed Carter's book and who had previously expressed a desire to debate Carter several times." Carter, however, was stunned by the proposal: "I don't want to have a conversation even indirectly with Dershowitz," Carter said. "There is no need to for me to debate somebody who, in my opinion, knows nothing about the situation in Palestine." Stockman and Bombardieri, "Carter Book Won't Stir Brandeis Debate."

13. See Alan Dershowitz, "Jimmy Carter Is a Liar," *Huffington Post*, March 12, 2007.
14. "Rice says Carter was warned against meeting with Hamas," *Associated Press*, April 22, 2008, www.breitbart.com/article.php?id=D90708G80&show_article=1.
15. Robert F. Worth, "Rice Suggests Carter Confused Peace Process," *New York Times*, April 23, 2008.
16. William Rubenstein, *Genocide: A History* (London: Pearson, 2004), pp. 305–306. See the French, British, Russian, and American joint declaration:

> Department of State, Washington
> May 29, 1915
> Amembassy [American Embassy], Constantinople.
> French Foreign Office requests following notice be given Turkish Government.
> Quote. May 24th
> For about a month the Kurd and Turkish populations of Armenia has [*sic*] been massacring Armenians with the connivance and often assistance of Ottoman authorities. Such massacres took place in middle April (new style) at Erzerum, Dertchun, Eguine, Akn, Bitlis, Mush, Sassun, Zeitun, and throughout Cilicia. Inhabitants of about one hundred villages near Van were all murdered. In that city Armenian quarter is besieged by Kurds. At the same time in Constantinople Ottoman Government ill-treats inoffensive Armenian population. In view of those new crimes of Turkey against humanity and civilization, the Allied governments announce publicly to the Sublime-Porte that they will hold personally responsible [for] these crimes all members of the Ottoman government and those of their agents who are implicated in such massacres.

> R.G. 59, 867.4016/67
> Available at www.armenian-genocide.org/Affirmation.160/current_category.7/affirmation_detail.html.

17. Jeffrey Goldberg, "What Would Jimmy Do? A Former President Puts the Onus for Resolving the Mideast Conflict on the Israelis," *Washington Post*, December 10, 2006, p. T03.
18. Carter, *Palestine: Peace Not Apartheid* (New York: Simon & Schuster, 2006), p. 190, n. 3.
19. Jimmy Carter, speech at Brandeis University, Waltham, Massachusetts, January 23, 2007, http://my.brandeis.edu/news/item?news_item_id=7816.
20. Irshad Manji, "Modern Israel Is a Far Cry from Old South Africa," *Australian*, February 9, 2007, www.theaustralian.news.com.au/story/0,20867,21194124–7583,00.html.
21. The quote was printed on the conference program for an anti-Israel hate-fest titled "The Apartheid Paradigm in Palestine-Israel," hosted at Boston's Old South Church in October 2007. Al-Fassed denies that he deliberately intended to mislead people but has been less than diligent in informing fellow anti-Israel radicals that the Mandela quote is make-believe.
22. "West 'Pandering to Darfur Rebels,' " BBC News, October 4, 2007, http://news.bbc.co.uk/1/hi/world/africa/7028267.stm.
23. Quoted in Eric Reeves, "Jimmy Carter's Shamefully Ignorant Statement on Darfur," *New Republic*, October 8, 2007, www.tnr.com/doc.mhtml?i=w071008&s=reeves100807.

24. Alan M. Dershowitz, "The World According to Carter," *New York Sun,* November 22, 2006.
25. Jimmy Carter, "A New Chance for Peace?" *Washington Post,* January 18, 2007.
26. He repeated variations of this statement elsewhere. In an interview with Tavis Smiley (December 11, 2006) he insisted, "The book is absolutely true, and it tells about the horrible, almost unbelievable abuse of Palestinians in their own land, where the land has been occupied, confiscated, and then colonized by the occupying powers." He told CNN's Soledad O'Brien on December 13, 2006, "I know what I'm talking about and the book in completely accurate." Committee for Accuracy in Middle East Reporting in America, *Bearing False Witness: Jimmy Carter's Palestine Peace Not Apartheid* (Boston: CAMERA, 2007), p. 7.
27. Carter, *Palestine: Peace Not Apartheid,* p. 59.
28. See "The Khartoum Resolutions, September 1, 1967," *Avalon Project* (Yale Law School), www.yale.edu/lawweb/avalon/mideast/khartoum.htm.
29. See, for example, Sam Pope Brewer, "11-Day Fight Over; 350 Israeli Combatants Are Captives—Hurva Synagogue Razed," *New York Times,* May 29, 1948.
30. Carter, *Palestine: Peace Not Apartheid,* p. 126.
31. Ibid., p. 148.
32. Ibid., pp. 198, 201. See also William J. Brennan, "The Quest to Develop a Jurisprudence of Civil Liberties in Times of Security Crisis," paper delivered in Jerusalem, December 22, 1987.
33. Geneva Convention Relative to the Treatment of Prisoners of War, entered into force October 21, 1950, www.unhchr.ch/html/menu3/b/91.htm.
34. "Jimmy Carter," *JewishVirtualLibrary.org,* www.jewishvirtuallibrary.org/jsource/US-Israel/presquote.html.
35. Rhoda Kadalie and Julia Bertelsmann, "Franchising 'Apartheid': Why South Africans Push the Analogy," *Z-Word.com,* March 2008, www.z-word.com/z-word-essays/franchising-%25E2%2580%259Capartheid%25E2%2580%259D%253A-why-south-africans-push-the-analogy.html.
36. Ibid., p. 2.
37. Michael F. Brown, "Dems Rebut Carter on Israeli 'Apartheid,'" The Nation.com, November 20, 2006, www.thenation.com/doc/20061204/brown.
38. *Hardball with Chris Matthews,* MSNBC television broadcast, November 28, 2006 (transcript on file with LEXIS).
39. Ibid.
40. Carter, *Palestine: Peace Not Apartheid,* p. 209.
41. Beshara Doumani, "Palestine versus the Palestinians? The Iron Laws and Ironies of a People Denied," *Journal of Palestine Studies* 26, no. 4 (Summer 2007): 62.
42. Alan Dershowitz, "Has Carter Crossed the Line?" *Jerusalem Post,* December 21, 2006, www.jpost.com/servlet/Satellite?cid=1164881943132&pagename=JPost%2FJPArticle%2FShowFull.
43. Transcript of *Larry King Live* interview with Jimmy Carter, CNN, November 27, 2006, http://transcripts.cnn.com/TRANSCRIPTS/0611/27/lkl.01.html.
44. Jimmy Carter, "Speaking Frankly about Israel and Palestine," *Los Angeles Times,* December 8, 2006, www.latimes.com/news/opinion/la-oe-carter8dec08,0,7544738.story.
45. Ibid.
46. Ibid.
47. *Meet the Press* with Tim Russert, NBC television broadcast, December 3, 2006.
48. Carter, speech at Brandeis, available at http://my.brandeis.edu/news/item?news_item_id=7816.

49. Suggestions of anti-Semitism dogged Carter from his first campaign for president; see Charles Mohr, "Carter Gets an Ovation after Assuring Jews in Jersey on His Religious Views," *New York Times*, June 7, 1976; George Cornell, "Carter Denounces Accusation That the Jews Killed Christ," *New York Times*, May 14, 1977. See also www.antisemite.org.

50. Andrew and Leslie Cockburn, *Dangerous Liaison: The Inside Story of the U.S.-Israeli Covert Relationship* (New York: HarperCollins, 1991), p. 313.

51. Douglas Brinkley, *The Unfinished Presidency: Jimmy Carter's Journey beyond the White House* (New York: Viking Press, 1998) pp. 328, 345.

52. See the Carter Center Annual Report for 1998–1999, p. 30 (www.cartercenter.org/documents/520.pdf); the Annual Report for 2006–2007 (www.cartercenter.org/documents/annual_report_07.pdf), p. 60; and each year in between under "Founders" (www.cartercenter.org/news/publications/annual_reports.html).

53. Rachel Ehrenfeld, "Carter's Arab Financiers," *Washington Times*, December 21, 2006, p. A23.

54. Jimmy Carter, Acceptance Speech in the United Arab Emirates, April 21, 2001, transcript available at www.cartercenter.org/news/documents/doc447.html.

55. Anti-Defamation League of B'nai B'rith, "ADL Backgrounder: The Zayed Center," www.adl.org/Anti_semitism/zayed_center.asp.

56. Carter, speech at Brandeis, available at http://my.brandeis.edu/news/item?news_item_id=7816.

57. Jimmy Carter, statement to UN Human Rights Council, March 29, 2007, www.cartercenter.org/news/pr/humanrightscouncil_032907.html.

58. Interview by Al-Jazeera with Jimmy Carter, January 14, 2007, www.memritv.org/clip/en/1355.htm. Note that the MEMRI translation omits the word *really*, which can be heard beneath the Arabic voice-over.

59. Ibid.

60. Joseph Lelyveld, "Jimmy Carter and Apartheid," *New York Review of Books*, March 29, 2007, www.nybooks.com/articles/19993.

61. Betty Glad, quoted in *American Experience: Jimmy Carter*, Public Broadcasting Service, transcript of documentary film, www.pbs.org/wgbh/amex/carter/filmmore/pt.html.

62. Joshua Muravchik, "Our Worst Ex-President," *Commentary*, February 2007, p. 17.

63. "Timorese Protest at July 4 Party at U.S. Mission," press release, East Timor Action Network, July 4, 2000, www.scoop.co.nz/stories/WO0007/S00012.htm.

64. Amnesty International, *Power and Impunity: Human Rights under the New Order*, 1994, www.amnesty.org/ailib/intcam/indopub/indoint.htm.

65. Martha Wenger, "Reagan Stakes Morocco in Sahara Struggle," *Middle East Report* (May 1982): 24.

66. Jimmy Carter, "The United States and China: A President's Perspective," inaugural Oksenberg lecture at Stanford University, May 6, 2002, transcript available at www.cartercenter.org/documents/1041.doc.

67. See Frank Litsky, "Carter, in Plea to Athletes, Is Firm on Olympic Ban," *New York Times*, March 22, 1980; Steven Weisman, "New Olympic Boycott Drive," *New York Times*, April 5, 1980; Steven Weisman, "Carter Weighing Economic Move to Enforce Boycott of Olympics," *New York Times*, April 10, 1980. Carter said that he'd prefer not to revoke passports, but never officially took the threat off the table.

68. "Carter's Unhelpful Freelancing," *Boston Globe*, April 21, 2008.

69. Muravchik, "Our Worst Ex-President."

70. Shimon Peres, on *The Charlie Rose Show*, November 30, 2006.

71. Carter, *Palestine: Peace Not Apartheid*, p. 32.

72. See Kenneth W. Stein, "My Problem with Jimmy Carter's Book," *Middle East Quarterly*, Spring 2007.

73. Carter, *Palestine: Peace Not Apartheid,* 143.
74. Brinkley, *The Unfinished Presidency.*
75. Joseph Lelyveld, "Jimmy Carter and Apartheid," *New York Review of Books,* March 29, 2007, www.nybooks.com/articles/19993.
76. Elaine Sciolino, "Self-Appointed Israeli and Palestinian Negotiators Offer a Plan for Middle East Peace," *New York Times,* December 2, 2003, p. A8.
77. "The Carter Version: A President Remembers," *Economist,* December 16, 2006, p. 86.
78. See Dennis Ross, "Don't Play with Maps," *New York Times,* January 9, 2007.
79. See Jennifer Siegel, "'Apartheid' Book Exposes Carter-Clinton Rift; Clinton: 'I Don't Know Where His Information Came From,'" *Jewish Daily Forward,* March 30, 2007.
80. Carter, *Palestine: Peace Not Apartheid,* p. 152.
81. World Conference against Racism NGO Forum Declaration, September 3, 2001, www-personal.umich.edu/~hfc/mideast/NGO_WCAR.htm.
82. "Racial Discrimination, Xenophobia and Related Intolerance," Daily Press Briefing, World Conference against Racism, Durban, South Africa, September 7, 2001, www.un.org/WCAR/pressreleases/db090701.htm.
83. Steven Emerson, "Money Laundering and Terror Financing Issues in the Middle East," testimony before the U.S. Senate Committee of Banking, Housing, and Urban Affairs, July 13, 2005, banking.senate.gov/_files/emerson.pdf.
84. Desmond Tutu, Keynote Address at Sabeel Conference, Old South Church, Boston, October 27, 2007.
85. Kadalie and Bertelsmann, "Franchising 'Apartheid': Why South Africans Push the Analogy."
86. Desmond Tutu, "An International Campaign: Build Moral Pressure to End the Occupation," *International Herald Tribune,* June 14, 2002, www.iht.com/articles/2002/06/14/edtutu_ed3_.php.
87. Desmond Tutu, "Apartheid in the Holy Land," *Guardian,* April 29, 2002, www.guardian.co.uk/world/2002/apr/29/comment
88. See also his op-ed agreeing completely with Carter's specious characterization: John Dugard, "Apartheid: Israelis Adopt What South Africa Dropped," *Atlanta Journal-Constitution,* November 29, 2006.
89. John Dugard, "Implementation of General Assembly Resolution 60/251 of 15 March 2006 Entitled 'Human Rights Council'—Report of the Special Rapporteur on the Situation of Human Rights in the Palestinian Territories Occupied since 1967," Human Rights Council, A/HRC/4/17, January 29, 2007, p. 20.
90. John Dugard, Report of the Special Rapporteur on the situation of human rights in the Palestinian territories occupied since 1967, January 29, 2007, UN Document A/HRC/4/17, pp. 6, 20, 23.
91. Speech at the Kennedy School of Government, moderated by Professor Duncan Kennedy, October 25, 2007.
92. John Dugard, Report of the Special Rapporteur on the situation of human rights in the Palestinian territories occupied since 1967, January 21, 2008, UN Document A/HRC/7/17, p. 6.
93. See Richard Falk, "Slouching toward a Palestinian Holocaust," *Transnational Foundation for Peace and Future Research,* June 29, 2007, www.transnational.org/Area_MiddleEast/2007/Falk_PalestineGenocide.html. This article also appeared on several other Web sites.
94. Jewish Telegraph Agency, "Poll Finds US support for Israel Soaring," *Jerusalem Post,* May 7, 2007, www.jpost.com/servlet/Satellite?cid=1178431587241&pagename=JPost%2FJPArticle%2FShowFull.
95. See, for example, Bernard-Henri Lévy, "The Sad End of Jimmy Carter," *Wall Street Journal,* April 25, 2008.

2. THE CASE AGAINST PROFESSORS JOHN MEARSHEIMER AND STEPHEN WALT

1. See Alan Dershowitz, *The Best Defense* (New York: Random House, 1982), pp. 3–84.
2. John J. Mearsheimer and Stephen M. Walt, "The Israel Lobby and U.S. Foreign Policy," John F. Kennedy School of Government Faculty Research Working Paper Series, March 2006, http://ksgnotes1.harvard.edu/Research/wpaper.nsf/rwp/RWP06–011/$File/rwp_06_011_walt.pdf.
3. Alan Dershowitz, "Debunking the Newest—and Oldest—Jewish Conspiracy: A Reply to the Mearsheimer-Walt 'Working Paper,'" April 2006, www.hks.harvard.edu/research/working_papers/dershowitzreply.pdf.
4. Mearsheimer and Walt, "The Israel Lobby and U.S. Foreign Policy" (2006), p. 18.
5. Ibid., p. 18.
6. Ibid., p. 23.
7. Ibid., p. 17.
8. Ibid., pp. 5, 6.
9. Ibid., pp. 9, 11, 12.
10. Ibid., p. 40.
11. Exodus 1:10 (King James Bible).
12. David Duke, "A Real Breakthrough in the Battle for Truth!" DavidDuke.com, March 20, 2006, www.davidduke.com/?p=501. As the old saying goes, "Even the devil knows the truth."
13. Eli Lake, "David Duke Claims to Be Vindicated by a Harvard Dean," *New York Sun*, March 20, 2006, p. 1.
14. John J. Mearsheimer and Stephen M. Walt, *The Israel Lobby and U.S. Foreign Policy* (New York: Farrar, Straus and Giroux, 2007), p. viii.
15. Ori Nir, "Professor Says American Publisher Turned Him Down," *Forward*, March 24, 2006; "In this case, the unsayable was punished with a book advance of three-quarters of a million dollars," in Michael Gerson, "Seeds of Anti-Semitism," *Washington Post*, September 21, 2007.
16. Alan Dershowitz, "A Challenge to Walt and Mearsheimer's Publisher," Huffington Post, November 3, 2006, www.huffingtonpost.com/alan-dershowitz/a-challenge-to walt-and-m_b_33191.html.
17. Ibid.
18. Charles A. Radin, "'Israel Lobby' Critique Roils Academe," *Boston Globe*, March 29, 2006; Lake, "David Duke Claims to Be Vindicated by a Harvard Dean."
19. Middle East/North Africa Weekend, Harvard University, November 30–December 1, 2007, www.harvardarabalumni.org/MENAweekend/speakers.htm.
20. The Investigative Project on Terrorism, "Groups and Networks: The Council on American-Islamic Relations (CAIR)," March 2008, www.investigativeproject.org/profile/172.
21. Mearsheimer and Walt cite Finkelstein on three separate occasions in their original essay to back their historical and political claims. In their book, however, they cite him only once—not as an academic authority but as a supposed victim of academic censorship. In truth, Finkelstein has been discredited because of his shoddy, vendetta-driven scholarship—as Mearsheimer and Walt themselves implicitly acknowledge by dropping him as a source for any other purpose.
22. Mearsheimer and Walt, *The Israel Lobby and U.S. Foreign Policy* (2007), p. 14.

23. Richard Benedetto, "Poll: Most Back War, but Want U.N. Support," *USA Today*, Sunday, March 16, 2003, www.usatoday.com/news/world/iraq/2003–03–16-poll-iraq_x.htm.
24. Dalia Sussman, "Poll Shows View of Iraq War Is Most Negative since Start," *New York Times*, Friday, May 25, 2007, www.nytimes.com/2007/05/25/washington/25view.html?_r=2&adxnnl=1&oref=slogin&adxnnlx.
25. Hofstadter wrote:

    In the history of the United States one finds it [paranoid-style politics], for example, in the anti-Masonic movement, the nativist and anti-Catholic movement, in certain spokesmen of abolitionism who regarded the United States as being in the grip of a slaveholders' conspiracy, in many alarmists about the Mormons, in some Greenback and Populist writers who constructed a great conspiracy of international bankers, in the exposure of a munitions makers' conspiracy of World War I, in the popular left-wing press, in the contemporary American right wing, and on both sides of the race controversy today, among White Citizens' Councils and Black Muslims.

    Richard Hofstadter, "The Paranoid Style in American Politics," http://karws.gso.uri.edu/jfk/conspiracy_theory/the_paranoid_mentality/the_paranoid_style.html. The essay is referenced and related to the Walt-Mearsheimer paper in Max Boot, "Policy Analysis–Paranoid Style," *Los Angeles Times*, March 29, 2006.
26. Mearsheimer and Walt, "Setting the Record Straight: A Response to Critics of 'The Israel Lobby,'" December 12, 2006, http://us.macmillan.com/CMS400/uploadedFiles/FSGAdult/Setting_the_Record_Straight.pdf.
27. Mearsheimer and Walt, "The Israel Lobby and U.S. Foreign Policy" (2006), p. 10.
28. Benny Morris, *Righteous Victims: A History of the Zionist-Arab Conflict, 1881–2001* (New York: Vintage, 2001), p. 169 (found in Alex Safian, "Study Decrying 'Israel Lobby' Marred by Numerous Errors," CAMERA.org, March 22, 2006).
29. Mearsheimer and Walt also ignore context, such as the fact that after both world wars, substantial "transfers" of populations from one country to another had been accepted almost universally as necessary to ensure a stable peace. Yosef Gorni, *From Binational Society to Jewish State: Federal Concepts in Zionist Political Thought, 1920–1990, and the Jewish People* (Boston: Brill, 2006), p. 66.
30. Mearsheimer and Walt, "The Israel Lobby and U.S. Foreign Policy" (2006), pp. 9, 43.
31. Mearsheimer and Walt, "Setting the Record Straight," http://us.macmillan.com/theisraellobbyandusforeignpolicy.
32. Ibid.
33. Ibid.
34. Mearsheimer and Walt, "The Israel Lobby and U.S. Foreign Policy" (2006), p. 16.
35. Mearsheimer and Walt, "Setting the Record Straight."
36. The Stephen Roth Institute for the Study of Antisemitism and Racism, "France 2006," www.tau.ac.il/Anti-Semitism/asw2006/france.htm.
37. Mearsheimer and Walt, "The Israel Lobby and U.S. Foreign Policy" (2006), p. 2.
38. Mearsheimer and Walt, "Setting the Record Straight."
39. Mearsheimer and Walt, *The Israel Lobby and U.S. Foreign Policy* (2007), pp. 234–236.
40. Yossi Alpher, "Sharon Warned Bush," *Forward*, January 12, 2007, www.forward.com/articles/sharon-warned-bush/.
41. Ibid.

42. Herb Keinon, "Sharon Warned Bush That Arabs 'Would Not Take Democracy,'" *Jerusalem Post*, January 12, 2007. See also Douglas Feith, *War and Decision: Inside the Pentagon at the Dawn of the War on Terror* (New York: Harper, 2008), pp. 207–208, for an account of the relative unimportance of Israeli interests to the arguments offered in favor of going to war.

43. Ori Nir, "Professor Says American Publisher Turned Him Down," *Forward*, March 24, 2006, www.forward.com/articles/7550.

44. See, e.g., Mearsheimer and Walt, *The Israel Lobby and U.S. Foreign Policy*, pp. 96 (Goldmann reference) and 172 (Frankel reference). Several years ago Norman Finkelstein accused me of "plagiarism," claiming (erroneously) that I had cited several quotations to original sources that I had actually (he believed) found in secondary sources. Mearsheimer and Walt did the very thing Finkelstein falsely accused me of doing (which does not amount to plagiarism in any case, according to the *Chicago Manual of Style* and independent inquiries by Harvard University, the *New York Times*, and others). Interestingly, Finkelstein has failed to probe the same accusation in the case of Mearsheimer and Walt, which indicates that he realizes the charge is patently ridiculous or that he has a double standard for his ideological bedfellows, or both—which he has virtually acknowledged.

45. Alan Dershowitz, "Debunking the Newest—and Oldest—Jewish Conspiracy: A Reply to the Mearsheimer-Walt 'Working Paper,'" April 2006, www.hks.harvard.edu/research/working_papers/dershowitzreply.pdf.

46. Ibid., pp. 21–22.

47. Mearsheimer and Walt, "Setting the Record Straight."

48. Mearsheimer and Walt, *The Israel Lobby and U.S. Foreign Policy* (2007), p. 96.

49. Alan Dershowitz, "Debunking the Newest—and Oldest—Jewish Conspiracy: A Reply to the Mearsheimer-Walt 'Working Paper,'" April 2006, www.hks.harvard.edu/research/working_papers/dershowitzreply.pdf. Conducting a simple Google search with the first line of the quote yields hundreds of Web sites, including explicitly anti-Semitic sites and blogs.

50. They leave the quote unchanged in *The Israel Lobby and U.S. Foreign Policy*. Indeed, one might question whether they have ever read Goldmann's memoir at all or simply cut-and-pasted the quote.

51. David Ben-Gurion, quoted in Efraim Karsh, "Benny Morris and the Reign of Error," *Middle East Quarterly* (March 1999), www.meforum.org/article/466.

52. Mearsheimer and Walt, "Setting the Record Straight."

53. Ibid.

54. Quoted in "Who Runs America? Forty Minutes with Noam Chomsky," *Boston Phoenix*, April 1–8, 1999, www.bostonphoenix.com/archive/features/99/04/01/NOAM_CHOMSKY.html.

55. Alexander Cockburn, "Bush as Hitler? Let's Be Fair," *Nation*, January 26, 2004, p. 8.

56. Robert Pape, *Dying to Win: The Strategic Logic of Suicide Terrorism* (New York: Random House, 2005).

57. Robert Pape, "Why the War on Terrorism Goes South?" lecture at the 2007 Middle East and Central Asia Politics, Economics, and Society Conference, University of Utah, Friday, September 7, 2007.

58. Mearsheimer and Walt, *The Israel Lobby and U.S. Foreign Policy* (2007), p. 85.

59. See Alan Dershowitz, *The Case for Israel* (Hoboken, NJ: John Wiley & Sons, 2003), p. 91.

60. Mearsheimer and Walt, *The Israel Lobby and U.S. Foreign Policy* (2007), p. 85, ns. 26–27.

61. Michael Oren, "Who Started It?" *Washington Post*, June 10, 2007, p. BW13. See also Michael Walzer, *Just and Unjust Wars: A Moral Argument with Historical Illustrations* (New York: Basic Books, 1977).

62. Lee Hamilton, in Mearsheimer and Walt, *The Israel Lobby and U.S. Foreign Policy* (2007), p. 117.

63. Mearsheimer and Walt attempt to dispute this point, but they cannot provide any proof that AIPAC pushed for a U.S. invasion. Instead, they argue that "AIPAC usually supports what Israel wants, and Israel certainly wanted the United States to invade Iraq" (p. 242). Not only is it untrue that Israel "certainly" wanted the war, but this fallacious reasoning exposes the weakness of the authors' case. They also cite an article in the *New York Sun* reporting that AIPAC executive director Howard Kohr said the organization had been "'quietly' lobbying Congress to approve the use of force in Iraq," but as John Judis noted in the *New Republic* ("Moran Down: The Groups Who Cried Anti-Semitism," October 3, 2007), "AIPAC's spokesman Josh Block insists that the organization did no lobbying and that Kohr was misquoted."

64. "In Dark Times, Blame the Jews," *Forward*, March 24, 2006, www.forward.com/articles/7532.

65. Mearsheimer and Walt, "Setting the Record Straight."

66. Ibid.

67. Non-Jews can also become citizens through ordinary immigration procedures.

68. Nationality Law (1952). Part One: Acquisition of Nationality.

69. Mearsheimer and Walt, "The Israel Lobby and U.S. Foreign Policy" (2006), p. 5.

70. Mearsheimer and Walt, *The Israel Lobby and U.S. Foreign Policy* (2007), p. 65.

71. Osama bin Laden, "Al Qaeda's Fatwa," *NewsHour with Jim Lehrer,* transcript: *Online Focus,* www.pbs.org/newshour/terrorism/international/fatwa_1998.html.

72. Mearsheimer and Walt, "The Israel Lobby and U.S. Foreign Policy" (2006), p. 8.

73. Benny Morris, "And Now for Some Facts," *New Republic,* April 28, 2006.

74. Ibid.

75. Morris, quoted in Mearsheimer and Walt, "Setting the Record Straight."

76. Mearsheimer and Walt, "The Israel Lobby and U.S. Foreign Policy" (2006), p. 10.

77. Benny Morris, *Righteous Victims* (New York: Vintage Books, 2001), p. 256.

78. Benny Morris, *1948 and After: Israel and the Palestinians* (Oxford: Clarendon Press, 1994), pp. 38–39.

79. Meansheimer and Walt, "Setting the Record Straight."

80. Mearsheimer and Walt, *The Israel Lobby and U.S. Foreign Policy* (2007), p. 12.

81. Mearsheimer and Walt, "The Israel Lobby and U.S. Foreign Policy" (2006), p. 10.

82. Mearsheimer and Walt, *The Israel Lobby and U.S. Foreign Policy* (2007), p. 93.

83. Gorni, *From Binational Society to Jewish State,* n. 30.

84. Mearsheimer and Walt, *The Israel Lobby and U.S. Foreign Policy* (2007), p. 93.

85. Mearsheimer and Walt, "The Israel Lobby and U.S. Foreign Policy" (2006), p. 11.

86. Dennis Ross, *The Missing Peace: The Inside Story of the Fight for Middle East Peace* (New York: Farrar, Straus and Giroux, 2004), p. 42.

87. Elsa Walsh, "The Prince: How the Saudi Ambassador Became Washington's Indispensable Operator," *New Yorker,* March 24, 2003.

88. For a refutation of Arafat's Bantustan lie, see Alan Dershowitz, *The Case for Peace: How the Arab-Israeli Conflict Can Be Solved* (Hoboken, NJ: John Wiley & Sons, 2005), chap. 3. Rick Richman also carefully dissects Walt and Mearsheimer's argument in "The 'Israel Lobby' and Academic Malpractice," *Jewish Press,* March 29, 2006, www.jewishpress.com/page.do/8758/The_%27Israel_Lobby%27_And_Academic_Malpractice.html.

89. Alan Dershowitz, "Debunking the Newest—and Oldest—Jewish Conspiracy: A Reply to the Mearsheimer-Walt 'Working Paper,'" April 2006, www.hks.harvard.edu/research/working_papers/dershowitzreply.pdf, p. 34.

90. Mearsheimer and Walt, "The Israel Lobby and U.S. Foreign Policy" (2006), pp. 5–6.
91. Mearsheimer and Walt, *The Israel Lobby and U.S. Foreign Policy* (2007), p. 282.
92. Daniel W. Drezner, "A Follow-Up on the Israel Lobby," DanielDrezner.com, March 21, 2006, www.danieldrezner.com/archives/002642.html.
93. "Rafsanjani Says Muslims Should Use Weapons against Israel," *Iran Press Service,* December 14, 2001, www.iran-pressservice.com/articles_2001/dec_2001/rafsanjani_nuke_threats_141201.htm.
94. Mearsheimer and Walt, "The Israel Lobby and U.S. Foreign Policy" (2006), p. 15.
95. Dershowitz, "Debunking the Newest—and Oldest— Jewish Conspiracy: A Reply to the Mearsheimer-Walt 'Working Paper,'" p. 34.
96. Mearsheimer and Walt, "The Israel Lobby and U.S. Foreign Policy" (2006), p. 23.
97. Mearsheimer and Walt, "The Israel Lobby and U.S. Foreign Policy" (2007), p. 22.
98. J. Lorand Matory, "Israel and Censorship at Harvard," *Harvard Crimson,* September 14, 2007.
99. J. Lorand Matory, "Why I Stood Up: The Case against Summers," *Harvard Crimson,* June 7, 2006, www.thecrimson.com/article.aspx?ref=513842.
100. Mearsheimer and Walt, "The Israel Lobby and U.S. Foreign Policy" (2006), p. 43.
101. Morris Amitay, quoted in ibid., p. 18; and Mearsheimer and Walt, *The Israel Lobby and U.S. Foreign Policy* (2007), p. 153.
102. John Mearsheimer and Stephen Walt, "Setting the Record Straight: A Response to Critics of 'the Israel Lobby'," at the Macmillan Web site, December 12, 2006, http://us.macmillan.com/CMS400/uploadedFiles/FSGAdult/Setting_the_Record_Straight.pdf.
103. Mearsheimer and Walt, *The Israel Lobby and U.S. Foreign Policy* (2007), pp. 207–208.
104. James Bennet, "Seized Arms Would Have Vastly Extended Arafat Arsenal," *New York Times,* January 12, 2002; Uri Dan, "'Godfather': Arafat's Lies about Terror," *New York Post,* January 27, 2002.
105. Ruth R. Wisse, "Israel Lobby," *Wall Street Journal,* March 22, 2006.
106. David Gergen, "An Unfair Attack," *U.S. News & World Report,* April 3, 2006, www.usnews.com/usnews/opinion/articles/060403/3edit.htm.
107. Ibid.
108. Mearsheimer and Walt, "Setting the Record Straight."
109. George P. Shultz, in Mearsheimer and Walt, *The Israel Lobby and U.S. Foreign Policy* (2007), p. 46.
110. George P. Shultz, in Abraham H. Foxman, *The Deadliest Lies: The Israel Lobby and the Myth of Jewish Control* (New York: Palgrave, 2007), p. 17.
111. E. B. Solomont, "Feminist Magazine Rejects Ad Featuring Israeli Women," *New York Sun,* January 11, 2008, www2.nysun.com/article/69338?page_no=1.
112. David Harris, "What Happens When the Shoe's on the Other Foot?" *Executive Director's Blog,* April 5, 2008, www.ajc.org/site/apps/nlnet/content2.aspx?c=ijITI2PHKoG&b=2818289&content_id={EBFDC0DD-5302-43AE-9CD5-6473EC1F8473}&notoc=1.
113. Mearsheimer and Walt, *The Israel Lobby and U.S. Foreign Policy* (2007), p. 14.
114. Mearsheimer and Walt, "Setting the Record Straight."
115. Mearsheimer and Walt, *The Israel Lobby and U.S. Foreign Policy* (2007), p. 113; Foxman, *The Deadliest Lies,* p. 90.
116. Mearsheimer and Walt, *The Israel Lobby and U.S. Foreign Policy* (2007), p. 350.

3. THE CASE AGAINST BOYCOTTING ISRAELI ACADEMICS AND DIVESTING FROM ISRAELI BUSINESSES

1. Diana Jean Schemo, "Mideast Strife Loudly Echoed in Academia," *New York Times,* July 11, 2002.
2. Ibid.
3. Diana Jean Schemo, "Rejecting Boycott, Researchers Gather in Israel," *New York Times,* October 6, 2002.
4. Steven and Hilary Rose, "The Choice Is to Do Nothing or Try to Bring about Change: Why We Launched the Boycott of Israeli Institutions," *Guardian,* July 15, 2002; Lucy Hodges, "Campus Ferment: Lucy Hodges on Why UK Universities Are Boycotting Their Israeli Colleagues," *Independent* (London), May 16, 2002.
5. Andy Beckett and Ewen MacAskill, "British Academic Boycott of Israel Gathers Pace," *Guardian,* December 12, 2002.
6. Patrick Healy, "Israeli Academics Hit Back against Boycott," *Boston Globe,* February 20, 2003; Oren Yiftachel and Asad Ghanem, "Understanding 'Ethnocratic' Regimes: The Politics of Seizing Contested Territories," *Political Geography* 23, no. 6 (August 2004): 647–676; also Andy Beckett, "It's Water on Stone—In the End, the Stone Wears Out," *Guardian* (London), December 12, 2002.
7. Beckett and MacAskill, "British Academic Boycott of Israel Gathers Pace."
8. Healy, "Israeli Academics Hit Back against Boycott."
9. Ibid.; also, see Jon Henley, "University Drops Israeli Boycott: Wave of Protest Forces Reversal of Plan by Administrators at Paris Institution to Scrap Academic Links," *Guardian,* January 7, 2003.
10. Healy, "Israeli Academics Hit Back against Boycott."
11. Julie Henry, "University Dons Call for Academic Boycott of Israel; Lecturers' Union to Debate Motion Branded by Critics as Anti-Semitic," *Sunday Telegraph* (London), May 4, 2003.
12. Will Woodward, "Lecturers Reject Call to Boycott Israel: Union Votes for Maintaining Links to Support Progressive Academics," *Guardian,* May 10, 2003.
13. Chris McGreal, "Anglican Group Calls for Israel Sanctions: Campaigners Inspired by Boycott of Apartheid South Africa," *Guardian,* September 24, 2004.
14. Polly Curtis, "Boycott Call Resurfaces: The Campaign by Some Academics against Israeli Universities Will Intensify at the Association of University Teachers' Annual Council This Month," *Guardian* (London), April 5, 2005.
15. Ibid.
16. "Don't Boycott Us, Plead Israeli Academics," *Guardian Unlimited,* April 19, 2005.
17. Lizette Alvarez, "Professors in Britain Vote to Boycott 2 Israeli Schools," *New York Times,* May 8, 2005.
18. Ibid.
19. Curtis, "Boycott Call Resurfaces."
20. Oliver Duff, "Architects Threaten to Boycott Israel over 'Apartheid' Banner," *Independent* (London), February 10, 2006.
21. Alan Cowell, "British Union Weighs Boycott of Teachers from Israel," *New York Times,* May 15, 2006.
22. Alan Cowell, "British Teachers Favor Call to Boycott Israelis," *New York Times,* May 30, 2006.
23. Ibid.
24. Jon Boone and Rebecca Knight, "Israeli Boycott 'Anti-Semitic,' Says Harvard President," *Financial Times,* June 1, 2006.

25. Ibid.
26. Alan Cowell, "Britain: Journalists Vote to Boycott Israeli Goods," *New York Times,* April 17, 2007.
27. Judy Siegel, "AJC Calls for Fight against Boycott of Israeli MDs," *Jerusalem Post,* May 24, 2007.
28. Jon Boone, "Academic Union Set to Vote on Boycotting Israel," *Financial Times,* May 29, 2007.
29. Ibid.
30. Alan Cowell, "British Academics' Union Endorses Boycott of Universities in Israel," *New York Times,* May 31, 2007.
31. Alan Cowell, "Britain: Biggest Union Backs Israel Boycott," *New York Times,* June 23, 2007.
32. See Alan Dershowitz, "Israel at 60: So Vilified, Yet So Deserving of Praise," *Christian Science Monitor,* May 8, 2008.
33. For example, Israel has eight Nobel laureates, five of which won for academic achievements (that is, not for peace). Egypt, which has the most prizes after Israel among the countries in question, has two for academic achievements: one for chemistry and one for literature. See http://nobelprize.org/nobel_prizes/lists/all/.
34. Jonny Paul, "UK Academic Boycott Backlash Grows: Dershowitz-Led Petition Reaches 1,000 Signatures in Seven Weeks," *Jerusalem Post,* July 30, 2007. See also Scholars for Peace in the Middle East, http://spme.net/cgi-bin/display_petitions.cgi?ID=9.
35. Paras Bhayani and Claire Guehenno, "Faust Condemns Boycott of Israeli Universities," *Harvard Crimson,* August 14, 2007.
36. "College Presidents, Nobel Laureates Protest British Academic Boycott," Hillel Web site, www.hillel.org, August 17, 2007. See also "Boycott Israel Universities? Boycott Ours, Too!" (advertisement), *New York Times,* August 8, 2007, available at www.ajc .org/site/apps/nlnet/content2.aspx?c=ijlT12PHKoG&b=854099&ct=4261829.
37. Jonny Paul, "Liberal Democrat Party Conference Calls Boycott 'Utterly Misguided,'" *Jerusalem Post,* September 18, 2007.
38. Alan Dershowitz and Anthony Julius, "The Contemporary Fight against Anti-Semitism," *Times* (London), June 14, 2007.
39. James Meikle, "Lecturers Drop Israeli Universities Boycott Call after Legal Advice," *Guardian* (London), September 29, 2007.
40. Scott Jaschik, "British Union Drops Boycott Call," *Inside Higher Ed,* October 1, 2007.
41. See Ronnie Fraser, "The Academic Boycott of Israel Is Back in the UK!" *Academic Friends of Israel* 7, no. 6 (March 27, 2008); Ronnie Fraser, "The Academic Boycott of Israel: A Review of the Five-Year UK Campaign to Defeat It," *Academic Friends of Israel* 7, no. 4 (March 5, 2008). See also the UCU's Web site regarding the boycott motion: www.ucu.org.uk/index.cfm?articleid=2622.
42. Meikle, "Lecturers Drop Israeli Universities Boycott Call after Legal Advice."
43. Jonny Paul, "Call for Boycott of Israeli Academia Once Again Rears Its Head in Britain," *Jerusalem Post,* March 30, 2008.
44. Ibid.
45. The full text of the motion (number 25) is available at the UCU Web site: www.ucu. org.uk/circ/html/ucu104.html.
46. "General Assembly Action Resolution on Israel and Palestine: Initiating Divestment and Ending Occupation," Presbyterian Church USA, www.pcusa.org/worldwide/ israelpalestine/israelpalestineresolution.htm.
47. See "What's with the Presbyterians?" *Jewish Week,* June 20, 2008.
48. Michael Lerner, "Divestment and More: A Strategy Exploration," *Tikkun,* March–April 2005, p. 42.
49. Robert Brustein passed his comments on to me and others via e-mail in March 2008, and he has authorized me to include this quote in this book.

4. THE CASE AGAINST THE ANTI-ISRAEL HARD LEFT AND HARD RIGHT

1. See George Michael, *The Enemy of My Enemy: The Alarming Convergence of Militant Islam and the Extreme Right* (Lawrence: University Press of Kansas, 2006).
2. See Fyodor Dostoyevsky, *The Diary of a Writer*, translated by Boris Brasol (Salt Lake City: Peregrine Smith Books, 1985), pp. 642–645.
3. Karl Marx, "On the Jewish Question," in Robert Tucker, ed., *The Marx-Engel Reader*, 2nd ed. (New York: W. W. Norton, 1978), pp. 48, 50, 52.
4. Ibid., p. 50.
5. Stephen J. Greenblatt, "Marlowe, Marx, and Anti-Semitism," *Critical Inquiry* 5, no. 2 (Winter 1978): 293.
6. Andrei Markovits in *Uncouth Nation* uses the term "litmus test." (Princeton, NJ: Princeton University Press, 2007.)
7. Israel Shahak, *Jewish History, Jewish Religion: The Weight of Three Thousand Years* (Boulder, CO: Pluto Press, 1994), pp. 48, 49.
8. Ibid., pp. 2, 3, 8.
9. Ibid., p. 100.
10. Ibid., pp. 1, 103.
11. Ibid., p. 1.
12. Ibid., pp. 29, 80.
13. See Vladimir Begun, Polzuchaia kontrrevoliutsiia [The encroaching counterrevolution] (Minsk: Izd-vo Belaru, 1974).
14. Shahak continues, "Indeed, the cabbalists believe that some of the sacrifices burnt in the Temple were intended for Satan. For example, the seventy bullocks sacrificed during the seven days of the feast of Tabernacles, were supposedly offered to Satan in his capacity as ruler of all the Gentiles, in order to keep him too busy to interfere on the eighth day, when sacrifice is made to God." This claim is footnoted, but instead of citing a legitimate Talmudic source, the footnote describes another alleged Jewish "custom" pertaining to devil worship that Shahak traced to *Shevet Musar*, a book published in 1712 that he claimed is still widely followed by Orthodox Jews. (Not surprisingly, Norman Finkelstein relies on Shahak's misreading of Jewish tenets in his own mischaracterization of Judaism: "I don't know about Judaism, but [Shahak] did. He knew it well. He took an interest in it and I have no doubt that what he wrote is accurate.") (Shahak must have been right about Judaism, according to Finkelstein, because he was an anti-Zionist!)
15. That title comes from Paul Robinson, "The Chomsky Problem: *Language and Responsibility* by Noam Chomsky," *New York Times*, February 25, 1979.
16. Noam Chomsky interview with Amy Goodman, *Democracy Now!* April 17, 2007, www.democracynow.org/2007/4/17/noam_chomsky_accuses_alan_dershowitz_of.
17. Some of it can also be traced to the bigotry of the Reverend Daniel Berrigan:

> In a highly publicized speech delivered on October 19, 1973—a speech that many people see as the original declaration of war by the radical American Left against Israel—the Reverend Daniel Berrigan described Israel as "a criminal Jewish community" that has committed "crimes against humanity," has "created slaves," and has espoused a "racist ideology" reminiscent of the Nazis, aimed at proving its "racial superiority to the people it has crushed." Berrigan also chastised the "Jewish people," whom he described as "so proud" and so "endowed with intelligence," but who "have in the main given their acquiescence or their support to the Nixon ethos," which has

led to the death, maiming, and displacement of "some six million Southeast Asians." Berrigan referred to the ironic figure of six million as "one of those peculiar facts which must be called free-floating" and concluded with a veiled threat to both American Jews and to Israel: "To put the matter brutally, many American Jewish leaders were capable of ignoring the Asian holocaust in favor of economic and military aid to Israel. . . . It is not merely we nor the Vietnamese who must live with the fact. So must Israel. So must the American Jews."

Reaction to Berrigan's polemic was swift and sharp, especially among lawyers who had represented left-wing causes and individuals. Battle lines were quickly drawn. Some, like William Kunstler, supported Berrigan. Others—among them lawyers who had represented Berrigan and Kunstler—were appalled at Berrigan's diatribe.

From Alan Dershowitz, "Can the Guild Survive Its Hypocrisy?" *American Lawyer,* August 11, 1978.

18. Alison Weir, "What Our Taxes to Israel Are Funding," *Greenwich Citizen,* April 4, 2008.
19. For the details of the dispute, see these articles: Alan Dershowitz, "Shahak, Best Proof of Freedom of Speech," *Boston Globe,* April 29, 1973, p. 5; Alan Dershowitz, "Dershowitz Replies," *Boston Globe,* May 25, 1973), p. 16; Noam Chomsky, "Shahak, a Man of Honor and Principle," *Boston Globe,* May 17, 1973, p. 18; and Noam Chomsky, "In Defense of Shahak," *Boston Globe,* June 5, 1973, p. 18.
20. Chomsky, "Shahak, a Man of Honor and Principle," p. 18. Chomsky criticized me for choosing to "distort beyond recognition what Shahak has said and done and to vilify him as a 'hate-monger' who 'spews forth (his) venom' against Israel." Thirty years later, Chomsky continues to be influenced by, and defend, Shahak. In his book *Middle East Illusions,* he praises Shahak's "courageous work as chairman of the Israeli League for Human and Civil Rights" and condemns my "falsehoods" pertaining to Shahak's removal as chairman. (My account of Shahak's short tenure as chairman was absolutely correct and is confirmed by court records.) See Noam Chomsky, *Middle East Illusions* (New York: Rowman and Littlefield, 2003), pp. 265–266, n. 47; Dershowitz, "Shahak, Best Proof of Freedom of Speech," p. 5; and Dershowitz, "Dershowitz Replies," p. 16.
21. See Robert Faurisson, "The Problem of the Gas Chambers," leaflet, Institute for Historical Review, www.ihr.org/leaflets/gaschambers.shtml; Robert Faurisson, "The Diary of Anne Frank: Is It Genuine?" 19 *Journal of Historical Review* 6 (November/December 2000), p. 2, www.ihr.org/jhr/v19/v19n6p-2_Faurisson.html.
22. "Faurisson est une sorte de liberal relativement apolitique." Robert Faurisson, *Mémoire en defense contre ceux m'accusent de falsifier l'Histoire. La question de chambres à gaz. Précédé d'un avis de Noam Chomsky* [Account in defense against those who accuse me of falsifying history. The question of the gas chambers. Preceded by an opinion of Noam Chomsky.] (Paris: A Vieille Taupe, 1980), xiv–xv; Pierre Vidal-Naquet, *Assassins of Memory: Essays on the Denial of the Holocaust* (New York: Columbia University Press, 1993), p. 67. Werner Cohn, "Chomsky and Holocaust Denial," in Peter Collier and David Horowitz, eds., *The Anti-Chomsky Reader* (New York: Encounter Books, 2004), p. 24.
23. For Chomsky's defense of this statement, see "Noam Chomsky: You Ask the Questions," *Independent* (UK), August 28, 2006, www.independent.co.uk/news/people/noam-chomsky-you-ask-the-questions-413678.html. The quote originally appeared in W. D. Rubinstein, "Chomsky and the Neo-Nazis," *Quadrant* (Australia), October 1981, www.paulbogdanor.com/rubinstein-chomsky.pdf.

24. Scot Lehigh, "Men of Letters," *Boston Phoenix,* June 16–22, 1989, p. 30.
25. See Cohn, "Chomsky and Holocaust Denial," pp. 124–133.
26. To read his "research" and "findings," visit the bizarre conspiracy theory Web site *Rense.com,* which tellingly reproduces Faurisson's paper in full. Robert Faurisson, "The Victories of Revisionism," December 11, 2006, www.rense.com/general74/revis.htm.
27. Chomsky published the French version of his *Political Economy of Human Rights* (written with Edward Herman) with La Vieille Taupe, the publisher of the Holocaust denier Robert Faurisson, although he could have published it with a commercial firm. See Cohn, "Chomsky and Holocaust Denial," pp. 124–133.
28. Paul L. Berman, reply to "Chomsky: Freedom of Expression? Absolutely," *Village Voice,* July 1–7, 1981, p. 13.
29. *La Jornada* (Mexico), September 15, 2001.
30. *Ethics,* October 1968.
31. Chomsky has said: "I would like to express the great joy that we feel in your accomplishments. . . . Your heroism reveals the capabilities of the human spirit and human will" (Radio Hanoi, Apr. 14, 1970). "The evacuation of Phnom Penh, widely denounced at the time and since for its undoubted brutality, may actually have saved many lives. It is striking that the crucial facts rarely appear in the chorus of condemnations." (*After the Cataclysm* [South End Press, 1979], p. 160.) Thanks to Paul Bogdanor for these quotes.
32. Noam Chomsky, *Fateful Triangle: The United States, Israel, and the Palestinians* (Cambridge, MA: South End Press, 1999), p. 208.
33. Interview, "Shmate: A Journal of Progressive Jewish Thought" (Summer 1988).
34. Ibid.
35. Chomsky's Ph.D. (University of Pennsylvania 1955) is in linguistics, according to MIT (http://web.mit.edu/linguistics/people/faculty/chomsky/index.html). His expertise is in "Linguistic Theory, Syntax, Semantics, Philosophy of Language."
36. President Clinton told me this directly and personally, and it is confirmed by Dennis Ross and others who were at Camp David, in their writings and interviews.
37. "Noam Chomsky v. Alan Dershowitz: A Debate on the Israeli-Palestinian Conflict," *Democracy Now!* December 23, 2005, www.democracynow.org/2005/12/23/noam_chomsky_v_alan_dershowitz_a.
38. Eric Pace, "UN Resolution the Key," *New York Times,* March 4, 1968.
39. "The Khartoum Resolutions, September 1, 1967," *Avalon Project,* Yale Law School, www.yale.edu/lawweb/avalon/mideast/khartoum.htm.
40. Tariq Ali, John Berger, Noam Chomsky, et al., "Israel, Lebanon, and Palestine," July 19, 2006, www.chomsky.info/letters/20060719.htm.
41. Associated Press, "Palestinian Militants Attack Israeli Army Post," *Washington Post,* June 25, 2006, A19.
42. An appearance on Amy Goodman's *Democracy Now!* (transcript at www.democracynow.org/2006/7/14/noam_chomsky_u_s_backed_israeli).
43. Josh Brannon, "IDF Commandos enter Gaza, Capture Two Hamas Terrorists," *Jerusalem Post,* June 25, 2006.
44. "Secretary-General's Briefing to the Security Council on the Situation in the Middle East," Secretary General, Office of the Spokesperson, New York, July 20, 2006, www.un.org/apps/sg/sgstats.asp?nid=2142.
45. Reuters, "Israel Makes First Gaza Arrest Raid Since Pullout," *Turkish Daily News,* June 25, 2006. Note particularly the first sentence: "Israeli forces detained two Palestinians, who the army said were Hamas militants, in the Gaza Strip on Saturday in what marked the first such arrest raid in the territory since Israel pulled out of Gaza a year ago."
46. Berger, Noam Chomsky, et al., "A Letter from 18 Writers," *Nation,* August 18, 2006.

47. Ibid.
48. I doubt that all who have signed the Chomsky letters were aware that they are disseminating provable falsehoods. The list of signatories, in addition to Chomsky, Pinter, and Saramago, now includes Tariq Ali, John Berger, Eduardo Galeano, Naomi Klein, Arundhati Roy, Giuliana Sgrena, and Howard Zinn. Even after being made aware of the lies contained in the letter, they refused to remove their names. They apparently don't realize or care how dangerous it is to their integrity and reputation it is to sign a Chomsky letter without checking its contents.
49. Speech at Harvard, December 2007. Joel Pollack, a student at Harvard Law School who attended the speech, took verbatim notes of this statement.
50. Chomsky, *Fateful Triangle*, pp. 468–469.
51. As reported in the *Washington Post:* "In a Eurobarometer poll by the European Union in November 2003, a majority of Europeans named Israel as the greatest threat to world peace. Overall, 59 percent of Europeans put Israel in the top spot, ahead of such countries as Iran and North Korea. In the Netherlands, that figure rose to 74 percent." See Robin Shepherd, "In Europe, an Unhealthy Fixation on Israel," *Washington Post,* January 30, 2005; and Peter Beaumont, "Israel Outraged as EU Poll Names It a Threat to Peace," *Guardian* (UK), November 2, 2003.
52. Transcript, "Noam Chomsky Accuses Alan Dershowitz of Launching a 'Jihad' to Block Norman Finkelstein from Getting Tenure at DePaul University," *Democracy Now!* April 17, 2007, www.democracynow.org/2007/4/17/noam_chomsky_accuses_alan_dershowitz_of), accessed April 20, 2008.
53. When I wrote my book *The Case for Israel,* I barely knew who Norman Finkelstein was. I cited him once or twice in the book and had a vague notion that he was an obscure academic who worshipped Chomsky and Shahak. As part of my publicity tour for *The Case for Israel,* I was asked to participate in a debate on the hard left radio show *Democracy Now!* I was told that my opponent would be either Chomsky or Edward Said, a prominent anti-Israel Columbia professor. I readily agreed, always relishing an intellectual encounter with a smart opponent. I was a bit surprised when Norman Finkelstein showed up instead to debate me. I later learned that the bait and switch was a carefully planned and well-coordinated ploy, organized by Chomsky, Finkelstein, and Alexander Cockburn (a hard-left, anti-Israel zealot and the owner of the radical Web site *Counterpunch*) with the full knowledge and cooperation of the show's host, Amy Goodman. Little did I realize at the time that this would be the beginning of a five year-long effort by the anti-Israel hard left to discredit my book *The Case for Israel* (as it had previously tried to discredit other pro-Israel books)—an effort that would end with Finkelstein being discredited and denied tenure at DePaul University, where he was then teaching.

   The attack against me began with the claim that I did not "write this book." (Finkelstein subsequently claimed that I don't write *any* of my books: "It's sort of like a Hallmark line for Nazis. . . . They churn them out so fast that he has now reached a point where he doesn't even read them." ("Norman Finkelstein 'Ambushes' Alan Dershowitz [Part II]," an original transcript from the *Experiment,* December 6, 2003, www.theexperiment.org/articles.php?news_id=1991.

   Their next charge was that if I did actually write my 2003 book in my own hand, I must have plagiarized it from a 1984 book by a woman named Joan Peters. The problem with their charge, in addition to its complete falsity, is that Peters's book was entirely demographic and historical, whereas more than 90 percent of my book deals with contemporary events that took place years *after* the publication of Peters's book in 1984. The other, even more serious, problem for them is that they could not come up with a *single* sentence, phrase, or idea in my book that was taken from another source and was used without quotation marks, attribution, and citation. I explicitly cited Peters's book numerous times, while disclaiming reliance on its conclusions because I disagreed with some of them. That, of course, means there was no plagiarism, as Harvard concluded when I asked it to investigate Finkelstein's charge. (See Alan Dershowitz, "Discredited Charges Should Not Be Repeated," *Harvard Crimson*, October 4, 2004.)

Moreover, Finkelstein has publicly stated that he does not take the issue of plagiarism seriously, virtually acknowledging that he uses it only as a tactic against his ideological enemies: "I'm a leftist and I don't get too excited about plagiarism, I have to admit it." Despite Finkelstein's lack of excitement about plagiarism and his own obvious realization that I had not engaged in it, he knew from his previous experience that the false charge of plagiarism, if leveled, would be more likely to garner media attention than would simple criticism of my conclusions. (I demolish Finkelstein's false charges elsewhere. See *The Case for Peace: How the Arab-Israeli Conflict Can Be Solved* [Hoboken, NJ: John Wiley & Sons, 2005], and sources cited therein.)

54. For a complete answer to these false charges, see Dershowitz, *The Case for Peace*, and Dershowitz, "Discredited Charges Should Not Be Repeated."

55. "Canadian Jewish Organizations Charged with Stifling Campus Debate," Washington Report on Middle East Affairs, April/May 1992.

56. "A Reply to Henry Kissinger and Fouad Ajami," *Link* (Americans for Middle East Understanding) 25, no. 5 (December 1992), www.ameu.org/page. asp?iid=116&aid=158&pg=1.

57. Norman Finkelstein, "A Reply to Michael Young," www.normanfinkelstein.com/ article.php?pg=4&ar=15#almanar.

58. Interview with Norman Finkelstein, "The Holocaust Industry," March 10, 2004, part 1 of DVD, www.snowshoefilms.com.

59. Don Atapattu, "How to Lose Friends and Alienate People: A Conversation with Professor Norman Finkelstein,"*Counterpunch*, December 13, 2001.

60. Bas Blokker, "*Joden zijn immuun voor elke vorm van Kritiek*" [Jews are immune against any sort of criticism], *NRC Handelsblad*, August 5, 2000, quoted in Leon de Winter, "Der Groll des Sohnes" [The Son's Anger], in Petra Steinberger, ed., *Die Finkelstein-Debatte* (München: Piper Verlag, 2001). Translated from German.

61. Interview with Norman Finkelstein, "The Holocaust Industry," Snowshoe Films (video), March 10, 2004, part 1 of DVD (found at www.normanfinkelstein.com/ content.php?pg=19; www.snowshoefilms.com/palestine.html; madison.indymedia. org/usermedia/video/7/16871_1.wmv; chicago.indymedia.org/usermedia/ video/10/finkelsteinmar0456k.wmv).

62. Catalyst Radio Interview with Dr. Finkelstein, March 1, 2005, www.grcmc.org/ catalystradio/mp3s/catalyst03042005.mp3.

63. Bas Blokker, "*Joden zijn immuun voor elke vorm van Kritiek.*"

64. Bryan Appleyard, "Stop, in the name of the Holocaust," *Sunday Times* (UK), June 11, 2000.

65. Finkelstein, *The Holocaust Industry*, p. 81.

66. Norman Finkelstein, "The Business of Death,"*Guardian* (UK), July 12, 2000.

67. Peter Novick, "*Offene Fenster und Tueren. Ueber Norman Finkelstein Kreuzzug*," [Open Windows and Doors. About Norman Finkelstein's Crusade.], in Petra Steinberger, ed., *Die Finkelstein-Debatte* [The Finkelstein Debate] (München: Piper Verlag, 2001), p. 159. (Translated from German.)

68. David Cesarani, "Finkelstein's Final Solution," *Times Higher Education Supplement*, August 4, 2000. See also *Tagesspiegel*, February 6, 2001. (Translated from German.)

69. "A Tale of Two Holocausts,"*New York Times*, August 6, 2000, p. 8.

70. "A Comment by Daniel Jonah Goldhagen on: A Nation on Trial: The Goldhagen Thesis and Historical Truth," www.goldhagen.com/csiz2.html.
71. "Holocaust Reparations,"*Commentary*, January 2001, p. 20.
72. Martin Dietzsch and Alfred Schobert, eds., *Ein "judischer David Iving"? Norman G. Finkelstein im Diskurs der Rechten—Erinnerungsabwehr und Antizionismus* [The "Jewish David Irving"? Norman G. Finkelstein in the Discourse of the Right—Defense against Remembrance and Antizionism] (Duisburg, Germany: DISS, 2001), p. 11. Another admirer of Finkelstein called him "the Jewish Ward Churchill." Portland Independent Media Center, http://portland.indymedia.org/en/2005/03/312868.shtml.
73. The cartoon can be seen here: www.indybay.org/newsitems/2006/08/10/18296109.php.
74. The letter in its entirety can be found on my Web site, www.alandershowitz.com.
75. His name initially appeared on the schedule (http://adelaideinstitute.org/2006December/contents_program1.htm) but immediately disappeared when I wrote about it (see www.huffingtonpost.com/alan-dershowitz/is-norman-finkelstein-in-b_36122.html).
76. He can be heard giving that reason on Iranian television at www.youtube.com/watch?v=YemOW3lVoAI, also stating that he didn't consider the conference to be "serious" enough.
77. For a list of Hezbollah's crimes, see the Council on Foreign Relations Web site, www.cfr.org/publication/9155/.
78. "Top 50 Most Influential Rabbis in America,"*Newsweek*, April 11, 2008, www.newsweek.com/id/131600.
79. Norman Finkelstein, "The Occupation's Spillover Effect,"*Tikkun*, March/April 2005, p. 14.
80. Norman Finkelstein, *Beyond Chutzpah: On the Misuse of Anti-Semitism and the Abuse of History* (Berkeley: University of California Press, 2005), p. 83.
81. Michael Lerner, "Alan Dershowitz! Stop Your Personal Attacks,"*Jerusalem Post*, October 24, 2006.
82. Michael Lerner, "There Is No New Anti-Semitism,"*Baltimore Chronicle and Sentinel*, February 2, 2007, http://baltimorechronicle.com/2007/020207LERNER.shtml.
83. Ibid.
84. Ibid.
85. See "Israel Section," *Tikkun* Web site, www.beyttikkun.org/article.php?story=israel.
86. Michael Lerner, "Murders at a Yeshiva in Jerusalem," *Tikkun*, March 6, 2008.
87. Ibid.
88. Ibid.
89. Amnon Rubenstein, "Reason for the Time Being Prevails Out of Africa," *Jerusalem Post*, August 7, 2007, p. 16.
90. Avi Shlaim, "A Debate: Is Zionism Today the Real Enemy of the Jews?"*International Herald Tribune*, February 4, 2005.
91. Ibid.
92. Ibid.
93. Richard Falk, "Slouching toward a Palestinian Holocaust," Transnational Foundation for Peace and Future Research, June 29, 2007, www.transnational.org/Area_MiddleEast/2007/Falk_PalestineGenocide.html. It also appeared on several other Web sites.
94. Ibid.
95. Ibid.
96. Tovah Lazaroff, "UNHRC Appointment Infuriates Israel,"*Jerusalem Post*, March 26, 2008, www.jpost.com/servlet/Satellite?cid=1206446111162&pagename=JPost%2FJPArticle%2FShowFull.

97. David Aaronovitch, "UN Expert? No, a Conspiracy Crank,"*Times Online,* April 15, 2008, www.timesonline.co.uk/tol/comment/columnists/david_aaronovitch/article3746592.ece.

98. Melanie Phillips, "The Club of Tyranny's Falked Tongue,"*Spectator* (UK), April 9, 2008.

99. Richard Falk, foreword to *The New Pearl Harbor,* by David Ray Griffin, June 16, 2004, www.transnational.org/SAJT/forum/meet/2004/Falk_GriffinForeword. html; and Richard Falk, "One of the Great Watersheds of Modern History," MERIP Reports, no. 75/76, *Iran in Revolution,* March–April 1979, pp. 9, 12.

100. Richard Falk, "International Law and the Al-Aqsa Intifada,"*Middle East Report* 217 (Winter 2000): 16.

101. Daphna Berman, "Speaker Accuses Israel of Committing Genocide," *New York Sun,* October 14, 2002, p. 3.

102. Ted Merwin and David Zax, "The Playwright's Politics,"*Moment,* October/November 2007; Andrea Levin, "Munich and the Kushner Connection," *CAMERA,* January 4, 2006, www.camera.org/index.asp?x_article=1048&x_context=8; Chris Jones, "Playwright Kushner Espouses Politics as Usual, but Globally,"*Chicago Tribune,* April 10, 2002.

103. Tony Kushner and Alisa Solomon, *Wrestling with Zion: Progressive Jewish-American Responses to the Israeli-Palestinian Conflict* (New York: Grove, 2003), pp. 2, 5.

104. Ibid., p. 6.

105. Tamara Traubman, "Haifa University President Calls on Dissident Academic to Resign," *Haaretz,* April 26, 2005.

106. Ilan Pappé, "Ilan Pappé on How Israel Was Founded on Ethnic Cleansing," *Socialist Worker Online,* July 29, 2006, www.socialistworker.co.uk/article.php?article_id=9307.

107. Ibid.

108. Ibid.

109. Ilan Pappé, "Genocide in Gaza,"*Electronic Intifada,* September 2, 2006, www.ilanPappé.org/Articles/Genocide%20in%20Gaza.html.

110. Pappé, "Ilan Pappé on How Israel Was Founded on Ethnic Cleansing."

111. Ilan Pappé, "The Israeli Recipe for 2008: Genocide in Gaza, Ethnic Cleansing in the West Bank,"*Independent,* June 23, 2007, www.indypendent.org/2007/06/22/the-israeli-recipe-for-2008-genocide-in-gaza-ethnic-cleansing-in-the-west-bank/.

112. Mohammed Iqbal, "Academic Slams Israel for Land Grab,"*Peninsula,* March 29, 2007, www.thepeninsulaqatar.com/Display_news.asp?section=local_news&month=march2007&file=local_news200703298205.xml.

113. Emanuele Ottolenghi, "The War of the Jews: Not One Voice,"*National Review Online,* September 20, 2006, http://article.nationalreview.com/?q=MDk4NTUxMDlmNTUxZDVjMDgxM2M4OGJiZTBjNWU5ZDE=.

114. Dostoyevsky, *The Diary of a Writer,* pp. 637, 642, 643, 645, 648.

115. Ibid., pp. 647, 650, 651.

116. Patrick Buchanan, "Where Are the Christians?"*Creators Syndicate,* July 18, 2006.

117. Patrick Buchanan, "A. M. Rosenthal Pins the Scarlet Letter on Me,"*Seattle Post-Intelligencer,* September 20, 1990:

> Confession time. From June of '67, when I was in Israel with Richard Nixon after the Six Day War, until I went back in the White House in 1985, I was an uncritical apologist of Israel, a Begin man, defending everything from the attack on the Iraqi reactor to the invasion of Lebanon. I thought they were terrific friends. And, yes, a change has taken place. For many reasons. Among them: The manipulation of the traitor Jonathan Pollard to systematically loot the secrets of the most generous friend Israel will ever have. The gratuitous

brutality against Palestinian old men, women, teen-agers and children. The Good Friday land grab at the Church of the Holy Sepulchre in Jerusalem. The shipment of cluster bombs to the Stalinist Mengistu regime in Ethiopia. The caustic, cutting cracks about my church and popes from both Israel and its amen corner in the United States. Finally, the hate mail and hate columns, every time some new fight breaks out.

These are among the most mendacious (and most stereotyped) rationalizations I have ever read for so complete an about-face on so important an issue.

118. See Alan Dershowitz, *The Vanishing American Jew: In Search of Jewish Identity for the Next Century* (New York: Touchstone/Simon & Schuster, 1997), p. 156, where Buckley said, "I find it impossible to defend Pat Buchanan against the charges that what he said and did during the period under examination amounted to anti-Semitism." Originally in William F. Buckley, *In Search of Anti-Semitism* (New York: Continuum, 1994), p. 44.

119. Alan Dershowitz, *Chutzpah* (New York: Simon & Schuster, 1991), p. 163, in Patrick Buchanan, "Healing . . . or Awakening at Auschwitz," *Washington Times*, September 25, 1989.

120. Dershowitz, *Chutzpah*, p. 165, in Shenon, "Washington Talk"; Philip Shenon, "The Buchanan Aggravation," *New York Times*, February 19, 1987: "I have come to believe that John Demjanjuk is not the bestial victimizer of men, women and children of the Treblinka killing ground but a victim himself of a miscarriage of justice," Mr. Buchanan wrote. "John Demjanjuk may be the victim of an American Dreyfus case." Dershowitz, *The Vanishing American Jew*, p. 156.

121. Alan Dershowitz, *Contrary to Popular Opinion* (New York: Pharaos Books, 1992), p. 371, quoting a "recent column by Buchanan."

122. Jacob Weisberg, "The Heresies of Pat Buchanan," *New Republic*, October 22, 1990, 27.

123. Ibid.

124. Ibid.

125. See Patrick J. Buchanan, "Nazi Butcher or Mistaken Identity?" *Washington Post*, September 28, 1986; Jonathan Alter, "Is Pat Buchanan Anti-Semitic?" *Newsweek*, December 23, 1991.

126. Joshua Muravchik, "Buchanan on Trial," *National Review*, November 29, 1993.

127. Philip Shenon, "Washington Talk: The Buchanan Aggravation," *New York Times*, February 19, 1987.

128. Ibid.

129. Buchanan has said, "If we can give 50 Phantoms [jet fighters] to the Jews [meaning Israel], and a multi-billion dollar welfare program for the blacks . . . why not help the Catholics save their collapsing school system." From a memo to President Reagan, as reported in the *Boston Globe*, January 4, 1992. Found at FAIR.org: "Pat Buchanan in His Own Words," *FAIR*, February 26, 1996, www.fair.org/index.php?page=2553.

130. For example, see Buchanan's recent syndicated column discussing "the Jews"—and birth control. Patrick J. Buchanan, "The Lost Tribes of Israel," *Human Events*, May 16, 2008, www.humanevents.com/article.php?id=26552. See also "Pat Buchanan in His Own Words."

131. See William A. Henry III, "Buchanan, the Biter, Bitten," *Time Magazine*, October 1, 1990. The full quote refers to "American kids with names like . . ."; Buchanan later argued, "The comment about McAllister and Murphy, Gonzales and Leroy Brown was in a . . . column where I was attacking The Economist magazine, which said the Americans are going to have to march all the way up to Baghdad. And I said, 'Just a minute, you elitists at The Economist, it's not going to be British kids. It's going to be American kids with names like McAllister, Murphy, Gonzales and

Leroy Brown who are humping up that road to Baghdad.'. . . People say, 'Well, isn't that anti-Semitic?' Why isn't it anti-Greek? Why isn't it anti-Polish? Why isn't it anti-Russian or anti-German?" ("Pat Buchanan on the controversy surrounding his new book, 'A Republic, Not an Empire,'" *Tim Russert* (CNBC show), Oct. 2, 1999.

132. See Alan M. Dershowitz, "U.S. Media Should Shun Buchanan," *Jerusalem Post,* October 16, 1990.

133. *McLaughlin Group,* June 15, 1990.

134. *Meet the Press,* September 5, 2004.

135. Patrick J. Buchanan, "Whose War?" *American Conservative,* March 24, 2003.

136. Ibid.

137. Ibid.

138. Patrick J. Buchanan, "No End to War," *American Conservative,* March 1, 2004.

139. Buchanan, "Whose War?"

140. Patrick J. Buchanan, "Where Are the Christians?" *Human Events,* July 18, 2006.

141. *The American Conservative,* "Mission Statement," www.amconmag.com/aboutus. html.

142. Taki Theodoracopulos, "Rich Rewards," *Spectator* (UK), February 24, 2001, www .takistopdrawer.us/2001/february/article_2001-Feb-24.html.

143. Ibid., www.spectator.co.uk/the-magazine/cartoons/8769/rich-rewards.thtml.

144. Robert Novak, "Carter's Clarity: End Occupation," *New York Post,* November 5, 2007, www.nypost.com/seven/11052007/postopinion/opedcolumnists/ carters_clarity__end_occupation_438102.htm?page=2#.

145. Ibid.

146. Robert Novak, "Worse Than Apartheid?" *Washington Post,* April 9, 2007, p. A31.

147. Ibid.

148. Robert Novak, "Hamas Talks Peace, but U.S. Not Listening," *Chicago Sun-Times,* April 17, 2007, p, 37.

149. Ibid.

150. Robert Novak, "American Politicians Are Lining Up in Support of Israel," *Chicago Sun-Times,* July 20, 2006, p. 33; Samuel Francis was another nationally syndicated conservative columnist who had been a contributor to Buchanan's *American Conservative* before he died in 2005.

Whereas Novak, as seen previously, is at least somewhat veiled in his criticism of Israel, in that he attempts to cloak his anti-Israel bias in the guise of "balanced" reporting, Francis clearly feels no compunction in proudly exhibiting his bigotry, as illustrated by a September 2004 article titled "How Far Does Israeli Spy Case Go?" In this article, a wild-eyed Francis excitedly explores various unsubstantiated conspiracy theories about a vast network of Israeli spies in Washington.

> Lawrence Franklin, the Pentagon analyst named as the subject of the investigation, works in the same office as his supervisor, Undersecretary of Defense for Policy Douglas Feith, who is himself part of the now-notorious "cabal" of neoconservative policy makers who promoted war with Iraq from at least the days after the 9/11 attacks.
>
> Along with Mr. Feith's own boss, Deputy Defense Secretary Paul Wolfowitz, former Defense Policy Board Chairman Richard Perle, and several others in the administration, they are all part of a group that has been extremely close to the Israeli government and especially to Ariel Sharon's Likud government. It is now clear that the investigation is interested in all of the above.
>
> And they are not alone. Yet another figure surfacing in the case is Michael Ledeen, also a prominent neoconservative, who was involved in the Iran-Contra Affair of the 1980s, when he served as the conduit between the Israeli

and U.S. governments in kicking off the whole covert business. Now, Mr. Ledeen is reported to have held meetings with Mr. Franklin and his old buddy from Iran-Contra days, Iranian Manucher Ghorbanifar.

It all gets curiouser and curiouser. . . . But the reaction to the whole story from both the subjects of the investigation and their buddies in the neoconservative media has been to deny everything and insinuate "anti-Semitism."

"Friends and associates of the civilian group at the Pentagon," the *New York Times* reported, "believe they are under assault by adversaries from within the intelligence community who have opposed them since before the war in Iraq."

The anti-Semitism card, always a favorite with neoconservatives, was played almost immediately by neocon David Frum, the ex-speechwriter for President Bush who gave the world the phrase "axis of evil" and who was the coauthor of a recent book with Mr. Perle.

The "Israel-controls-Washington" theme is continued in another article by Francis, titled "Bush Is Right, Sharon (and Assorted Neocons) Wrong." In this piece, Francis seeks to perpetuate the myth of "Israel's journalistic fifth column inside the United States":

And it is that demand that lies behind the Big Lie being purveyed by virtually all of Israel's journalistic fifth column inside the United States that the Sept. 11 attack had nothing to do with U.S. support for Israel and the Palestinian issue but was driven by Osama bin Laden's hatred of "democracy," the "West," or just plain hatred pure and simple—"the haters need no reason to hate us," columnist Paul Greenberg glibly assures us. By denying that U.S. support for Israel plays a major role in precipitating terrorism against American targets, they hope not only to divert attention from Israel but also to arouse and manipulate America counter-hate against Israel's regional enemies.

That claim is a lie that has been blatantly contradicted by almost every public statement and communiqué from bin Laden himself, including his statement after the U.S. air raids against Afghanistan recently. Bin Laden and his henchmen never hesitate to make plain that there are three major reasons for their war against America: U.S. military bases in Saudi Arabia, "the land of Mohammed," as bin Laden calls it; U.S. policy against Iraq and the devastation of its people; and U.S. support for Israel and the repression of the Palestinians. To enumerate these reasons is not to endorse them as being morally or factually correct, but only to emphasize that they are the reasons bin Laden himself offers—and he could hardly offer them if they had no resonance in the Arab world.

In an article written shortly after the 9/11 attacks, Francis takes up the (unfortunately) familiar "Israel-is-responsible-for-9/11" refrain in an article called "On Novak, Podhoretz, Israel, and Terrorism."

151. Joseph Sobran, "Chutzpah and Hubris," *Sobran's*, March 23, 2004, www.sobran .com/columns/2004/040323.shtml.
152. Joseph Sobran, "For Fear of the Jews," *Sobran's*, September 2002, www.sobran .com/fearofjews.shtml.

The Israelis complain about the Arabs' refusal to acknowledge Israel's "right to exist." But if any state can be said to have a right to exist, it must be because it treats its subjects justly. If Israel's "right to exist" means the Jews' right to oppress Arabs—to impose a double standard to the disadvantage of the Arabs—then why on earth should the Arabs assent to it? Like Sharon, the Israelis feel persecuted when they are denied the right to persecute.

153. Ibid.
154. Ibid. He goes on to say:

> The fear of the label *anti-Semitic* is a fear of the power that is believed to lie behind it: Jewish power. . . .
>   The "fear of the Jews," to use the phrase so often repeated in the Gospel according to John, seems to have wrought a reorientation of the tone, the very principles, of today's conservatism. The hardy skepticism, critical intelligence, and healthy irony of men like James Burnham, Willmoore Kendall, and the young Buckley have given way to the uncritical philo-Semitism of George Will, Cal Thomas, Rush Limbaugh, and of course the later Buckley—men who will go to any lengths, even absurd and dishonorable lengths, to avoid the terrorizing label *anti-Semite*.

> . . .

> The Holocaust stands as the historical objectification of all the world's gentiles' eternal "anti-Semitism." Jewish life is an endless emergency, requiring endless emergency measures and justifying everything [Israel] does in the name of "defense." Jews and Israel can't be judged by normal standards, at least until Israel is absolutely safe—if even then.

155. Joseph Sobran, "The Jewish Faction," *Sobran's,* May 2004, www.sobran.com/articles/faction.shtml.
156. Ibid.
157. David Duke, "Israeli Terrorism and Sept. 11: How Israeli Terrorism and American Treason Caused the September 11 Attacks," DavidDuke.com, October 23, 2004, www.davidduke.com/general/israeli-terrorism-and-sept-11_13.html.
158. David Duke, "Ariel Sharon: The Terrorist behind the 9–11 Attack!" DavidDuke.com, May 2, 2002, www.davidduke.com/general/ariel-sharon-the-terrorist-behind-the-9–11-attack_114.html?page=1.
159. Ibid.
160. Allison Kaplan, "Baker Denies Using Obscenity in Comment on American Jews," *Jerusalem Post,* March 8, 1992.
161. The late David Bar-Illan, a world-class pianist and the former editor of an Israeli newspaper, reported that.
162. Rafael Medoff, "Ed Koch Still Pulls No Punches," *Jewish Press,* February 27, 2008.
163. Herb Keinon, "Israel Should Embrace, Not Fear, James Baker," *Jerusalem Post,* November 21, 2006.
164. Ibid.
165. Daniel Pipes, "James Baker's Terrible Iraq Report," Danielpipes.org, December 12, 2006, www.danielpipes.org/article/4192.

5. THE CASE AGAINST ISRAEL'S SUICIDAL ENEMIES

1. In Christopher Hitchens, "Jefferson's Quran," *Slate,* January 9, 2007, www.slate.com/id/2157314/.
2. Robert Worth, "Hezbollah Threatens Attacks on Israeli Targets," *New York Times,* February 15, 2008.
3. Memri.org, January 4, 2006.
4. Benny Morris, *1948: A History of the First Arab-Israeli War* (New Haven, CT: Yale University Press, 2008), p. 210.

5. Memri.org, Special Report No. 24, December 26, 2003.
6. Mudhafer al-Husaini and Richard Oppel, "Suicide Bomber Is Spotted and Shot, but Kills 3 in Baghdad," *New York Times,* February 18, 2008.
7. See "Plotters Made Martyrdom Videos," *BBC News,* April 4, 2008.
8. Jesus Rangel, "Fall River Jury Finds 2 More Defendants Guilty of Rape in Bar," *New York Times,* March 23, 1984.
9. A *New York Times* article stated, "For the last three days, Israel has been telling the residents of southern Lebanon, through leaflets, radio broadcasts, taped telephone messages and conversations with the local authorities, to leave these villages and move north." Steven Erlanger, "Troops Ready, but Israel Bets on Air Power," *New York Times,* July 23, 2006.
10. Amos Harel and Roni Singer-Heruti, "Explosives Belt for Yom Kippur Suicide Bombing Found in TA," *Haaretz,* September 23, 2007.
11. Steven Erlanger, "Israel Closes All Gaza Border Crossings," *New York Times,* January 19, 2008.
12. "Pro-Sderot Ad Spiked as Unbalanced," *Jewish Week,* April 11, 2008, p. 3.
13. "U.N.: 100,000 More Dead in Darfur Than Reported," CNN.com, April 24, 2008.
14. Buber stated:

> It does not seem to me convincing when you base your advice to us to observe satyagraha in Germany on these similarities of circumstance. In the five years I myself spent under the present regime, I observed many instances of genuine satyagraha among the Jews, instances showing a strength of spirit in which there was no question of bartering their rights or of being bowed down, and where neither force nor cunning was used to escape the consequences of their behaviour. Such actions, however, exerted apparently not the slightest influence on their opponents. All honour indeed to those who displayed such strength of soul! But I cannot recognise herein a watchword for the general behaviour of German Jews that might seem suited to exert an influence on the oppressed or on the world. An effective stand in the form of non-violence may be taken against unfeeling human beings in the hope of gradually bringing them to their senses; but a diabolic universal steamroller cannot thus be withstood.

Martin Buber, "Letter from Martin Buber to Mahatma Gandhi," Jerusalem, February 24, 1939, www.jewishvirtuallibrary.org/jsource/History/BuberGandhi.html.

15. Gandhi's selfishness and singular concern only for his own people dates back to his earliest activism in South Africa, when he refused to lift a finger or raise his voice on behalf of Black South Africans. Indeed, he justified the lower status of blacks on pseudo-racial grounds, claiming that "both the English and the Indians spring from a common stock, called the Indo-Aryan." (Quoted in G. B. Singh, *Gandhi, Behind the Mask of Divinity* [Amherst, NY: Prometheus, 2004], p. 183).

Maureen Swan, in her book *Gandhi: The South African Experience* (Johannesburg: Raven, 1985), p. 112, summarizes Gandhi's role in relation to blacks as follows:

> Gandhi facilitated the implementation of the divisive segregationist policies, which helped ease the task of white minority rule in South Africa. Indeed, where the Transvaal whites insisted on separate facilities for themselves, Gandhi demanded further subdivision to separate Indians from other blacks. In fact, in his eagerness to compromise, to conciliate, to ensure the white South Africans their predominant position, he was sometimes even ahead of them in advocating separate facilities for whites and others. . . . Gandhi was a racial purist, and proud of it.

Quoted in Singh at pp. 200–201.

16. Arun Gandhi, "Jewish Identity Can't Depend on Violence," *Washington Post*, "On Faith" blog, January 7, 2008, http://newsweek.washingtonpost.com/onfaith/arun_gandhi/2008/01/jewish_identity_in_the_past.html.
17. Ibid.
18. Ibid.
19. "Chapter VII: Action with Respect to Threats to the Peace, Breaches of the Peace, and Acts of Aggression," Article 51, *Charter of the United Nations*, www.un.org/aboutun/charter/chapter7.htm.
20. See Alan Dershowitz, *Preemption: A Knife That Cuts Both Ways* (New York: W. W. Norton, 2006).
21. Ibid.
22. According to the Committee for a Secure Sderot, "more than 6,000 Kassam Rockets have been fired against the settlements of the western Negev" since 2001. See http://www.matesderot.co.il/info_en.asp?id=536365928.
23. Associated Press and JPost.com Staff, "Abbas: IDF Action Worse Than Holocaust," *Jerusalem Post*, March 1, 2008.
24. "Abbas Slams Israel's Gaza 'Holocaust,' " Agence France-Presse, March 1, 2008.
25. Griff Witte, "Gaza Fighters Attack Fuel Depot Inside Israel," *Washington Post*, April 10, 2008. See the Israeli Ministry of Foreign Affairs Web site for more information: www.mfa.gov.il/MFA/Terrorism-+Obstacle+to+Peace/Hamas+war+against+Israel/Gaza-+Israeli+aid+and+Hamas+attacks+8-Apr-2008.htm.
26. "Learning the Lessons of the Katyusha War," *Jerusalem Post*, September 1, 2006.
27. "Hezbollah Leader Apologizes for Attack's Child Victims," CNN, July 21, 2006, www.cnn.com/2006/WORLD/meast/07/20/nasrallah.interview/index.html; "Nazareth Arab Absolves Nasrallah of Blame for Sons' Death after Rocket Attack," *BBC Monitoring International Reports*, July 23, 2006; Sonia Verma, "They Weren't Supposed to Die: After Two Arab Boys Are Killed by Hezbollah Missile, Arabs in Israel Learn They're Not Immune from Conflict," *Newsday*, July 22, 2006; "Siding with the Enemy," *Jerusalem Post*, July 23, 2006.
28. Chris McGreal, "Arafat Mourns Arab Shot in Error," *Jerusalem Post*, March 22, 2004.
29. Ibid.
30. Anthony Shadid, "Hezbollah Chief Warns Israel of Wide War," *Washington Post*, February 15, 2008.
31. Quoted in Alan M. Dershowitz, *Why Terrorism Works: Understanding the Threat, Responding to the Challenge* (New Haven, CT: Yale University Press, 2002), p. 82.
32. A *New York Post article* reported:

> Last week, a suicide bombing in the port city of Ashdod claimed a dozen lives. The next day, Israeli forces at a checkpoint caught an 11-year-old Palestinian boy, Abdallah Quran, with a 20-pound bomb. Hamas was using him as a mule to sneak the device through. When the bomb was discovered, the terrorists tried to detonate it remotely. Fortunately, it didn't go off. But this is Hamas—first, using an 11-year-old boy as an unwitting accomplice in a plot to cause death and injury. Then ready to kill their innocent tool. The Israelis released the boy when they ascertained he was blameless.

Robert A. George, "Slaying the Past," *New York Post*, March 23, 2004.
33. Alan M. Dershowitz, *Preemption*, p. 247.
34. Asa Kasher and Amos Yadlin, "Military Ethics of Fighting Terror: An Israeli Perspective," *Journal of Military Ethics* (2005). See also Jonathan S. Sar, "Framework for Targeted Killing: Hit or Miss," third-year paper, Harvard Law School, 2008.
35. Kasher and Yadlin, "Military Ethics of Fighting Terror," p. 2.
36. Paul Richter and Laura King, "Warfare in the Middle East; Israel to Halt Bombing for 48 Hours," *Los Angeles Times*, July 31, 2006; Yaakov Katz, "Kana Collapse Was Hours after Attack," *Jerusalem Post*, July 30, 2006; "Burden of Civilian Deaths Sits

with Hezbollah, Not Israel," *Chicago Sun-Times*, July 31, 2006; Steven Erlanger and Hassan Fattah, "Israel Suspending Lebanon Air Raids after Dozens Die," *New York Times*, July 31, 2006; Liz Sly and Joel Greenberg, "Israel Suspends Air Raids," *Chicago Tribune*, July 31, 2006.

37. The *Los Angeles Times* reported: "The Israeli military concluded its inquiry into the Qana killings Thursday and said its forces were unaware that there were civilians in the building. 'Had the information indicated that civilians were present . . . the attack would not have been carried out,' the military said in a written statement." Kim Murphy, "Officials Say 28 Died in Qana, Not 54," *Los Angeles Times*, August 4, 2006. See also Greg Myre, "Offering Video, Israel Answers Critics on War," *New York Times*, December 5, 2006; Jonah Goldberg, "Israel's Lose-Lose Proposition," *Chicago Tribune*, August 3, 2006.

38. "UN Official Calls Hizballah Cowards," *Israel Today*, July 26, 2006. See also Uri Dan, "Hezbollah 'Cowards' to Blame for Civilian Slaughter: U.N. Big," *New York Post*, July 25, 2006.

39. "Israel/Lebanon: Deliberate Destruction or 'Collateral Damage'? Israeli Attacks on Civilian Infrastructure," Amnesty International, August 2006, www.amnesty.org/en/library/asset/MDE18/007/2006/en/dom-MDE180072006en.pdf.

40. H. W. Koch wrote:

> Indicative of this attitude is his letter of 8 July 1940 to Lord Beaverbrook, then minister of aircraft production: "We have no Continental army which can defeat the German military power. The blockade is broken and Hitler has Asia and probably Africa to draw from. . . . But there is one thing that will bring him back and bring him down, and that is an absolutely devastating, *exterminating* attack by very heavy bombers from this country upon the Nazi home-land." Unless this happened, Churchill could "not see a way through". That Churchill's use of the phrase "exterminating attack" was not a mere expression of temper, uttered in a moment of stress, but represented the policy he expected to pursue is substantiated by his remark to Stalin on 12 August 1942. Referring to the German civilian population, he said "we looked upon its morale as a military target. We sought no mercy and would show no mercy. . . . If need be, as the war went on, we hoped to shatter almost every dwelling in almost every German city". For even more drastic statements the Yalta documents provide ample evidence. As late as 28 March 1945 he admitted his policy of terror and extermination when he minuted his change of mind to the chiefs of staff com-mittee and to Portal: "It seems to me that the moment has come when the question of bombing German cities simply for the sake of terror, though under other pretexts, should be reviewed." [Emphasis in original.]

"The Strategic Air Offensive against Germany," *Historical Journal* 34, no. 1 (March 1991): 134.

41. Steven Erlanger and Jad Mouawad, "2 Leaders Want Peacekeepers to Be Sent to Lebanon," *New York Times*, July 17, 2006.

42. David Bernstein, "The Decline of Amnesty International," *Volokh Conspiracy* (blog), August 22, 2006, www.volokh.com/posts/chain_1156298269.shtml.

43. "Israel/Lebanon: Hizbullah's Deliberate Attacks on Israeli Civilians," Amnesty International, Sep. 14, 2006, MDE 02/026/2006 (Public). Also: "Under Fire: Hizbullah's Attacks on Northern Israel," Amnesty International, Sept. 2006, MDE 02/025/2006.

44. "AI: Israel Committed War Crimes," Al-Jazeera, August 27, 2006, http://english.aljazeera.net/English/archive/archive?ArchiveId=35357.

45. "Israel/Lebanon: Deliberate Destruction or 'Collateral Damage'?" Amnesty International, August 23, 2006 (MDE 18/007/2006): 3, www.amnesty.org/en/library/info/MDE18/007/2006.

46. "Israel/Lebanon: Deliberate Destruction or 'Collateral Damage'? Israeli Attacks on Civilian Infrastructure," Amnesty International, August 5, 2006, www.amnesty.org/en/library/asset/MDE18/007/2006/en/dom-MDE180072006en.pdf.
47. Ibid.
48. Press Release, "Israel/Occupied Territories: Women and Conflict, the Untold Story," Amnesty International, March 31, 2005, www.amnesty.org/en/library/info/MDE15/020/2005/en. Similarly, see Hillel Fendel, "Heb. U. Paper Finds: IDF Has Political Motives for Not Raping," *Arutz Sheva*, December 23, 2007, www.israelnationalnews.com/News/News.aspx/124674.
49. Alan M. Dershowitz, "Amnesty International's Biased Definition of War Crimes: Whatever Israel Does to Defend Its Citizens," Huffington Post, August 29, 2006. See also "Israel/Occupied Territories: Women and Conflict, the Untold Story," press release, Amnesty International, March 31, 2005, www.amnesty.org/en/library/info/MDE15/020/2005/en.
50. "Fatal Strikes: Israel's Indiscriminate Attacks against Civilians in Lebanon," *Human Rights Watch* 18, no. 3(e) (August 2006): 3, www.hrw.org/reports/2006/lebanon0806/lebanon0806web.pdf.
51. Ibid.
52. Sabrina Tavernise, "Christians Fleeing Lebanon Denounce Hezbollah," *New York Times*, July 28, 2006.
53. John Lee Anderson, "The Battle for Lebanon," *New Yorker*, August 8, 2006.
54. Sonia Verma, "Hezbollah's Deadly Hold on Heartland," *National Post*, August 5, 2006.
55. Charlie Gillis, "Diplomacy under Fire," *Maclean's*, August 7, 2006.
56. Steven Edwards, "UN Contradicts Itself over Israeli Attack," *Vancouver Sun*, July 27, 2006.
57. "United Nations Interim Force in Lebanon (UNIFIL), Naqoura, July 28, 2006" (press release).
58. Chris Tinkler, "Human Shields—How Terrorist Fighters Hezbollah Have Drawn Helpless Civilians into the Carnage," *Sunday Mail* (Australia), July 30, 2006.
59. Kenneth Roth, "Indiscriminate Bombardment," *Jerusalem Post*, August 18, 2006.
60. Greg Myre, "Offering Video, Israel Answers Critics on War," *New York Times*, December 5, 2006.
61. Ibid.
62. Ibid.
63. Ibid.
64. Ibid.
65. See Isabel Kershner, "Israel's Tactics Thwart Attacks, with Trade-Off," *New York Times*, May 3, 2008, pp. 1, A6.
66. See Kasher and Yadlin, "Military Ethics of Fighting Terror."
67. Uli Schmetzer, "Storm of Criticism Follows Airstrike," *Chicago Tribune*, July 25, 2002.
68. Colin McMahon, "Co-founder of Hamas Injured by an Israeli Bomb; 15 Others Hurt in Attack on Gaza Building," *Chicago Tribune*, September 7, 2003; Molly Moore and John Ward Anderson, "Israeli Jet Bombs Hamas Meeting, Injuring Spiritual Leader," *Washington Post*, September 7, 2003.
69. Amos Harel, "Pinpointed IAF Attacks in Gaza More Precise, Hurt Fewer Civilians," *Haaretz*, December 30, 2007.
70. As reported in *B'Tselem* (which uses questionable criteria in defining "civilians" and "minors"):

> A comparison between 2007 and 2006 reveals a decrease in Palestinians killed by Israeli forces, and a decrease in those cases that raise the suspicion of arbitrary killing. However, the figures for 2007 still give cause for concern. In 2007 (up

to 29 December), Israeli security forces killed 373 Palestinians (290 in Gaza, 83 in the West Bank), 53 among them minors. By comparison, in 2006, 657 Palestinians were killed, including 140 minors: 523 in Gaza, 134 in the West Bank. In 2007, about 35 percent of those killed were civilians who were not taking part in the hostilities when killed. This is a reduction in comparison with the number of casualties who did not participate in the hostilities in 2006, which was 54 percent, (348 persons). Palestinians killed seven Israeli civilians (three in a suicide attack in Eilat, two in Sderot by Qassam attacks, and two by gunfire in the West Bank). This is the lowest number of Israeli civilian casualties since the beginning of the Intifada. Palestinians also killed six Israeli security forces. In 2006, Palestinians killed 17 Israeli civilians.

"31 Dec. 2007: 131 Palestinians Who Did Not Participate in the Hostilities Killed by Israel's Security Forces in 2007," *B'Tselem*, December 31, 2007, www.btselem. org/english/press_releases/20071231.asp.

71. See Alan M. Dershowitz, *The Case for Israel* (Hoboken, NJ: John Wiley and Sons, 2003), pp. 125–126.

72. Ian Fisher, "Pope's Prayer Omits Israel, and Words Fly," *New York Times,* July 26, 2005.

73. Stephanie Holmes, "Taut Times for Israel and Vatican," *BBC News,* July 29, 2005.

74. The *New York Times* reported: "The Egyptian Organization for Human Rights, a nongovernmental group, reported in May 2004 that it had uncovered 292 cases of torture between 1993 and 2003, of which 120 led to death." David Johnston, "Terror Suspects Sent to Egypt by the Dozens," *New York Times,* May 12, 2005.

75. Nicholas Watt, "Turkey: EU Demands Action to End Torture of Prisoners," *Guardian* (UK), November 10, 2005.

76. Ian Fisher, "Vatican Denounces Israeli Reprisals," *New York Times,* July 29, 2005.

77. Glenda Cooper, "British Charge 11 Suspects in Airliner Plot," *Washington Post,* August 22, 2006.

78. Chuck Morse, *The Nazi Connection to Islamic Terrorism* (New York: iUniverse, 2003), p. 28. Another source argues that the perpetrators were already agitating for violence before hearing the mufti's speech and makes no reference to any order: Zvi Elpeleg, *The Grand Mufti: Haj Amin al-Hussaini, Founder of the Palestinian National Movement* (London: Frank Cass, 1993), pp. 21–22. Still another—Philip Mattar, *The Mufti of Jerusalem: Al-Hajj Amin al-Husayni and the Palestinian National Movement* (New York: Columbia University Press, 1988), pp. 46–47—argues that the mufti tried to calm and disperse the crowd with his speech more than once while other militant sheiks incited them to violence.

79. See Alan M. Dershowitz, *Why Terrorism Works* (New Haven, CT: Yale University Press, 2002).

80. Shmulik Hadad, "Qassam Hits Kindergarten; 2 Children Lightly Wounded, Eight More People Suffered Shock," Ynetnews.com, July 28, 2006.

81. See Alan M. Dershowitz, "Can the Guild Survive Its Hypocrisy?" *American Lawyer,* August 11, 1978, p. 30.

6. THE CASE AGAINST MAHMOUD AHMADINEJAD AND IRAN'S GENOCIDAL NUCLEAR WEAPONS PROGRAM

1. *Daily Star,* October 23, 2002, found in Deborah Passner, "Hassan Nasrallah: In His Own Words," *CAMERA,* July 26, 2006, www.camera.org/index .asp?x_context=7&x_issue=11&x_article=1158.

2. Jeffrey Goldberg, "In the Party of God," *New Yorker,* October 14, 2002, found in Deborah Passner, "Hassan Nasrallah: In His Own Words," *CAMERA,* July 26, 2006, www.camera.org/index.asp?x_context=7&x_issue=11&x_article=1158. *New Yorker* article available at www.newyorker.com/archive/2002/10/14/021014fa_fact4.
3. Goldberg, "In the Party of God."
4. "Argentina Charges Iran, Hezbollah in 1994 Jewish Center Bombing," Agence France-Presse, October 25, 2006, www.spme.net/cgi-bin/articles.cgi?ID=1346.
5. Reuters, "U.S. Sees Iranian Role in Buenos Aires Blast," *New York Times,* May 9, 1992; Allison Kaplan, "U.S. Says Iran behind Embassy Bombing," *Jerusalem Post,* May 8, 1992; Barry Schweid, "U.S. Intelligence Links Iran to Israeli Embassy Bombing," *Chicago Sun-Times,* May 8, 1992; Anthony Faiola, "Argentina Links Iran to Terror Bombings; Blast at Israeli Embassy, Jewish Center Killed 110," *Washington Post,* May 21, 1998.
6. Yaakov Katz and Herb Keinon, "Iran Smuggling Arms into Gaza by Sea," *Jerusalem Post,* April 18, 2008; Herb Keinon, "US Official: Iran Wants to Turn Hamas into Hizbullah," *Jerusalem Post,* February 27, 2006; Nicholas Blanford, "Palestinian Ties to Iran, Hizbullah Look Firmer," *Christian Science Monitor,* January 18, 2002. This is nothing new; see Jonathan Landay, "Terrorism's Sponsors Aim at Mideast, U.S.," *Christian Science Monitor,* May 16, 1995.
7. "Biography of H. E. Dr. Ahmadi Nejad, Honourable President of Islamic Republic of Iran," Presidency of the Republic of Iran Web site, www.president.ir/eng/ahmadinejad/bio/.
8. Ali Ansari, "Chapter Two: The Triumph of the Authoritarians," *Adelphi Papers* 47, no. 393 (2007): 23–40.
9. Ibid.
10. Doug Saunders, "The Revenge of Red Ken," *Globe and Mail* (Canada), October 2, 2004.
11. Ansari, "Chapter Two: The Triumph of the Authoritarians," p. 29.
12. Ibid., pp. 30, 31, 32. The Guardian Council is "the powerful body charged with checking that legislation conforms to Islamic law and vetting candidates for election. . . . They barred over 3,000 candidates from running, many of them sitting deputies, in a process that took place entirely behind closed doors; barred candidates were not told the reasons for their disqualification, other than a sudden assessment that they were 'un-Islamic.'" See also Anoushiravan Ehteshami and Mahjoob Zweiri, *Iran and the Rise of Its Neoconservatives: The Politics of Tehran's Silent Revolution* (London: I. B. Tauris, 2007), pp. 37–41.
13. Ibid., pp. 30, 31, 32, 42–44.
14. Ibid., pp. 33, 36–38. "It is important to recollect that, as late as a week before the second-round voting, Ahmadinejad barely registered on the electoral radar." See also ibid., pp. 45–47.
15. Aparisim Ghosh, "Iran's New Hand," *Time,* July 4, 2005.
16. Ali M. Ansari, "Chapter Three: The Ahmadinejad Presidency: Image and Foreign Policy," *Adelphi Papers* 47, no. 393 (2007): 41.
17. Ghosh, "Iran's New Hand."
18. Nazila Fathi, "Iran's New President Says Israel 'Must Be Wiped Off the Map,'" *New York Times,* October 27, 2005.
19. "Iranian President Says Israel Should Be 'Wiped Off the Map,'" *Los Angeles Times,* October 27, 2005.
20. Michael Slackman, "A New Face in Iran Resurrects an Old Defiance," *New York Times,* January 30, 2006.
21. Steven Weisman, "Western Leaders Condemn the Iranian President's Threat to Israel," *New York Times,* October 28, 2005.

22. Nazila Fathi, "Iranian President Stands by Call to Wipe Israel Off Map," *New York Times,* October 29, 2005.

23. Warren Hoge, "Annan, Citing Talk on Israel, Drops Iran Trip," *New York Times,* November 5, 2005. Annan condemned the remarks, saying, "Under the United Nations charter, all members have undertaken to refrain from the threat of use of force against the territorial integrity or political independence of any states."

24. Reuters, "Move Israel to Europe, Iran Leader Suggests," *New York Times,* December 9, 2005.

25. Ibid.

26. Associated Press, "Iran's President Clarifies His Stand on Holocaust: It's a European Myth," *New York Times,* December 15, 2005.

27. Ibid.

28. Associated Press, "Iran Chief Says Israel Exists for Genocide," *New York Times,* January 2, 2006.

29. Nazila Fathi, "U.N. Scrutiny Won't Make Iran Quit Nuclear Effort, President Says," *New York Times,* January 15, 2006.

30. Nazila Fathi, "Iranian Leader Renews Attack on Israel at Palestinian Rally," *New York Times,* April 15, 2006.

31. "Ahmadinejad's Letter to Bush," *Washington Post,* May 9, 2006.

32. Warren Hoge, "Iran Leader, at U.N., Skirts Issue of Hezbollah's Disarmament," *New York Times,* September 22, 2006.

33. Nazila Fathi, "Iran Invites Scholars to Assess Holocaust as History or Fiction," *New York Times,* December 6, 2006.

34. Nazila Fathi, "Israel Fading, Iran's Leader Tells Deniers of Holocaust," *New York Times,* December 13, 2006.

35. Consider, for example, the *fatwa* placed on Salman Rushdie by the Ayatollah Khomeini in 1989 for "un-Islamic" material in his novel *The Satanic Verses.*

36. Helene Cooper, "Ahmadinejad, at Columbia, Parries and Puzzles," *New York Times,* September 25, 2007.

37. Phillip Mattar, *The Mufti of Jerusalem: Al-Hajj Amin al Husayni and the Palestinian National Movement* (New York: Columbia University Press, 1988), p. xiii.

38. David G. Dalin and John F. Rothmann, *Icon of Evil: Hitler's Mufti and the Rise of Radical Islam* (New York: Random House, 2008), p. 35.

39. "The selection of the mufti was in recognition of his enormous popularity in Palestine as well as in many Arab countries." Mattar, *The Mufti of Jerusalem,* p. 121.

40. Chuck Morse, *The Nazi Connection to Islamic Terrorism: Adolf Hitler and Haj Amin al-Husseini* (New York: iUniverse, 2003), p. 33. To that end, he organized in 1941 an unsuccessful pro-Nazi coup in Iraq which resulted in the murder of 110 Jews, with hundreds more wounded and thousands left homeless. David G. Dalin and John F. Rothmann, *Icon of Evil: Hitler's Mufti and the Rise of Radical Islam* (New York: Random House, 2008), pp. 39–40; 43–44.

41. Morse, *The Nazi Connection to Islamic Terrorism,* p. 33.

42. According to Eichmann: "Nazi flags fly in Palestine and [Palestinians] adorn their houses with Swastikas and portraits of Hitler." Morse, *The Nazi Connection to Islamic Terrorism,* p. 46.

43. Zvi Elpeleg, *The Grand Mufti: Haj Amin al-Hussaini, Founder of the Palestinian National Movement,* David Harvey, trans. (London: Frank Cass, 1993), p. 36.

44. See Dalin and Rothmann, *Icon of Evil,* pp. 29–34; Morse, *The Nazi Connection to Islamic Terrorism,* pp. 44–45; Elpeleg, *The Grand Mufti,* pp. 37–44, 47.

45. Dalin and Rothmann, *Icon of Evil,* pp. 32–34; Morse, *The Nazi Connection to Islamic Terrorism,* pp. 44–45; Elpeleg, *The Grand Mufti,* pp. 37–44, 47.

46. Morse, *The Nazi Connection to Islamic Terrorism,* pp. 43, 47, 49, 56, 58, 60; Elpeleg, *The Grand Mufti,* p. 65.

47. Morse, *The Nazi Connection to Islamic Terrorism*, pp. 44, 71, 74–76.

48. Ibid., p. 46.

49. Benny Morris, *Righteous Victims: A History of the Zionist-Arab Conflict, 1881–2001* (New York: Vintage Books, 2001), p. 137.

50. See Dalin and Rothmann, *Icon of Evil*, pp. 49–52. Al-Husseini lived a life of luxury in Berlin, courtesy of the Nazis:

> The Nazi government spared no expense in offering him their hospitality, providing al-Husseini with a luxurious home . . . a full staff of servants, a chauffeured Mercedes limousine, and a monthly stipend in excess of $10,000, as well as four other residences and suites in two of Berlin's most luxurious hotels. The mufti was also given a monthly food budget, which would enable him to lavishly entertain the many leaders of radical Islam residing in or visiting Nazi Germany.

Dalin and Rothmann, *Icon of Evil*, p. 47. This money came from the *sonderfund*—"money confiscated from Jews on their way to concentration camps." Morse, *The Nazi Connection to Islamic Terrorism*, p. 56.

51. Elpeleg, *The Grand Mufti*, p. 70; Morse, *The Nazi Connection to Islamic Terrorism*, p. 55.

52. Dalin and Rothmann, *Icon of Evil*, p. 5. "One Nazi officer . . . noted in his journal that al-Husseini wanted to see the Jews 'preferably all killed.'" Morse, *The Nazi Connection to Islamic Terrorism*, p. 66.

53. Sarah Honig, "Fiendish Hypocrisy II: The Man from Klopstock St.," *Jerusalem Post*, April 6, 2001.

54. Morse, *The Nazi Connection to Islamic Terrorism*, p. 59.

55. Ibid., p. 60.

56. Dalin and Rothmann, *Icon of Evil*, p. 53.

57. Morse, *The Nazi Connection to Islamic Terrorism*, p. 66; Elpeleg, *The Grand Mufti*, p. 179.

58. Dalin and Rothmann, *Icon of Evil*, p. 54.

59. Ibid., pp. 54–55.

60. Ibid., p. 55.

61. "A police report said that these ten containers [found in the possession of the paratroopers] held enough poison to kill 250,000 people." Dalin and Rothmann, *Icon of Evil*, p. 61; Morse, *The Nazi Connection to Islamic Terrorism*, p. 84.

62. Elpeleg, *The Grand Mufti*, pp. 56–62, 69; Morse, *The Nazi Connection to Islamic Terrorism*, pp. 50–52, 70–80; Dalin and Rothmann, *Icon of Evil*, pp. 43–44; 55–59.

63. Germany, Auswärtiges Amt., *Documents on German Foreign Policy, 1918–1945, from the Archives of the German Foreign Ministry*, series D, vol. 13, no. 515 (Washington, DC: U.S. Government Printing Office, 1949), pp. 881–885; www.psych.upenn.edu/~fjgil/muftihitler.htm.

64. Ibid.

65. Dalin and Rothmann, *Icon of Evil*, pp. 61–62; Morse, *The Nazi Connection to Islamic Terrorism*, pp. 57, 67, 68–69; Elpeleg, *The Grand Mufti*, pp. 72–73.

66. Morse, *The Nazi Connection to Islamic Terrorism*, pp. 64, 66.

67. Ibid., p. 62; Mattar, *The Mufti of Jerusalem*, p. 105.

68. Morse, *The Nazi Connection to Islamic Terrorism*, pp. 62–63. He also may have prevented more from leaving Bulgaria, asking the Italians for help; see Dalin and Rothmann, *Icon of Evil*, p. 59.

69. Dalin and Rothmann, *Icon of Evil*, pp. 56–59; Morse, *The Nazi Connection to Islamic Terrorism*, pp. 70–79.

70. Ibid., pp. 48–49, 59–62; Morse, *The Nazi Connection to Islamic Terrorism*, pp. 62–63, 66. For example, he worked with the Nazis to create a "special Einsatzgruppe

Egypt, a mobile SS squad, under the supervision of Adolf Eichmann, which was to carry out the mass murder of Palestinian Jewry." The group was attached to the Afrika Korps, ready to begin murdering as soon as the Nazis conquered the Middle East. He also urged the Nazis to bomb Jerusalem and Tel Aviv. Dalin and Rothmann, *Icon of Evil,* p. 60.

71. Dalin and Rothmann, *Icon of Evil,* pp. 58, 61, and 62.
72. Morse, *The Nazi Connection to Islamic Terrorism,* p. 61; Mattar, *The Mufti of Jerusalem,* pp. 108–109.
73. Elpeleg, *The Grand Mufti,* pp. 76–79; Mattar, *The Mufti of Jerusalem,* p. 110; Morse, *The Nazi Connection to Islamic Terrorism,* pp. 93–95.
74. See also Dalin and Rothmann, *Icon of Evil,* pp. 91–94.
75. Nor was there any grand plan by the Israelis to force the Arabs to leave. The Israeli government was prepared to live with a substantial Arab population. But during the course of the war, evacuation of hostile Arab villages, from which snipers and terrorists embarked and then returned, became a military necessity. To be sure, once the Arab populations had left their villages—some by choice, some by fear, some by pressure, some by expulsion—the Israeli policy was not to permit the return of a hostile population, led by former Nazis sworn to their destruction. This is a very different account of the Nakba from the one being peddled on university campuses today and in the op-ed pages of newspapers around the world. But it is the truth, as documented by historical records and eminent historians, including Benny Morris, the dean of "Israel's new historians."
76. Dalin and Rothmann, *Icon of Evi,* pp. 81–86; Elpeleg, *The Grand Mufti,* p. 180.
77. Dalin and Rothmann, *Icon of Evil,* p. 105; Elpeleg, *The Grand Mufti,* pp. 180–181.
78. Elpeleg, *The Grand Mufti,* pp. 179–180.
79. Ibid., p. 179.
80. Dalin and Rothmann, *Icon of Evil,* p. 84.
81. Ibid., p. 142.
82. Benny Morris, *1948: A History of the First Arab-Israeli War* (New Haven, CT: Yale University Press, 2008), pp. 410–411.
83. Morris, *1948,* p. 407.
84. Timothy Ryback, "Dateline Sudetenland: Hostages to History," *Foreign Policy,* no. 105 (Winter, 1996–1997): 165–166. It wasn't until the collapse of the Austro-Hungarian Empire at the end of World War I and the redrawing of borders that followed that the Sudeten Germans "found themselves an ethnic German minority in a belligerently nationalistic Slavic state."
85. Chauncy Harris and Gabriele Wulker, "The Refugee Problem of Germany," *Economic Geography* 29, no. 1 (January 1953): 12.
86. Ibid., pp. 12–13.
87. Ryback, "Dateline Sudetenland: Hostages to History," p. 164; Harris and Wulker, pp. 17–23. The Czechs even decreed, as they put the Sudetens in camps for deportation, that all Germans must wear swastikas for identification. MacAlister Brown, "The Diplomacy of Bitterness: Genesis of the Potsdam Decision to Expel Germans from Czechoslovakia," *Western Political Quarterly* 11, no. 3 (September 1958): 623. Some compared the expulsion—particularly in its early stages, as administered by the Czechs—to a "death march." Joseph Schechtman, "Postwar Population Transfers in Europe: A Survey," *Review of Politics* 15, no. 2 (April 1953): 155.
88. Ryback, "Dateline Sudetenland: Hostages to History," p. 164. That number is from Sudeten German sources; Czech sources put the number at thirty thousand.
89. Morris wrote:

> In Arabic, before Arab audiences, [al-Husseini] was often explicit. With Westerners, he was usually evasive, but one cannot doubt his meaning. In

January 1937, for example, in his testimony before the Peel Commission, al-Husseini was asked: "Does his eminence think that this country can assimilate and digest the 400,000 Jews now in the country?"

Al-Husseini: "No."

On which the commissioners commented: "We are not questioning the sincerity or the humanity of the Mufti's intentions . . . but we cannot forget what recently happened, despite treaty provisions and explicit assurances, to the Assyrian [Christian] minority in Iraq; nor can we forget that the hatred of the Arab politician for the [Jewish] National Home has never been concealed and that it has not permeated the Arab population as a whole.

. . .

In 1974, just before his death, he told interviewers: "There is no room for peaceful coexistence with our enemies. The only solution is the liquidation of the foreign conquest in Palestine within its natural frontiers and the establishment of a national Palestinian state on the basis of its Muslim and Christian inhabitants and its Jewish [inhabitants] who lived here before the British conquest in 1917 and their descendants."

1948, pp. 408–409.

90. Ibid., p. 409.
91. Morris continued:

These expulsions by the Arab regular armies stemmed quite naturally from the expulsionist mindset prevailing in the Arab states. The mindset characterized both the public and the ruling elites. All vilified the Yishuv and opposed the existence of a Jewish state on "their" (sacred Islamic) soil, and all sought its extirpation, albeit with varying degrees of bloody-mindedness. Shouts of "Idbah al Yahud" (slaughter the Jews) characterized equally street demonstrations in Jaffa, Cairo, Damascus, and Baghdad both before and during the war and were, in essence, echoed, usually in tamer language, by most Arab leaders.

Ibid., pp. 409–410.

92. Morris wrote:

Already before the war, Iraq's prime minister had warned British diplomats that if the United Nations decided on a solution to the Palestine problem that was not "satisfactory" to the Arabs, "severe measures should [would?] be taken against all Jews in Arab countries. A few weeks later, the head of the Egyptian delegation to the United Nations, Muhammad Hussein Heykal, announced that "the lives of 1,000,000 Jews in Moslem countries would be jeopardized by the establishment of a Jewish State."

Morris documents the pogroms against the Jews of nearly every Arab country. See ibid., pp. 412–415.

93. Ibid., pp. 412–413.
94. Laurie Goodstein, "Ahmadinejad Meets Clerics, and Decibels Drop a Notch," *New York Times,* September 27, 2007.
95. Nazila Fathi, "Ahmadinejad Says A-Plant Will Open in a Year and Belittles Israel," *New York Times,* January 31, 2008.
96. "Iran to Defy West on Nuclear: Ahmadinejad," Agence France-Presse, April 9, 2008.
97. Nazila Fathi and William Broad, "Iran Says It's Installing New Centrifuges," *New York Times,* April 9, 2008.
98. Parisa Hafezi, "Iran Warns West of 'Bloody Nose' over Nuclear Issue," Reuters, April 9, 2008.

99. "Iran's Ahmadinejad Targets 'Corrupt World Leadership,'" Agence France-Presse, April 10, 2008.

100. "Ahmadinejad: 'Israel Is Collapsing and Nothing Will Be Able to Save It,'" *Jerusalem Post*, April 10, 2008.

101. Slackman, "A New Face in Iran Resurrects an Old Defiance." Also in Neil MacFarquhar, "How Iran's Leader Keeps the West Off Balance," *New York Times*, December 17, 2006: "The economy is so decrepit that Iran, a leading oil producer, has to import an estimated 40 percent of its gasoline."

102. Michael Slackman, "In the Streets, Aid to Hezbollah Stirs Iranian Fear and Resentment," *New York Times*, July 23, 2006. Other quotes include: "We Iranians have a saying. We should save our own house first and then save the mosque. A lot of people think this way. The government should help its people first, and then help the people in Lebanon." "Iranians want our money to stay in the country and be spent for Iranians to solve their problems." "One percent of our budget has been approved by my Parliament to give to Palestine. Why should I not get angry about this?" "Radio and television broadcast so many programs about Arab countries that I sometimes wonder if it is the Iranian TV or an Arab TV. Such a vast and big propaganda has caused a kind of indifference and even negative sense toward Arab nations."

103. Anne Penketh, "Iran Enters New Year in Somber Mood as Economic Crisis Bites," *Independent* (London), March 24, 2008. Julian Borger, "Conservative Wins in Iran Poll Show Sanctions Are Failing," *Guardian* (London), March 22, 2008. "[Inflation] is officially 20 percent, although estimated to be 10 per cent higher," in Penketh, "Iran Enters New Year in Somber Mood as Economic Crisis Bites."

104. Neil MacFarquhar, "How Iran's Leader Keeps the West Off Balance," *New York Times*, December 17, 2006. See also "Shutting Down Zanan," *New York Times* editorial, February 7, 2008, which describes how Ahmadinejad shut down Iran's leading women's magazine. "Today, Iran is experiencing the most severe crackdown on social behavior and dress in years, and women are often barred from smoking in public, let alone attending a stadium event," according to Michael Slackman, in "U.S. Focus on Ahmadinejad Puzzles Iranians," *New York Times*, September 24, 2007.

105. *New York Times* editorial, "Shutting Down Zanan."

106. Julian Borger, "Ahmadinejad's Hand Strengthened in Poll," *Irish Times*, March 17, 2008; Scott Peterson, "Iran Election: Hard-Liners Hold On, Despite High Inflation," *Christian Science Monitor*, March 17, 2008; Nazila Fathi, "Iran Reformists Question Conservative Gains," *New York Times*, March 18, 2008.

107. Thomas Erdbrink, "Allies of Iran's President Heading for a Majority in Parliament," *Washington Post*, March 17, 2008.

108. Peterson, "Iran Election: Hard-Liners Hold on, Despite High Inflation"; Nazila Fathi, "Iran Reformists Question Conservative Gains," *New York Times*, March 18, 2008; also Penketh, "Iran Enters New Year in Somber Mood as Economic Crisis Bites."

109. Peterson, "Iran Election: Hard-Liners Hold On, Despite High Inflation"; Fathi, "Iran Reformists Question Conservative Gains"; Nazila Fathi, "Conservatives Prevail in Iran Vote, but Opposition Scores Too," *New York Times*, April 27, 2008. Of the 82 seats nationwide decided by the runoff, conservatives won almost 70 percent, giving them 198 of the 290 seats in the parliament. Still, the reformists and unaffiliated candidates made gains; the reformists now control 47 seats, up from 40, and the unaffiliated candidates won more than 40 seats. See Fathi, "Conservatives Prevail in Iran Vote, but Opposition Scores Too."

110. Peterson, "Iran Election: Hard-Liners Hold on, Despite High Inflation."

111. Ibid.

112. Fathi, "Iran Reformists Question Conservative Gains."

113. Amir Taheri, "In Iran Vote, a Silent Dissent," *New York Post*, April 13, 2008. The average urban turnout was a little more than 30 percent.

114. Anne Penketh, "Rival's Victory Is a Blow for Ahmadinejad," *Independent,* March 17, 2008.

115. Editorial, "A Bell Tolls for Ahmadinejad," *Boston Globe,* June 2, 2008; Yaniv Berman, "Analysis: Ahmadinejad Loses Power as Larijani Elected Speaker," *Jerusalem Post,* May 28, 2008.

116. Slackman, "U.S. Focus on Ahmadinejad Puzzles Iranians."

117. MacFarquhar, "How Iran's Leader Keeps the West Off Balance"; Ethan Bronner, "Just How Far Did They Go, Those Words against Israel?" *New York Times,* June 11, 2006.

118. "Ahmadinejad Says Israel Will 'Disappear,'" *New York Times,* June 2, 2008.

119. Office of the Director of National Intelligence, *National Intelligence Estimate: Iran: Nuclear Intentions and Capabilities,* November 2007.

120. Alan Dershowitz, "Stupid Intelligence," *Jerusalem Post,* December 18, 2007.

121. Valerie Lincy and Gary Milhollin, "In Iran We Trust?" *New York Times,* December 6, 2007.

122. Ibid.

123. Gary Hart, "The NIE Iran Report and Alan Dershowitz," Huffington Post, December 7, 2007, www.huffingtonpost.com/gary-hart/the-nie-iran-report-and-a_b_75894.html.

124. Ibid.

125. Adrian Croft, "Panel Warns of Nuclear Iran by 2015," *Boston Globe,* March 2, 2008.

126. Ibid.

127. William Broad and David Sanger, "Vienna Meeting on Arms Data Reignites Iran Nuclear Debate," *New York Times,* March 3, 2008.

128. Alan Dershowitz, "British Intelligence Is Smarter Than Ours—and Than Gary Hart," Huffington Post, March 4, 2008.

129. Rafsanjani claimed, as was mentioned earlier in the chapter, that mutual destruction of Iran and Israel via nuclear exchange would result in a negligible loss—meaning in Iran—to the Muslim world as a whole. See Alan Dershowitz, "Amend International Law to Allow Preemptive Strike on Iran," *Forward,* August 20, 2004.

130. Alan Dershowitz, "How the UN Legitimizes Terrorists," *Chicago Tribune,* July 25, 2006.

131. Ewen MacAskill, "Thousands Would Die in US Strikes on Iran," *Guardian* (London), February 13, 2006.

132. News of the Week in Review, *New York Times,* June 1, 2008, pp. 1, 8.

133. Ibid.

134. Nazila Fathi, "Iranian Leader Renews Attack on Israel at Palestinian Rally," *New York Times,* April 15, 2006.

135. Suzanne Fields, "Confronting the New Anti-Semitism," *Washington Times,* July 25, 2004.

136. A "hardened" site is one that is hidden underground (such as within a mountain or beneath rock) or otherwise fortified strongly so as not to be easily destroyed by a missile attack. Such difficult targets have led to the controversial development of both conventional and nuclear "bunker buster" missiles that are capable of penetrating rock and concrete to destroy hardened sites underground.

CONCLUSION

1. Jeffrey Goldberg, "Unforgiven," *Atlantic,* May 2008.

2. Associated Press, "Hamas Chief Sees Truce as a 'Tactic,'" *New York Times,* April 27, 2008.

INDEX